Praise for *The Affair of the Veiled Murderess*

"Adler's painstaking research demonstrates that Robinson's murder trial is more than a sensational historical tale … this remains a fascinating story, one that will be of interest to scholars of urban life, crime, politics, and gender in nineteenth-century America."

— *New York History*

"Adler deftly navigates an abundance of primary source material to recreate the facts of Robinson's sensational murder trial in this enjoyable page-turner. *The Affair of the Veiled Murderess* is an … excellent entry to the subject for the general reader."

— *H-Net Reviews, H-Law*

"…a must-read for mystery fans or anyone who enjoys the culture of mid-nineteenth century New York."

— *Hudson River Valley Review*

THE AFFAIR OF THE VEILED MURDERESS

THE AFFAIR OF THE VEILED MURDERESS

An Antebellum Scandal and Mystery

JEANNE WINSTON ADLER

excelsior editions
State University of New York Press
Albany, New York

Published by
STATE UNIVERSITY OF NEW YORK PRESS, ALBANY

Printed in the United States of America

For information, contact
State University of New York Press, Albany, NY
www.sunypress.edu

Excelsior Editions is an imprint of State University of New York Press

Production, Ryan Morris
Marketing, Fran Keneston

Library of Congress Cataloging-in-Publication Data

Adler, Jeanne Winston, 1946–
The affair of the veiled murderess : an antebellum scandal and mystery / Jeanne Winston Adler.
p. cm.
Includes bibliographical references.
ISBN 978-1-4384-3547-3 (hardcover : alk. paper) 978-1-4384-3548-0 (paperback : alk. paper)
1. Robinson, Henrietta, b. 1827. 2. Murder—New York (State)—Troy. I. Title.

HV6534.T76A35 2011
364.152'3092—dc22 2010031626

10 9 8 7 6 5 4 3 2 1

CONTENTS

PART FOUR
TRIAL, MAY 1854

PART FIVE
THE VEILED MURDERESS, JUNE 1854–AUGUST 1855

PART SIX
IRISH ANSWER, 1851 AND THE DEEPER PAST

PART SEVEN
LATER LIFE AND LEGEND, SEPTEMBER 1855–MAY 1905

PART EIGHT
CONCLUSION

ACKNOWLEDGMENTS

My thanks go to Lady Frances Eliott of Haworth, Scotland (of the Eliott family) and to Dennis Apedaile of Calgary, Canada, and William Reeve of Dunmow, Essex, England (of the Wood family) who kindly answered queries about William Francis Augustus Eliott and his wife Charlotte Wood Eliott (the alleged-by-some Murderess) and also shared their own family research and papers with me. In the same generous way, Kim Burdick of Wilmington, Delaware, a descendant of John C. Mather, supplied me with historical materials on the Mather family. And Charles Rommelt of Probst Investigations, Albany, donated his important handwriting analysis to the project—as a gift to Albany-Troy history.

Independent researcher Sylvie Tremblay of Quebec City, Canada, and the librarians of the Troy Public Library, Sage College Libraries, Emma Willard School, Rensselaer County Historical Society, Rensselaer County Court House, New York State Library and Archives, Albany Hall of Records, Albany Public Library, and Family Research Center of the Church of Latter-Day Saints in Loudonville all helped in tracking down the long-ago people and events described here.

A New York State Writer's Institute workshop, led by poet and nonfiction writer Ed Sanders, taught me to organize my information chronologically and present the story mainly that way. This approach allowed me to write up my research (mainly gathered in the 1990s!) at last. Thanks also go to Stacy Pomeroy Draper of the Rensselaer County Historical Society, Troy, and to Lucinda Carnahan of New York City for both reading several manuscript versions of the current book and offering valuable advice, and to James Peltz and Ryan Morris of SUNY Press for persevering with the publication of *The Affair of the Veiled Murderess* through many revisions. Finally, I must express my gratitude to author and editor Field Horne for his early confidence in this work. His continuing belief that it contains interesting and valuable material *quite outside the mystery of Henrietta Robinson's life* has been a special support.

INTRODUCTION:

TROY, NEW YORK, 1853

The city is in the early summer of its prosperity and industrial might. Located on the east bank of the Hudson River, six miles north of Albany, Troy faces the great river's meeting point with the Champlain and Erie canals. Since completion of the canals in 1825, raw produce from the North and West flows to Troy where it is "milled" and then re-shipped.

The Hudson itself and two tributaries, the Poestenkill and the Wynantskill, power many of the city's manufactures. There are planing mills for lumber, flouring mills for grain, and plastering mills that process chalky mounds of gypsum and lime. Live cattle disappear into Trojan packinghouses and reappear as barrels of salt beef bound for the warehouses of Troy's provision merchants. The hides head to the city's tanneries, and later to its boot and shoe factories. Animal pelts from Canada and the West supply factories devoted to the making of fur caps alone.

The endless stream of raw materials creates an almost endless number of industries in the city, though by 1853, Troy already takes its chief fame from two: iron and textiles. Troy's foundries, fed by canal barge-loads of coal and iron ore, make stoves, steam engines, railroad spikes, safes, iron fences, and many other things. The cotton and woolen factories get their bales of wool and some cotton from the canal route, too, though cotton also comes up the Hudson from New York City's seaport.

Visitors admire Troy's wide, straight streets and new brick and stone buildings. Reservoir water runs through iron pipes beneath the streets to corner hydrants as well as to fountains in private gardens and public squares. And after a disastrous experiment with an explosive substance called "camphene," the Troy Gas Company now supplies a reliable coal gas light to street lanterns and some houses in the central wards. But most visitors, and residents too, save their greatest admiration for the sheer bustle of the streets, in particular the riverfront commercial district forming the western edge of the Second and Third Wards. Here, canal-boat goods, Troy manufactures, and luxury imports are all offered up for sale along a six-block stretch of River Street. Storefronts and warehouses deal in coal, cotton, wire, rope, ploughs, shovels, ready-made clothing, "sheetings, shirtings, and rich calicos,"[1] looking glasses, feather beds, cornhusks and straw, French and Indian china, German violins and microscopes, gold watches, silver pens, and much more. Grocers and provision merchants dispense almonds and "Madeira Nuts," grapes and figs, oil, pickles, flour, salt meat and fish, butter, cheeses, tea, sugar, rum and whiskey. They crowd the sidewalks before their stores with boxes and barrels and hams hung from awning posts. Rafts of logs, tied up along the docks, make a floating lumberyard of much of the river, while steamboats and other craft disembark crowds of passengers at the Ferry Street and State Street boat landings, including parties of dazed Irish and Germans led along by "emigrant runners."

The mill-owners join with an older elite of Dutch merchants and landowners to support important educational and cultural ventures: the Rensselaer Institute, a college devoted to the sciences; Emma Willard's Troy Female Seminary, the nation's first academic high school for girls; and the Troy Young Men's Association, a lecture and debating society that also maintains an impressive lending library and art collection.

The new elite is very proud of the city's success, which they generally attribute to special qualities in their own Yankee blood. The fact of Troy's location at one end of the Erie Canal often seems to escape them. But they are not a complacent elite. They worry in print over the future of Troy's boom and urge fellow citizens to strive onward with "unwearied perseverance," "constant activity," and "untiring vigilance."[2]

Yet all their efforts can't prevent a period of crisis from overtaking the city in 1853. It's partly a crisis born out of success, the creaking and shifting of a growing community's tectonic plates, for Troy will go on to even more industrial and commercial achievements in the 1860s and 1870s. But the creaking and shifting, shared by other antebellum cities too, is definitely unpleasant. In Troy it means a bad cholera epidemic in the spring and summer of 1853—a direct result of overcrowding caused by a bounding population—off-and-on-again strikes by ironworkers from the summer of 1853 through the fall of 1855, and a factory fire in the summer of 1854 that destroys eight city blocks as undisciplined volunteer fire companies fight each other at the scene. It also means tensions between the old and new elites, evident in a bitter January 1853 struggle for leadership of the Young Men's Association.

The creaking and shifting of the state and nation press on the city, too. Hot-button issues of the day—slavery, immigration, temperance—split the established Whig and Democratic parties into factions, and in the spring of 1853 political infighting threatens one of Troy's leading citizens. This is John Cotton Mather, one of three New York State Canal Commissioners, as well as a possible Democratic candidate for New York State governor in

1854. In April 1853 a faction of his own party seeks his indictment and impeachment on charges of "dereliction" and "corruption." The Mather impeachment story fills the Troy newspapers into September.

In the middle of this slow-motion earthquake of change, something else happens. The new event—actually a series of events—springs from the environment of transition. The affair couldn't have taken shape anywhere else but in one of the United States' new industrial cities of the 1850s—at least, it couldn't have taken shape in the same way or to the same degree. Within a twelve-hour span on May 25–26, 1853, two Irish immigrants die in a riverfront neighborhood of Troy's Tenth Ward, after drinking poisoned beer. Suspicion falls on their drinking companion and neighbor, a single woman known as Mrs. Henrietta Robinson. After her arrest one explosion of scandal follows another. Robinson is the mistress or ex-mistress of John Cotton Mather, then just beginning to battle for his political life against the corruption charges.

As if this isn't sensation enough, little more than a week into June 1853, a rumor about another facet of Robinson's identity breaks into print. Mrs. Emma Willard of the Troy Female Seminary writes to the *Troy Daily Whig* newspaper to deny that Robinson is one of her former pupils: specifically that she is not one of four sisters, the Misses Wood, who attended the school in the 1830s and 1840s.

Everything seems to grow curiouser and curiouser as the imprisoned Henrietta Robinson, who proclaims her innocence, takes to wearing a heavy veil over her face—even within her jail cell—and her trial is repeatedly postponed.

What a situation! Today's *National Enquirer* and *The Star* would have been all over it, and Troy's papers and others farther afield in the 1850s did give the case a lot of play, especially throughout Robinson's trial in May of 1854 (at which she was found guilty) and then during renewed questions about the Wood family link which lasted at high intensity from end of trial through the summer of 1855. But for a range of reasons, reporters of the 1850s weren't all that thorough. They certainly didn't dig out the truth of the Veiled Murderess affair, as the scandal became known.

Sentenced to death in July of 1855, Robinson escaped hanging at almost the last moment thanks to a governor's reprieve. She then lived out her life in a series of New York prisons. She was very long-lived for her day, reaching either 79 years or 89 years—according to different accounts of her age—and she survived every other principal of her trial, except one: her most active defense counsel, Martin I. Townsend.

Up until Robinson's death in 1905, her story resurfaced from time to time in the newspapers with the focus always on the identity issue. Who was the Veiled Murderess? By the 1890s, an early (1855) rumor had crystallized into widely accepted fact. This rumor named the convicted woman as Charlotte Wood Eliott, Wood daughter No. 3 as well as runaway wife of Sir William Francis Augustus Eliott, Seventh Baronet of Stobs, Roxburghshire, Scotland. Rutherford Hayner, author of *Troy and Rensselaer County, N.Y.: A History* (1925), reconfirmed this view[3] though he also included a more cautious account of the affair in his three-volume work. Mrs. Della E. Stuart penned this second piece:

> In 1851 a woman calling herself Mrs. Henrietta Robinson came to Troy ostensibly looking for a position as teacher, which she failed to procure. She dressed well, but made few friends, living much by herself. After a few years of residence she was arrested for the peculiar murder of her grocer and his young woman clerk. Throughout her subsequent trial she aroused much curious comment by insisting on wearing a heavy blue vail [sic] which she refused to remove and came to be known as "the veiled murderess" . . .She served fifty-two years in Sing Sing prison, in Auburn State Hospital for the Insane and at Mattewan and at no time revealed her identity. It is said she never wrote a letter and never signed her name, but spent her days in reading, making fine lace and playing with much talent on the prison musical instruments. She died in 1905 and was buried in the Potter's Field at Mattewan. Her grave is marked only by a pine stake bearing the number "88" and the mystery of her life has never been solved.[4]

Stuart's paragraph represents the ultimate "tidying up" of the Veiled Murderess affair, with *all the sex* and *all the politics* edited out. But behind her vanilla-bland narrative, as behind Hayner's spicier legend, the real story still lives. And we can uncover it, in all its meaning and in most details, by operating like police detectives: gathering background information about players in the affair while working to establish a clear timeline. The timeline will hold important clues. We are police detectives with a difference. Our field of operations lies in a foreign country, the past, and the help of "local authorities" is absolutely necessary. These authorities are modern-day historians of antebellum society who supply insights into the world of the investigatees.

In the end, we see how political divisions, unease about women's changing roles, and just the "slipperiness" of identity in new urban centers combined to bloom one shocking crime into a half-century-long scandal and mystery. The sources of the crime itself come clear as well. A desperate situation, alcohol abuse, and (perhaps) past trauma overwhelmed one woman, semi-predictably in a way, but always *against* and *shaped* by the exotic nineteenth-century backdrop.

Yet this woman's, Robinson's, personal story actually recedes before the struggles of those around her: John C. Mather; Emma Willard and her son, John; earnest Canadian gentleman William Wood; feisty Troy editor John Francis; feminist celebrity Elizabeth Oakes Smith; and, as a shadowy presence, all-powerful Albany political boss Thurlow Weed; plus still more eminent people (the trial lawyers and doctors, in particular). The responses of these VIPs to the scandal make the chief drama, the scene that holds our eyes.

PART ONE

HENRIETTA ROBINSON

SPRING 1852–SPRING 1853

Henrietta Robinson, from David Wilson, *Henrietta Robinson*
(New York & Auburn: Miller, Orton & Mulligan, 1855)

The conveniently raised veil may be the lace mantilla of one of the "Spanish" dancers then popular, like Lola Montez—and thus, this picture was just a stock image available to the publishers. But there is some resemblance (eyes and nose, mostly) between this portrait and Robinson's late photograph (See page 222.)

1

RIVER STREET

In the spring of 1852 Henrietta Robinson was 26 years old—according to her own account.[1] Perhaps she was really as much as ten years older. She had a round, pretty face and vivid coloring: ink-black hair, blue eyes which sometimes looked black, and rosy, almost ruddy, cheeks. A late-in-life photograph hints that at this time, the early 1850s, Robinson may have worn her hair in an old-fashioned way, with crimped puffs or curls above the temples and the rest of the "glossy"[2] mass pulled into a high bun.[3] The up-to-date woman's hairstyle of the 1850s called for flat wings of hair curving down and back to a low bun. But Robinson dressed very fashionably. Wasp-waisted gowns with the skirts falling in a bell over layers of starched petticoats flattered her "fine form"[4] of the "middle height."[5]

Her wardrobe at about this time held three black silk dresses plus "one plaid silk dress, one embroidered silk dress, three satin dresses, one green rule silk, one linen traveling dress, one velvet dress, three morning wrappers, two velvet cloaks, three shawls, twenty-four handkerchiefs, and other articles of apparel in proportion."[6] In her expensive clothes, she moved and spoke with the "air and appearance of an accomplished lady."[7]

Sometime in early 1852, Henrietta Robinson arrived "at the Dam" in Troy, New York. "At the Dam" meant the riverfront district of the Tenth Ward close to the State Dam that spanned the Hudson River at the city's northern end. It was an area of large factories, strung out along the Hudson's high eastern shore and crowded round with poorly-built wooden houses for workers, most of them new immigrants from Ireland.[8] The district lay eight long blocks from the northern edge of the city's central core in the First, Second, and Third Wards. These wards held many of Troy's fine houses and churches and all of its fine shops—along with its courthouse, library, theaters, banks, main boat landings, and busy wholesale district. But some affluent people lived in the Tenth Ward, too, alongside their poorer neighbors (a situation soon to change). Troy of the 1850s was still mostly a "walking city,"[9] and mill owners as well as millhands lived near their workplaces. Oliver Boutwell, owner of a large flour mill which backed on the river and fronted on the north-south highway of River Street, was one of the wealthy Tenth Warders.[10] He occupied a three-story brick house on the northwest corner of River and Rensselaer Streets only a few lots south of his mill. Just north of Boutwell's home, a white-painted cottage, No. 627 River, perched on the riverbank, too.

In March or April (probably) Henrietta Robinson came to live at No. 627, accompanied by a single maid. She soon employed an outside gardener as well, to take care of No. 627's large front yard. The one-and-a-half-story cottage sat farther back from the street than Boutwell's house or the one or two dwellings then separating the cottage from Boutwell's mill. With its columned front porch and green lawn, Robinson's new home looked quaintly rural.

In 1855 after No. 627 River had become notorious, a journalist was surprised to find the address "a little abode of modesty," one which a stranger might "regard . . . as the home of humble and unpretending innocence." He noted the "tasty yard" and the pleasant, breezy location atop the river bluff. The journalist, David Wilson, an 1840 graduate of Schenectady's Union College as well as a recent state assemblyman (1852–1854) commented on the cottage's seclusion: "A large brick edifice [Boutwell's] hides it entirely from view as you approach from the south." Wilson suggested, fancifully—and given his knowledge of later events—that the house "had shrunk back from the street in order to avoid observation."[11]

He wrote of the interior: "It was furnished with taste and elegance." Wilson must have been guessing, since by the time he saw it, most of the furniture had been removed and "a poor family" lived there. But during Robinson's stay these furnishings included an upholstered sofa, a half-dozen upholstered or "sofa-bottomed" chairs, wooden rocking chairs, tables, looking glasses, a wardrobe, and the Victorian equivalent of wall-to-wall carpeting, wool rugs tacked down to within an inch or two of the walls. Henrietta Robinson also owned silver forks and at least one piece of ornamental silver, a fancy serving dish of pierced silver called a "cake-basket."[12]

She hardly ventured from her comfortable home for many months. It wasn't until the winter of 1852–53, perhaps after losing her lady's maid, that the mistress of No. 627 began to step out into the North River Street neighborhood. She frequented a grocery store and bar, Lanagan's, on the southeast corner of Rensselaer and River Streets. She bought groceries and liquor there and made friends with the owners, Timothy and Ann Lanagan, who had only arrived in the neighborhood that year as well. Soon Robin-

Oliver Boutwell & Son's Mills.

son was stopping daily at the corner store, and Ann Lanagan and her four children, whose ages ranged from six to twelve, paid visits to their attractive neighbor. The house at No. 627 River must have appeared fine to the eyes of the young Lanagans. Their own home, No. 622 River, was an unpainted wooden building of just two rooms: a front room, facing the street, which held the bar counter and grocery stock (barrels and boxes of tea, sugar, crackers, and a handful of other commodities) and a back "kitchen" where meals were prepared and where the family of six ate, slept, and carried out all other indoor activities.

The Lanagans belonged to a large clan that had arrived in the city at least six years earlier, though some members, including Timothy, had left their native Tipperary years before. His eldest son, William, had been born in England in 1840.[13] Timothy, who had craftsman's training as a shoemaker, was a man of some education.[14] He could read and write and keep accounts—no ordinary accomplishments for a Roman Catholic Irishman at this time, since most schools in Ireland educated Protestants only. His grocery and bar, opened in October of 1852, immediately played a lively part in the life of the Dam neighborhood. In March of 1853 the Lanagans held a dance there, the second one they had hosted since coming to River Street.

It wasn't a big affair; that was hardly possible in their two rooms. A single musician played for the dancers. A year later Mrs. Lanagan couldn't remember whether this man had been a piper or a fiddler, but it was one or the other. She did remember most of those present had been relatives or friends. We can imagine the scene: the sawdust or straw on the bare boards of the grocery and barroom floor; the smoke from the pipes of the men, who surely didn't waste money on more-expensive cigars; the warmth and firelight radiating from the dwelling's sole hearth or stove in the backroom.

Cheap oil lamps or tallow candles probably supplied more light—and more smoke and smell, too.

Henrietta Robinson came "to trade" on this evening and made her way past the swirling petticoats of the female dancers and the stamping boots of the male ones. After completing her purchases, she lingered, standing in the doorway between the kitchen and the public room. Her fine clothes and her bonnet—she never left home without one—set her apart from the Irish women present. They wore shawls or went bareheaded, according to one native-born Trojan observer of the day.[15] A young man named David Smith approached the fashionable lady in the doorway and asked her to dance. Ann Lanagan, behind the bar counter, heard Robinson refuse Smith. The pair proceeded to the counter where they continued to exchange remarks, more or less face to face with Mrs. Lanagan. Yet the mistress of the grocery-bar failed to hear any more of their conversation—or so she claimed—except its close. This was Henrietta Robinson's angry cry that Smith had insulted her.

"And she pulled her pistol out," said Ann Lanagan of the incident, "and said if he ever insulted her again she would blow his brains out. My husband came and said he didn't want any noise in the place—that they must leave from there. I went to her and told her to go home. I went along with her to her own door—told her to keep in her own place and nobody would insult her."[16]

But Robinson re-crossed the muddy or frozen cobbles of River and Rensselaer Streets that night and returned to the dance. Ann Lanagan remembered: "She called for the young man that insulted her. She asked if Smith was in there. She knocked at the door and asked the person who opened it. Smith went out and I heard nothing further." No one witnessed what then happened between Robinson and the young man, but we know David Smith was a bully and a troublemaker. A year later, in February of 1854, he and a companion would go to "the private ball at Harmony Hall . . . and not being admitted, commenced a tremendous row. They knocked down and badly injured the doorkeeper . . . and also struck Mr. Wm. Buswell and others. They were finally got rid of, and warrants have been issued for their arrest."[17]

One or two mornings later, very early, Mrs. Robinson stormed into the grocery and confronted Ann Lanagan. "She abused me very much then. She said I was a very mean woman, and that I kept rowdies in my house to insult her. She said she would get us turned out of the place and would not let us get any license to sell." The Troy Common Council issued licenses to grocers. The Council had denied licenses outright to all "foreigners" up until 1840, but this was no longer the case.[18] Also, Timothy Lanagan had probably become a naturalized citizen in 1851[19] (though his naturalization papers no longer survive) so the Lanagans may not have been overly afraid of Robinson's threat.

"I told her that I didn't want any bother with her—to go home. But she kept still talking. My husband got out of bed in the back room and told Mrs. Robinson that he wouldn't stand such noise, and that she must leave the house.

"She asked him if he wanted to turn her out when she was so good a customer.

"He said he didn't want her custom. He wanted to have her go away.

"She said she wouldn't leave, that he would have to get a constable to turn her out."

In the end Ann Lanagan convinced her one-time friend to return the short way across the River and Rensselaer intersection to her white cottage. But the incident marked the beginning of a string of troubled dealings between Robinson and her neighbors. She boycotted Lanagan's for at least three weeks after the dance, patronizing Peter Cox's grocery instead, which was located a little farther away, two "short" blocks to the east on North Second Street. (Troy was a "modern," planned city; in 1786 Jacob Vanderheyden, owner of the ferry crossing where the city would rise, laid out this part of his farmland in uniform lots forming rectangular, north-south-running blocks.) Cox sold hard liquor as well as beer, and Robinson may have begun to drink more heavily at this time.

"I expect she has got the worse for liquor sometimes," said Cox. "She generally got the best liquor I had: brandy. Sometimes she bought beer. Sometimes she would buy a half a pint of brandy, and at others a quart of beer—sometimes not so much."

Around this time Robinson tried to make a friend of Mary Jane Dillon, a pretty sixteen-year-old who worked as a dressmaker from her family home

Lock at State Dam, Troy.

at the corner of North First and Rensselaer. Robinson gave the girl sewing work and encouraged her to linger at the white cottage for long sessions of conversation. The older woman did most of the talking, seated on her sofa or on one of the "sofa-bottomed" chairs or perhaps even lounging atop the bed in her first-floor bedroom. She complained about her next-door neighbors, the Boutwells. Oliver Boutwell, himself, and members of his family had slandered her, she said, and a man had threatened "to lay violent hands upon her" at the house of Patrick Galvin, a Boutwell employee who lived close to the flour mill. Robinson also confided details of a romantic past life—though some of the details appeared to contradict one another. At one time she told Mary Jane Dillon she was the daughter of an Irish lord. At another time she said her father was a French lord.[20] She first claimed a cruel stepmother had driven her from her father's castle-door. Later she stated her own mother had wished her goodbye and given her a memento when her father had banished her for marrying a poor man. Dillon had a chance to examine the memento, a daguerreotype portrait, and found it odd. This example of the near-brand-new (1840s) technology of daguerreotypy showed a young woman, perhaps thirty years old, holding a bouquet of flowers. Yet Robinson maintained the woman was her mother and the flowers had been "gathered in the garden of the King of France."

She even gave two different accounts of a middle-aged man the young girl had once glimpsed inside the house at No. 627. At one point, Henrietta Robinson referred to this man as her husband, Mr. Robinson, a "contractor on the railroad." But at some later time, she identified him as Dr. Potter, a clergyman from Albany. Dr. Horatio Potter, a well-known minister of the day, became Episcopal bishop of New York in 1855.

Dillon generally enjoyed Mrs. Robinson's company, both her stories and her lively, often emotional manner. Henrietta Robinson had cried on producing the daguerreotype of the woman with the flowers, but then moments later had turned to lighter subjects and laughed and even danced about her carpeted parlor.

"The days I passed at her house were very pleasant a part of the time," remembered the young girl. But sometimes Robinson's conversation turned coarse. "It consisted of such language as ladies do not often use," said Dillon. And more plainly, "She used obscene words."

Doubtless Robinson used the words when talking about Oliver Boutwell and about another neighborhood man, Dr. G. E. Buswell. She had taken a violent dislike to Buswell, too, and told Dillon a disturbing story—especially disturbing in view of later events—about him. Buswell had given her some medicine, she said, which she suspected of being poison. She gave the potion to a neighbor's dog who died within half an hour. As a bizarre footnote to the story: "She then said she put the cork in the bottle and threw it in the river; that someone found it and brought it back to her . . . [and] she paid $5 for the dog."

The social relationship between Dillon and Robinson didn't last long—not more than a few weeks. The older woman's increasingly troublesome behavior was one cause of the break. Oliver Boutwell witnessed some of this bad behavior in mid- to late April: "I used to often see her in the streets, prior to May '53, when I thought she was the worse for liquor." The Dillon family had a closer view of Robinson's more and more disordered condition. She appeared at their door one night between eleven and twelve o'clock, first wanting one of Mary Jane's sisters to fetch Dr. Buswell for her husband who, she said, had arrived home ill. But she soon revealed her real purpose was "to get him [Dr. Buswell] to blow his brains out, as he was at her house the night before and insulted her." On one of the last days of April she arrived at the Dillons' again, early in the morning, wearing her nightgown and requesting the loan of a dress so she could "go down street and purchase a revolver and take out a warrant for Dave Smith." Mary Jane supplied the dress, which she sent a sister to retrieve later in the day.

In her agitated and apparently friendless condition, Henrietta Robinson reached out for help to city officials. On a rainy Sunday evening in late April, she walked eleven long blocks south to the Rensselaer County Courthouse at the corner of Congress and Second Streets in the Second Ward. This was a long, dirty, and slightly dangerous walk for a lone woman in 1853 Troy. Ladies' shoes were then most often delicate slippers tied onto the feet and ankles with ribbon. Wearing these with leather gaiters fastened over them to guard the shoe uppers and her stockinged ankles, Robinson had to pick her way around pools of foul mud at the street crossings. In addition to horse manure, Troy mud of the era often contained a fraction of human waste, slopped from the buckets and carts that regularly emptied "vaults" or privies of the still sewer-less city. Robinson also took care to avoid the knots of street toughs—called "short-boys" or "soap-locks" according to hair length (the long-haired used soft tallow soap to fix or "gel" their curls)—as well as the sometimes very large pigs ambling freely in their role as street cleaners. Gentlemen carried walking sticks, not to help them walk, but to deal with hoodlums or threatening animals, if necessary. Workingmen wore knives or whips tucked into their belts or boot-tops for the same reason, and women rarely walked unescorted. In fact, the simple act of walking alone constituted grounds for a woman's arrest on suspicion of prostitution at this time, with two women walking together not judged much better in the public eye.[21]

But Robinson reached the courthouse in safety and, after failing to find the Chief of Police, poured out her troubles to Edwin Brownell, Overseer of the Poor, who kept an office in the basement of the building.

"She said there had been a lot of rowdies about her house, that they had broke in, and they were going to attempt it again. She wished me to tell Mr. Copp [Amasa Copp, Chief of Police] to send up a policeman to protect her house.

"After she told me this, I went over to the residence of the Chief of Police, saw Mr. Copp, and returned. I had considerable conversation with Mrs. Robinson after I returned and told her she had better go home. The Chief of Police promised to send someone up to protect her. It was the request of the Chief of Police that I should try to get her home.

"She sat there nearly an hour. It rained quite hard and was dark, and she would not consent to go unless I went with her. She talked about a great many things after I returned to the office. She made a great many complaints, complained of rowdies attacking her. She said she had not been well attended to of late.

"I asked her who had neglected her.

"She replied, 'John C. Mather.' " This was John Cotton Mather, formerly a cotton wholesaler and now part owner of a brand-new Troy bank as well as a New York State canal commissioner. "She said she had not seen him for some time. She inquired of me if I was acquainted with him."

"I told her I was.

"She then asked me if I had heard he was going to be married to Judge Geer's daughter, attending the Seminary." The Troy Female Seminary, the first academic high school for women in the nation, had been founded by Connecticut-born Emma Willard in the 1820s and stood at this time very close to the courthouse building. The school's buildings occupied the west side of Second Street between Congress and Ferry Streets—closer to the Ferry Street end.

"I told her I had not. She said she was his lawful wife. I think she said she was married at his father's house, and he would have to avow it when he came back, or she would take his life. She asked me what I thought was the reason of his being away so long. I told her he was probably attending to breaks in the Canal. She declared herself devoted to him. I think she said she had not seen him in a week or two. During all this conversation Mrs. Robinson appeared to be laboring under a good deal of excitement. When I first saw her, I thought she was slightly intoxicated, and thought she was not entirely sober when I left her. I think she told me who the rowdies were who had been there. One of them was this David Smith. I went up home with her to the cottage next to Boutwell's. She showed me a revolver and two single-barreled pistols. I loaded them with powder and wad; she had powder and ball in her house. She showed me nothing particularly about the room but pointed me to some shirts she had done up; they were men's shirts. I think she stated they were Mr. Mather's. The shirts lay on a chair.

They were in the room connected with the parlor by folding doors in which there was a bed. She said that Mather had not been home in a week or two.

Henrietta Robinson told a different story to Brownell than to her neighbors. She didn't claim a "Mr. Robinson" for her husband but John C. Mather. Was Mather the middle-aged man seen at No. 627 by Mary Jane Dillon? Except for Henrietta Robinson's claim of a *legal* tie to Mather, everything else in the new story explained her situation perfectly. The comfortable home in the out-of-the-way neighborhood was a love nest. The important John C. Mather kept his mistress there. And Robinson's growing problem with "insults" stemmed, at least partly, from a growing recognition of her "fallen" state by her neighbors. The recent absence of her protector and economic lifeline, Mather, had only added to her worry and anguish.

It's not surprising Brownell took her fears of rowdies seriously enough to load her revolver and two pistols. In fact it's not surprising Henrietta Robinson owned the guns and had already brandished one in Lanagan's store. In cities of pre-Civil War America, workingmen often assaulted prostitutes or women they judged to be leading immoral lives. These were rarely sexual assaults. Typically the men just broke into the women's houses, beat them, and destroyed property.[22] The danger was real for women like Henrietta Robinson as, basically, there was no police force in the daytime. Only ten constables, one for each ward, worked to keep the peace in a community of nearly 30,000 persons. After dark, Amasa Copp's night police force of 60 non-uniformed men patrolled the streets—their only badges of office special city-issued hats—but newspaper editors regularly noted the timid behavior of solitary night police officers.[23]

Sometime after Mrs. Robinson's nightgowned visit to the Dillon house, she called there again and Mary Jane turned her away. Three days later the woman appeared once more. "She came in and said she had a warrant for me, that I had slandered her. I asked her what I had said about her. She made no reply, but came up and kissed me and asked me to forgive her."

Henrietta Robinson had employed Mary Jane's father, Henry Dillon, as a gardener. But now after the break with the family, she hired another elderly neighborhood man, a Mr. Haley, to take charge of the "tasty yard." Her maid was long gone, and she took Haley to live with her in the house, probably as an added security measure.

On Saturday night, May 21, Robinson walked the eleven blocks south to Congress Street again. She went on the arm of the white-headed Mr. Haley, but still did not present a very respectable appearance. A 24-year-old druggist, John H. Knickerbocker, encountered her on the corner of First and Congress Streets, between ten and eleven o'clock according to his later recollection. "My attention was drawn to her as acting like a very droll woman; she was with an old man and walking very slow. She asked me to direct her to Mrs. Brewster's boarding house." Knickerbocker knew Mrs. Brewster's well. He boarded there himself, as did John C. Mather. He gave Robinson directions to the house that stood on the corner of Second and Ferry Streets, directly across Second from the Troy Female Seminary.

Edwin Brownell, the official Robinson had spoken with about a week earlier, spotted her and overheard the conversation with Knickerbocker, though he put the time of the exchange at nine o'clock. "She was dressed rather in disguise, as I thought," recalled Brownell. "She had a white sun bonnet on. She was rather negligently dressed—had a loose dress." He reacted by quickly ducking out of sight. "I then passed along [in]to the hall of Seymour & Romeyn's office . . . she was going in the direction of his [Mather's] boarding house on the corner of Ferry and Second Streets." Even if Troy's overseer of the poor did not jump to the conclusion Robinson was on her way to shoot John C. Mather, as she had threatened in his office, Brownell evidently feared a scene or trouble of some kind.

The same sense of coming drama sparked a different reaction in Knickerbocker. The younger man followed Robinson to Second Street to take in any "droll" events about to happen there. "I turned down that street to the east, a little way—not so but what I could see Mrs. Brewster's door. I think the old man first went up and rang the bell. Afterwards, she went up. She then stepped back and met me and told me, 'You see I am prepared not to be followed!' and drew out a pistol . . . I had an opportunity of seeing Mrs. Robinson's countenance, I suppose by the gaslight, as there is a lamp on that corner. Her countenance was very much excited and unsettled in appearance." The incident ended here. Knickerbocker backed off, and Robinson and her companion walked homeward with her mission, whatever it had been, unfulfilled.

Knickerbocker didn't see Mather at all that night. The canal commissioner had been in Washington, D. C., for the past ten days, along with other Troy Democrats—all of them petitioning the new Democratic administration of President Franklin Pierce over local patronage jobs. (In the nineteenth century, new administrations didn't take office until March 25, the archaic New Year's date of Annunciation Day). Pierce's new secretary of state was William Marcy, onetime Troy lawyer and newspaper editor and the man who famously said, "to the victor belong the spoils of the enemy" to justify political or party appointments. In mid-May Mather and others essentially camped out in and around Marcy's office to win jobs for their friends and supporters.

The canal commissioner may have consulted Marcy about his own political troubles, too. Since April a faction of New York Democrats had made moves to impeach Mather in the New York State Senate, charging him with "dereliction" and "corruption" in his handling of canal affairs. Basi-

Rensselaer and Saratoga Railway Bridge.

cally, one wing of the Democratic Party wanted to stop new cash outflows on the canal system—expenditures already voted into law under a Whig state administration in 1851. But the partly impersonal origins of the charges didn't help the immediate target, and Mather had to fight for his political life through most of 1853.

Moses Warren, Democrat and Troy police court judge,[24] ran into Mather in Washington, and though they didn't travel together, the two men took the same train home, arriving at Troy on Saturday evening, the 21st. Knickerbocker believed Mather had spent the night at Mrs. Brewster's, though interestingly, he thought "Mather occupied the room formerly occupied by Mr. Root on that evening. Mr. Root was then absent on a foreign tour." And "he [Mather] left soon after his returning." Had John C. Mather returned home after Henrietta Robinson's visit, and then made a point of not sleeping in his usual room and quitting the boarding house as soon as possible?

In the mid-1840s Troy newspapers had carried many stories about Amelia Norman, a young woman who had stabbed her middle-class seducer on the steps of the fashionable Astor Hotel in New York City. At about this same time, a similar attack went terribly wrong in Troy—or at least that was the story told many years later. An unknown assailant struck down and killed a well-respected man as he walked home one evening, and "B., the painter" left town right afterwards. As an old man explained towards the end of the century: "B. was not the murderer, but he had compromised himself with a very energetic female, and he went away about that time to avoid trouble with her. She had, in company with her brother, threatened him with violence and he feared her. Just before going he called . . . and as he looked so haggard and worried, I could not help asking him the cause of it, and this drew from him the secret of his escapade. As he was leaving, he turned to ask me the question if I thought he looked like the murdered man . . . Did it ever occur to you how much he resembled the murdered man?"[25]

So there were frightening precedents for Mather to consider in his relations with his well-armed mistress. But though Knickerbocker hinted otherwise, Mather may have acted without any thought of Henrietta on the 21st and 22nd, simply falling into whatever bed Mr. and Mrs. Kittle, the actual operators of "Brewster's," offered him on his late-night return home and then hurrying away the next morning on business. A great deal of pressing business hung over John C. Mather as Troy papers now carried almost daily articles about his impeachment.

Years and years later, someone noted of Henrietta Robinson "read[s] but a very little."[26] Maybe if she'd been more of a reader, she wouldn't have feared Mather was leaving her for Miss Geer in the spring of 1853. Throughout the spring Troy newspapers not only ran accounts of his trips to Washington—he'd spent a good deal of time there in March, too—but discussed the growing impeachment crisis. (The Senate would formally indict Mather on June 22, citing fourteen separate "high crimes and misdemeanors.") So he had much to occupy him and keep him away from No. 627 River Street—even if he wanted to visit his Henrietta.

2

MAY 25

In 1853 Troy experienced an unusually cold, wet spring. A chill rain fell on Sunday, May 22, the day after Robinson's visit to the boarding house, and again heavily on Monday night. Tuesday began clear and fine, but another storm swept in later that day. On Wednesday morning at six o'clock, drizzle still dampened the city as Henrietta Robinson left her house and walked to Lanagan's. It was one hour past dawn, and wagons loaded with country produce clattered down River Street on their way to the city markets at Fulton and River and, a block farther south, in triangular Washington Square, formed by the meeting of Broadway, Second, and River Streets. Though the factory hands, both men and women, didn't begin their 12-hour workday until 7:00 A.M., some workers already moved along the roadway, outside the path of teams and wagons, but clear of the miry gutters at each verge.[1] Clothed in the homespun linen or wool of the Irish and Yankee countrysides, they called out to one another in loud, carrying country voices. Henrietta Robinson, in her more upscale garb, proceeded more sedately (we imagine) among them. At Lanagan's grocery she bought a quart of "strong beer" and a pound of soda crackers that she carried home. About two hours later she sent the old man, Haley, to the grocery to ask for a loan of two dollars.

"Mrs. Robinson kept an account with us," remembered Ann Lanagan. "She paid her bills when requested to. She used to borrow money of us and always paid it again." Yet on this occasion: "I did not let him [Haley] have it. I had the money in the house, but did not want to let her [Robinson] have it."

As Lanagan spoke with Haley, Mrs. Robinson suddenly appeared. "She asked the old man Haley what kept him so long?"

"I answered that I had delayed him." And then, lying: "that I had no money in the house, and that I thought I would send and see if I could not borrow some."

Washington Square, 1845.

"She asked me was I so scarce of money?"

"I said yes."

"She said she was sorry, but that she would lend me a hundred dollars tomorrow. She left the place then and went away."

During their conversation, Haley had told Mrs. Lanagan his employer "had everything in the house that she wanted." He didn't know why she had sent him for the two dollars. So the request must have been a test—to see if the Lanagans would still oblige her in this way. And Henrietta Robinson came up empty-handed. She tried once more for sympathy or some acknowledgment a little later:

"I saw her again on that day about eleven o'clock [A.M.]" said Ann Lanagan. "She came in the grocery again. She told me she was in great trouble; that she had a telegraph a few minutes ago that Robinson got hurt on the cars." People then referred to railroad trains casually as "the cars." Later Ann Lanagan made it plain her neighbor was talking about a fatal accident. Was this an attempt to explain "Mr. Robinson's" absence as well as a bid for sympathy? If so, Henrietta Robinson had now given up hope of her lover's return and had decided to claim the status of a widow. But her story of the accident met an insulting wall of disbelief.

"There was a man stood by who told her not to fret; that his wife was in the west, and that if she was dead he would not fret until he saw her." This man implied, pretty openly, he considered "Mr. Robinson" an imaginary husband.

"She then turned away from the counter and went inside to the kitchen off the grocery. She stopped in the kitchen some time. There was a lot of men sitting on the inside there when she went in, and there was loud talking. I do not know who the men were that was talking. I could hear Mrs. Robinson's voice. I did not hear what was said." As on the night of the dance, Ann Lanagan strangely failed to hear the words of dramatic, or at least loud, confrontations in her two-room home and place of business.

"She [Robinson] went into the kitchen again before she left. I told her to go home. It was no place for her to be there among such a lot of men. She left after a little time."

Henrietta Robinson remained within her cottage for some two hours, her thoughts surely dwelling on the rebuff and slights of the morning.

"I saw her [Mrs. Robinson] again that day about one o'clock," recalled Ann Lanagan. "She came through the grocery into the kitchen. My husband and Catharine Lubee was in the kitchen at this time. Catharine's sister was married to a brother of mine. Miss Lubee had been at our house seven or eight days. She was twenty-five or twenty-six years of age, unmarried, and resided, when at home, in Albany. She did not lodge with us; she stopped in the daytime with me and went to Mr. James Lanagan's [Timothy's cousin] to lodge nights, as I had no bed for her. Mrs. Robinson knew Miss Lubee; she got acquainted with her at my place." Catharine Lubee, who worked as a maid, was between jobs in May of 1853.

"She [Robinson] said, 'Are you at dinner?' "

"I said, 'Yes.' "

"There was an egg on the table and she asked whose egg that was. My husband said it was hers if she wanted it. She took the egg in her hand and my husband stood up and went into the grocery. She set down to the table and eat [*sic*] the egg, and I peeled a potato for her."

"She said we should have a glass of beer from her."

"I declined and Miss Lubee said she didn't like beer." Clearly, Henrietta Robinson was an unwelcome guest, yet the Lanagans treated her very gingerly. Were they already afraid of her—of her sometime threats and of the revolver she waved about? "She said she would not leave the house until we had the beer. She then asked me if I had got any sugar in the house."

"I told her I thought she did not want any, as she had got nine pounds during the week."

"She said she didn't want to take it home; she wanted to put it in the beer to make it good."

"I took a saucer and went into the store and brought in some sugar. It was white, powdered sugar. After I brought in the sugar, I went out for the beer; I brought some in a quart measure. I poured it into two glasses."

"Mrs. Robinson was walking the floor with her saucer in her hand when I came in with the beer. Mrs. Robinson said she would have the two glasses full."

"I went back and brought in some more beer from the grocery. When I came in with the second beer, Mrs. Robinson was pouring the sugar in the two glasses. I poured in the remainder part of the beer and filled the glasses." These were big drinks; each glass must have held at least two pints. But the beer the women were preparing to drink was "small beer" (according to one later newspaper report) not the "strong beer" purchased that morning by Mrs. Robinson.

"I sat down to the table to take my glass of beer," said Ann Lanagan. "Mrs. Robinson was standing beside me. There were two glasses of beer. The other stood before Catharine. I noticed a little foam that was upon the top of the beer, and I thought it was some dust from the sugar. I took a teaspoon in my hand to take it off."

"She [Mrs. Robinson] took the spoon out of my hand and said, 'Don't you do so; that is the best of it.' Mrs. Robinson, when invited to partake of the beer, said she didn't feel like taking any at present."

"My beer was already to drink, when my husband called me and I went to wait upon him. He wanted to go downtown as far as Mr. Morrison's. I went into the grocery [as Timothy Lanagan returned back into the kitchen]. I turned round to the door and saw the glass of beer in my husband's hand; he was just putting it to his lips to take it. Mrs. Robinson left a few minutes after."

Before Timothy Lanagan departed for Morrison and Lord's, a wholesale grocery and liquor dealer near the corner of Federal and River Streets, both he and Catharine Lubee were already feeling slightly ill.

Burr Lord, co-owner of Morrison and Lord's, saw Lanagan between 1:30 and 2:00 P.M. "He came down, I suppose, to look at some beef. I think he stayed about five or ten minutes; he didn't make a purchase. He said he was very sick; he looked sick. His eyes looked bad and his lips looked blue."

Lanagan made his way home alone where he found Catharine Lubee also very ill, lying upon the one bed in the kitchen. Henrietta Robinson had returned yet again and was hovering nearby. Catharine had already directly accused the woman of having "put something in the beer."

"Mrs. Robinson [had] answered that she put nothing in it but something that would do her good," remembered Ann Lanagan.

"At that time," Mrs. Lanagan continued, "my husband came in and laid down on the sofa. He was very bad, hardly able to speak. My husband said to send for the doctor as he was 'done for.' I sent a man named William Buckley. I turned round and asked Mrs. Robinson, 'What have you done? You have killed the father of my children!' "

"She said, no, she would do no such thing. She thought to go over to speak to him."

"I put my hand against her and told her to go away. Lanagan's mother also came in and helped put her outdoors. My husband put up his hands and said, 'Go, woman, go!' "

Catharine soon tottered away to her bed at James Lanagan's house. Then, said Ann Lanagan, "My husband was so sick that Buckley had to take him in his arms and lay him in bed. I was crying and he told me not to fret. I must make the best of it now that he was 'done for.' "

As Mrs. Lanagan tried to help her stricken husband, she heard from Henrietta Robinson one more time. Mr. Haley brought an urgent request that the grocery-bar's proprietress visit his employer at the cottage as soon as possible. "I told him I could not go," said Ann Lanagan, not surprisingly. Her husband "rolled" upon his bed in pain in a crowded sickroom.

"His wife, mother, father, brother, sisters, and children were in the room," recalled Dr. Adams who arrived to attend Lanagan at about 3:30 P.M. By 5:00 P.M., Dr. A. J. Skilton had joined Adams in the fight to save the grocery-bar owner. Skilton encountered "a great number of people" in the house—both family and friends of the sick man. A French Catholic clergyman was also present. Lanagan was in a bad way from the first. His symptoms struck the doctors as particularly violent.

According to Adams: "He complained of pain in the stomach and bowels, a burning sensation in the throat. Other symptoms were vomiting and severe evacuations of the bowels. Mr. Lanagan told me he thought he should not recover. [His] expression was that 'the villain had destroyed him' and he should not recover."

"I had no expectation after seeing him of his recovery. [Yet] I told him I thought he ought not to despair—he might recover. I was then adapting remedies for his relief. None of them as I could perceive relieved the pain."

"He continued to take my medicine and I continued to labor for his recovery. He helped himself in and out of bed until within a half hour previous to his death; he continued to converse until within a few minutes of his death. His mother knelt down by the bed and prayed; this was a half hour before his death. His decease was very sudden."

Both doctors had hurried to James Lanagan's a short distance away at about 5:30 P.M. to see Catharine Lubee. She then showed milder symptoms than Lanagan, and the two medical men remained with her for only about twenty minutes—until after Timothy Lanagan's death at 6:30 or 7:00 P.M. when they returned. On their second visit they lingered at the woman's bedside for just ten minutes. Everyone seemed to think Catharine would recover.[2]

Very near the time of Timothy Lanagan's death, Henrietta Robinson entered Ostrom's drugstore at the corner of River and Federal Streets—

"considerably south of Mrs. Robinson's," commented one of the store's owners, William Ostrom.

"Between five and seven o'clock, when I came in from tea, I found her in the store, very much excited," recalled Ostrom. "She looked around apprehensively. She was very nervous and was not in one position any length of time, but walking all over the store. Her dress was in disorder." Robinson wore a short, loose wrap called a "Jenny Lind" above her skirt, a garment antebellum women usually saved for at-home use when relaxing without corsets.

"She said she was in trouble and had been charged with poisoning a couple of persons. I think she mentioned Lanagan's name, for one, and said they resided opposite where she did.

"I asked her why they should suspect her of the crime.

"She said she supposed it was out of revenge because she would not lend them a hundred dollars; she did not want to draw that amount out of the bank in the absence of Mr. Robinson. She said she had gone over to the grocery in search of her gardener, and that while there she was about drinking beer with Mrs. Lanagan and others. There was some confusion about the handling of tumblers and Mr. Lanagan was taken sick and they accused her of putting poison in the beer. She said she was very much in fear of the neighborhood and wanted my advice as to what she should do to be protected." (How smoothly and plausibly Robinson twisted the interchange about the hundred dollar loan!)

"She had a revolver with her. I probed it with the handle of a pen. I found at least one barrel loaded. There were three or four percussion caps on the hammer of the pistol, but the lock was so rusty that I doubt if it could be fired off."

Robinson left the drugstore within half an hour and went into a neighboring shop, Perkins Cabinet Store. Here, "between six and seven o'clock that afternoon," Officer Charles Burns arrested her.

"I did not observe what she was doing particularly in Perkins' shop," said Burns. "When I went into the store, she asked me if I was a police officer. I told her I was. I took her to jail on foot.

"She said nothing in relation to this difficulty. She excused herself on the way to jail for appearing in the dress she did—it being a wet, muddy day. I mean to say, she talked somewhat lightly. She asked me if I was not going to take her to the Recorder's office." The recorder, a kind of vice-mayor, who like Poormaster Edwin Brownell had an office in the courthouse, served partly as a police court judge dealing with minor infractions.

"I told her, yes. I brought her down Albany to Fifth and to the jail. This was a course nearly opposite that [leading to] the Recorder's office, but she made no remarks as to the course I took her. When I got on the corner of Ferry and Fifth Streets, I told her there was the place. I supposed she thought it was the courthouse."

But Henrietta Robinson now recognized her shameful destination and took measures to avoid any scornful public notice.

"The corner opposite the jail is known as Murphy's corner," explained Charles Burns. "There was quite a number of boys standing on [this] corner.

"She asked me if she could not walk up the hill a little ways [alone]. She went up as far as the first brick house and then she came back again so as not to be seen going into jail with me. When she passed by the jail [the second time], she stood into the hall—just so as I could see her. She seemed quite surprised when she went into the jail."

Inside the jail building Burns found Henrietta Robinson carried two pistols or revolvers "in her bosom"—the one Ostrom had just examined plus another. She resisted handing them over and the jailer, John Price, and one of his men, George Kennedy, had to help Burns wrestle them away. At this time Burns also took a small piece of "white wrapping paper" from one of Robinson's pockets. The paper bore no markings of any kind, and Burns judged it of no importance. He promptly threw it away.

At 9:00 P.M. Rensselaer County coroner, 29-year-old Dr. Reed Bontecou, met with a hurriedly-called coroner's jury at James Lanagan's. There the all-male panel took a bedside deposition from Catharine Lubee. Her story was chilling—and quite damning for Robinson. Catharine described how she first "refused to drink, but being pressed, drank, and was urged to take the sugar." According to Lubee, Mrs. Robinson showed particular concern she consume every bit of sugar from the glass: "Mrs. Robinson took the spoon which contained the dregs of the tumbler and forced it into the mouth of the witness [Catharine Lubee]."[3]

From James Lanagan's on North First Street, Bontecou went back downtown to the jail, located a block south and three blocks east of the courthouse. Though Officer Burns had taken the revolvers and the scrap of paper from Robinson earlier, he evidently didn't think it proper to search her clothing further. This job awaited Bontecou, a medical doctor. Bontecou didn't make a very thorough or intimate search by modern standards. He just patted down her clothing in a room filled with a small crowd of policemen and jailers ("Francis Bowman, Charles Burns, Nathan Camp, and the officers of the prison, and there may have been other persons present").

"I told her I had come to search her person," remembered Bontecou. "I forget what reply she made.

"She was laughing at that time. She replied to the remark, but it [her reply] was not touching the subject. She facilitated the search by raising her hands. She offered no resistance.

"I considered her dressed rather unusually at that time; her eyes had an unnatural, wild appearance; her countenance an unusual expression."

While some of Troy's public buildings contained interior gaslights in 1853, the then thirty-year-old jail was not one of them. Lanterns and "tallow dips" served as the only lighting in the first-floor cells.[4] Did Bontecou's encounter with the wild-eyed Robinson take place in one of these shadowy cells? Or did the new prisoner wait in some brighter reception room, lit by kerosene lamp?

Anyway, it was a dark and eerie journey Dr. Bontecou soon made through the streets of Troy. His frisking of Mrs. Robinson had turned up her house key. So Bontecou and the night policemen, Burns, Bowman, and Camp, set out immediately for the home of the suspected murderess. If they traveled by carriage, they soon left the illuminated central district behind, and with raised lanterns and occasional shouts to warn other street traffic, plunged into the sleeping thoroughfares of North Troy. At No. 627 River, they entered Robinson's quiet home, lantern light bouncing against the walls and excited voices sounding through the cottage's rooms.

Charles Burns: "We searched in the garret, and from the garret to the cellar, and all through the house. I found some arsenic there under the corner of the carpet; it was done up in a piece of white paper. Dr. Bontecou took it. It was found in a middle room of the house where there was a bed [Bontecou described this room as the "back parlor"]. It was about four inches under the edge of the carpet, near the corner of the room, laid up close to the wall. The carpet was tacked down.

"I believe there was a paper of Spanish flies found there, and a box of jewelry and a locket. Also at the same place—under the carpet—I found a watch and chain. The watch and chain, I think, was in the box; I am not certain as to the locket. There were several other articles of jewelry, breastpins, earrings, and other articles."

The arsenic hidden under the carpet looked incriminating, plain and simple. The paper of Spanish flies signaled to contemporaries that Robinson was a courtesan or prostitute. Spanish fly or *cantharides* had been acclaimed as an aphrodisiac since ancient times—falsely so, according to modern science. Antebellum apothecaries ground up quantities of the small, bright-green beetle, native to Mediterranean Europe, to produce a green powder often converted into little green pills. Burns' "I believe there was a paper of Spanish flies . . ." expresses some doubt, so perhaps the night policeman only conjured up this packet to jibe with his opinion of Mrs. Robinson and her house. If there *was* a packet of *cantharides* in the downstairs bedroom of No. 627, Robinson could have used it for a non-aphrodisiac purpose. Instead of slipping love stimulants to the canal commissioner, she might have taken the stuff herself as a contraceptive. A popular marriage manual of the day, Hollick's *Marriage Guide* (1850) recommended Spanish fly as a birth control pill for women.[5] (Modern science rejects this, too.)

What about the jewelry under the carpet? Anyone might hide their valuables under their bed—Burns later made it clear the "room . . . where there was a bed" was Henrietta Robinson's first-floor bedroom—but the searchers first judged these valuables to be guilty loot. Two days later, on Friday, May 27, the editor of the *Troy Daily Whig* would write: "We learn that a large number of stolen goods were found in her [Robinson's] residence, consisting of silverware, boots, shoes, &c., to the value of over one thousand dollars. From this it would seem that her house was a rendezvous for thieves and blacklegs [swindlers] . . ."

3

THE NEW PRISONER

On Thursday morning, the 26th, Coroner Bontecou held a second inquest over the bodies of Lanagan and the now-deceased Lubee, who had died at 5:00 a,m, that morning. "Quite a number were present," commented Bontecou later. "The jury and Drs. Skilton and Seymour." Either both bodies now lay at the late Timothy Lanagan's or else the jury first visited James Lanagan's house where Catharine had expired. At 9:00 a.m. they began work on Catharine's remains and then moved on to Timothy's.

"I took the stomach from the body [of Timothy Lanagan] myself," said Bontecou. As the jurymen and other doctors watched the operation, Dr. Seymour found "a white powder mixed up in the muca [*mucosa*] of the stomach of the man." The stomachs of both Lanagan and Lubee were placed in jars for examination by Dr. Bontecou at his own home-office. The coroner also took charge of the grocery-bar's sugar box, found on a shelf behind the bar counter, and packed this away for later analysis. He didn't bother to carry away any sample of the beer.

"I tested the beer at Lanagan's by drinking it," he later stated. "It produced no very unpleasant effect. It did not kill me. I think there was no poison in it." Ann Lanagan drew drafts from the beer barrel for several of the jurymen, too. They must have been pretty sure the liquid straight from the barrel was poison-free. Still, their casual approach surprises today. And the fact Ann Lanagan drew the beer makes us wonder where she was during the home-autopsy.

On the heels of this second inquest, as after the previous night's inquest, Bontecou visited Henrietta Robinson in the Ferry Street jail. His visit took place late in the "forenoon," likely at the same time Sheriff John Price, Deputy Sheriff Dr. William Hegeman, and a lawyer named Richard Jennyss also saw the prisoner. Jennyss claimed to be on a private mission that had nothing to do with his professional life:

Orrs & Co's Paper Mills.

"I went to see Mrs. Robinson as a friend of Mr. Mather. I [had] heard his name made use of in connection with hers prior to the arrest. I had also heard that she had letters of his, and to avoid the scandal that might arise from an exposure of these letters, I went to her to see if I could get them."

Jennyss found Robinson "excited and strange" and unable to "converse connectedly." Was Robinson too disturbed to communicate with Jennyss at all? Perhaps, but perhaps not. Jennyss later admitted that, though he never got any of Mather's letters, Robinson agreed to hand them over, and possibly gave her agreement on this very day.

"I asked her if she would sign an order for the letters," remembered Jennyss.

"She wanted to know what that was, and then started off on something else. She said she could not write her name."

"I asked her if she would consent that I should write her name for her. She consented that I might. I am not certain whether I did or not. I think I or Dr. Hegeman wrote the name—wrote Henrietta Robinson. I can't tell how the order read. It was given I think on the Coroner or some other officer. It was written to the bearer, but the order was protested. My impression is, this was written a week after the arrest; don't know but it was the first day after."

Jennyss' first visit accomplished one purpose. It alerted jailors and coroner to Robinson's special status as friend of Troy's most powerful Democrat—or at least confirmed that status for them.

"She [Henrietta Robinson] stayed in the room usually occupied by women the first night she entered," reported Hegeman. But, "On the morning of the 26th, I saw her, and the Sheriff or myself asked if she would not like to have another room? She was then placed upstairs in the room she now occupies." Bontecou offered to bring clothes to the disheveled prisoner and furniture from No. 627 River to make the new, private cell comfortable. The second-floor room was sizable for it soon held much of her furniture: at least three tables, a rocking chair and five other chairs, a bed, a wash-stand, a wardrobe—along with trunks, carpets, dishes, and other items. This was special treatment and no doubt about it. Hegeman even left the door of Robinson's room unlocked during daylight hours, only locking it about 8:00 or 9:00 P.M.

Hegeman and Bontecou also judged Robinson to be disturbed on the morning of the 26th. "Her dress was very disordered," remembered Hegeman, "hanging loose on her, muddy and dirty. Her eyes had an unnatural appearance; her countenance seemed to be expressionless. She did not seem to realize her condition." While admitting he "had no conversation to any extent with her at that time," Hegeman found "her remarks whenever she did make any were disconnected; she seemed irritable, solemn. When she was sitting she would apparently be very quiet; when she got up her movement seemed quick and impulsive."

According to Bontecou: "The state of her mind was much the same as the evening before; she acted very strangely at this time; her answers to the questions put to her were not satisfactory." And: "there was a wild, unnatural appearance to her eyes." Yet unlike Deputy Sheriff Hegeman, Dr. Bontecou did not see anything odd in her movements: "Her actions were not very peculiar—I mean her gesticulations."

All three men, Jennyss, Hegeman, and Bontecou, gave their descriptions of Robinson during the same window of time: her week-long trial for murder in May of 1854, as defense lawyers argued for acquittal on the grounds of insanity. Maybe significantly, the first published reports of the crime contain no mention of insanity. On the afternoon of the 26th, news of the North Troy deaths reached the city as a whole through the pages of at least two afternoon papers. The *Northern Budget*'s Page Two headline shouted: "Poisoning Case! Two Persons Dead!" (Page Two was the chief news page in the four-page newspapers of the day.) The *Budget* reporter wrote of "a woman of bad character named Robinson" and "Mrs. Robinson, as she calls herself" in an article outlining most of the known facts in the case. He (without question the writer was a he) drew a picture of the accused as a low, criminal culprit: "It is not known what induced the woman Robinson to commit this double murder. A report is current that she had an 'old grudge' against Lanagan, and she thought it about time and this a good way to obtain revenge! . . . She is said to be a married woman, but it is not generally believed. She was well known in the neighborhood as being a woman of very bad reputation and of desperate character; and it is a matter of surprise that Lanagan, who knew her well, did not have some suspicion of her purpose when she was giving him the fatal dose. She is about 30 years of age, has a very good appearance, but seems to be indifferent as to what she has done or what may be her own fate."

The *Troy Daily Times* ran a longer article under the headline, "Horrible; Double Murder by Poisoning," but presented Robinson and her case in the same way. The *Times* even added to the "low and criminal" portrait of Robinson. Their writer noted "the quantity of goods supposed to be stolen" found in Robinson's home and also raised the issue of her probable drunkenness on May 25: ". . . she was evidently laboring under the effects of strong drink." The *Times* article gave a slightly fuller, slightly more hostile description of Robinson: "She is about forty years of age, rather good looking, and has a foreign air. She claims to be French, but is undoubtedly English by birth." The *Times* confirmed Robinson's earlier complaints about community attacks:

"She has lived at the place mentioned ["nearly opposite Lannigan's in a cottage adjoining the residence of O. Boutwell"] something over a year, apparently private, but she was generally supposed to be a public woman. Her manner of late had attracted the attention of the neighborhood, and attempts have been made to drive her out of it. She manifested considerable spirit in resisting their efforts and frequently threatened to use her revolvers with which she was well supplied."

On the 27th a morning paper, the *Troy Daily Whig*, ran an article half again as long as the *Times*'s Thursday piece. Their soberly-titled "Poisoning Case in This City; Coroner's Verdict; Statement of Facts" repeated the stolen goods charge and also mentioned the battles between Robinson and her neighbors:

"Mrs. Robinson is a woman of the most ungovernable temper and high spirits which she has very frequently manifested to the injury of her neighbors. Her character was not, until recently, discovered by those residing in her immediate vicinity, and several attempts have recently been made to expel her from the neighborhood, but all these she has repelled."

The *Whig* introduced one new fact: "*The spite borne by Mrs. Robinson was against Mrs. Lanagan* [modern italics] and she had no reason for injuring either of the unfortunate victims of her fiendish designs."

The *Whig* reporter thanked "Mr. G. W. Vallance" for "assisting us to collect the . . . facts." Vallance lived two long blocks south of the Rensselaer and River Streets intersection, where he owned and operated a "Butt Factory" on the riverbank (these "butts" were metal door-hinges). Timothy Lanagan's uncle, Dennis, and at least three of Timothy's cousins, James, William, and Richard, all worked as "buttmakers" at Vallance's.[1] Timothy, himself, had worked there briefly in 1851, before leaving the factory to open his grocery-bar. Thus Vallance had likely gotten his information from the Lanagans or from their friends and co-workers at the factory. And the Lanagan family was in a position to know the details of the quarrel with Robinson.

The coroner's jury had gathered again on Thursday evening, the 26th, to deliberate and issue a verdict. The Whig, rushing to press that night, just squeaked the verdict finding into their morning edition story of the 27th: ". . . that the deceased, Timothy Lanagan and Catharine Lubee came to their death by the effects of poison administered to them by Mrs. Robinson, with the premeditated intention of causing their death."

Coroner Bontecou, aided by Professor Francis Dakin of the Albany Normal School, had recovered forty grains of arsenic from Timothy Lanagan's intestines, the same type of arsenic found in the packet under Robinson's rug. Their tests of the sugar from the grocery-bar showed it to be poison-free, and in a homely note Dakin reported: "Dr. Bontecou's family used the sugar afterwards."

As the community began to condemn Henrietta Robinson and tell one kind of story about her, the prisoner suffered a dramatic bout of hallucinations. Called "delirium tremens" by the *Troy Daily Times* three days after the fact and "feigned lunacy" by others a year later, the episode would serve as evidence for Robinson's insanity defense. On Friday night, the 27th, the close of Robinson's second full day in jail, Deputy Sheriff Hegeman "watched the door" of her cell for many hours.

"The reason of my doing so," said Hegeman, "[was] she seemed to be raving and called for assistance to protect her, and passing violently from one end of the room to the other; this conduct continued until nearly daylight."

In the morning Hegeman went to her cell with the lawyer, Jennyss. Robinson met the two men with frenzied pleas for help.

"She said she had heard people at her door [coming] to destroy her; she had heard them grinding knives, and that she had a kettle of hot water to scald them; she wanted me to assist her," recalled Hegeman.

"I told her the adjoining rooms were dark cells, where no one was placed.

"She said she knew better. They were people who had tried to slander her. They could not get at her any other way than by coming to the jail. And she wished me to bring her revolver to her, and she would try to protect herself.

"I could not convince her to the contrary.

"She said her pursuers were Mr. Boutwell's people, that they had got into the jail. She took hold of me very violently, laughing immoderately, saying I must assist her and protect her.

"I told her there was no occasion for it, nobody could harm her.

"She said she knew better, and I disengaged myself by force, pushing her away."

Jennyss remembered a more intriguing statement by the prisoner:

"She told me she was going to be killed, that they had tried to kill her the night previous.

"I asked her who?

"She said a mob of two or three hundred persons had broken into the jail during the night, and that just as they had got to the door, the Sheriff came and stopped them. 'But,' she said, 'I shall be killed for a man and woman uptown have caused a complaint to be entered against themselves in order to get in jail next to me, and during the night they heated a cauldron of boiling water, came to my cell, broke it open, began to abuse me, and gave me a choice, either to get in or they would put me in.' She said she told them she knew she had got to die, and if they wouldn't abuse her, she would get in. Said at that time a noise was heard at the door and they ran away.

"During the relation of this story her eyes were distended, the pupils very much dilated, and she had a wild and frightened look." Then, "immediately placing her hands on her dress, she said, 'Don't I look shabbily?' and began to laugh.

Robinson probably indirectly and subconsciously admitted her guilt in the poisonings when she spoke of the man and woman and cauldron of boiling water and the fact "she knew she had got to die." But she refused or was unable to speak directly about the events of May 25—a refusal which would last through more than a year's imprisonment.

Jennyss: "I could get no intelligent response from her."

Bontecou: "I told Mrs. Robinson once [in late May or early June 1853] that I heard Mr. Lanagan was dead. She took no notice of the remark. I think as far as I am able to judge that she did not know what I meant. I did on one occasion charge her with poisoning these persons; it was in the second or third week of my visits to her. The expression made by me was, 'You know you have poisoned these people. I want you to tell me all about it.' She made no answer, but went clattering away with the same incoherent jumble she had at other times."

Deputy Sheriff William Hegeman, who lived at the Ferry Street Jail during Robinson's time there, recounted: "I spoke to her about Lanagan's funeral; it was the same day it occurred. I think I said the funeral of the man and the woman whom it was supposed had taken poison was taking place. The answer she made to that was 'It's queer, isn't it?' She then commenced talking about some article of her dress." Robinson's words weren't unintelligible or incoherent—just oddly detached.

Coroner Bontecou remembered another instance: "I asked her if I should give up certain articles of cooking utensils to Mrs. Lanagan, and a bonnet. I told her Mrs. Lanagan wanted those things. I asked whether I should not let her have them."

"Mrs. Robinson replied, 'Why not?' This is all she said about it."

Then, "she talked about dresses. I do not recollect distinctly what she said about her dresses. I regarded her remark as to the dresses irrational. The irrationality consisted in the want of connexion with the subject."

Her own dress and appearance were evidently Topic No. 1 for Henrietta Robinson at most times. But was it strange she dodged references to the Lanagans and attempted to change the subject? To our minds, Mrs. Lanagan's request for Robinson's belongings seems almost stranger, especially the widow's wish for a bonnet once worn by Robinson, her husband's killer.

But some of the alleged murderess's behavior was definitely unusual. The young coroner noted Robinson's high spirits during the month of June, 1853: "At almost every visit, she [Robinson] appeared laughing and full of levity." In May of 1854, Bontecou would label this levity "insane."

Bontecou explained his at-least-twice-weekly visits to the prisoner in June of 1853 as necessary to settle Robinson's property affairs. He had charge of her house and all her belongings until early July when he gave the key to the River Street cottage to Hegeman. Jennyss cited the business of Mather's letters to explain his early visits. He also claimed, not very convincingly,

Corner SIXTH AND ALBANY Streets.

TROY, N. Y.

curiosity alone kept him returning to the jail after Robinson had agreed to release the letters. Jennyss practiced law in partnership with Samuel Stover who also called upon Robinson, at least once or twice, during June 1853, and Stover would represent Robinson, along with four other lawyers, at her trial the following spring.

Both Jennyss and Stover belonged to the same political faction as Mather—all three were "Hard" Democrats—and the two lawyers were probably already in Mather's employ. But they didn't manage to help their client much in the pre-trial period. They failed to protect his name anyway. By June 20 the scandal surrounding him had grown so public, the minister and elders of the Second Street Presbyterian Church named a special committee to investigate "reports . . . in circulation seriously affecting the moral and religious character of John C. Mather, a member of this church."[2]

We must mount our own intensive investigation of Mather. As Henrietta Robinson's chief *known* intimate, his life forms the main access road into her case.

PART TWO

JOHN C. MATHER

BIRTH (1813)—SPRING 1853

John C. Mather
(Courtesy Rensselaer County Historical Society)

4

INTRODUCING JOHN C. MATHER

In the spring of 1853 the canal commissioner was forty years old, slim and upright, with blue eyes in a boyish face. His lifted chin and direct gaze, in a portrait of about this time,[1] speak of energy and pride. The pride had at least one source: John Cotton Mather descended from the nearest thing to an aristocratic New England family, the clan of seventeenth and eighteenth-century ministers that included Increase Mather (1639–1723) and his son, Salem witch trial judge Cotton Mather (1663–1728).[2]

About 1803 Thaddeus Mather—a descendant of Increase's brother, Timothy—left Connecticut to settle in south-central New York State. By 1813, the year Thaddeus's wife Sarah gave birth to John Cotton, the couple's fourth child and second son, the family was living in the Broome County village of Deposit on the Delaware River.[3]

Thaddeus never owned more than about a thousand largely-unimproved acres,[4] and he practiced medicine to boost his family's farm income.[5] Yet Thaddeus had *status*, serving as executor of the giant estate of Joseph Cannon of nearby Cannonsville in 1826,[6] and probably benefiting from his blood tie with two of the region's richest men, Binghamton merchants Richard and Henry Mather.[7]

Deposit was a frontier area during John Cotton's childhood, dependent on lumbering and with its woods full of bears, panthers, and wild bee trees.[8] But by 1830 the village supported an academy or high school which John C. must have attended for a year or two.[9] He steps into clear view for the first time on October 16, 1834, at age 21, when he wrote Whig gubernatorial candidate William Seward on behalf of the Deposit "Town Whig Com[mittee]."[10] Then within months, the young Whig left home to seek his fortune in Troy.[11]

He may have speeded his rise in the city by marrying an heiress. On June 22, 1836, he wed one-year-younger Aloa Porter, a Connecticut Yankee like his parents.[12] She and an older sister, Sophrona, both married in Troy almost simultaneously—Sophrona wedding Massachusetts-born merchant Daniel Wight in March of 1836—and with no sign of either Porter parent in Troy documents. Aloa brought conservative religion into the marriage. She was an "Old Light" Presbyterian, a group opposed to religious "enthusiasm" as well as, generally, political "enthusiasms" like abolition and temperance. In 1834 Aloa and Sophrona had been among the founding members of the Second Street Presbyterian Church which broke away from Troy's First Presbyterian Church after the original congregation became a hotbed of emotional, reforming "New Lights."[13] John C. joined Aloa's church in 1838.[14]

Following their marriage the young couple lived in Berlin, a country town east of Troy. Mather would later (August 1843) represent Berlin at a Rensselaer County Democratic convention.[15] But from 1840 he had a Troy address, too, appearing in city directories as a "bookkeeper" at 265 River Street—the business of Aloa's sister's husband, Daniel Wight, "commission merchant"—and a householder on Ferry Street with his seven-years-younger brother, Calvin, boarding in his home.[16]

George R. Davis, a longtime Democratic legislator and speaker of the State Assembly in 1831 and again in 1842–43, had a home and political base in Pittstown, close to both Berlin and Troy City, and became an early political friend: ". . . Davis, 'his [Mather's] guide, philosopher, and friend,' his political father and mentor in the chicanery of intrigue and party management."[17]

Jolly George R. Davis, "more famous for his wit and humor than any other feature of his character,"[18] and Mather, a "social gentleman"[19] despite his Old Light Presbyterianism, got on well together, and Davis apparently "mentored" Mather right out of the Whig Party and into the Democratic one by August of 1843.[20] And that fall Democratic Governor William Bouck appointed Mather one of two county "Loan Commissioners."[21] These officials gave out money, as mortgage-holders for properties, from the "United States Deposite Fund," a kind of politicized federal aid program.[22]

Job Pierson, another county Democrat, played a role in Mather's political progress, too. Pierson, who would coordinate Henrietta Robinson's defense in 1854, had homes in Troy and Schaghticoke, a town north of the industrial city. Like both Davis and Mather, he went to the August 1843 Rensselaer County Democratic Party convention. This body chose Pierson as a delegate to the national convention in Baltimore, where he would join other conservative Democrats in derailing the renomination of President Martin Van Buren, Andrew Jackson's heir.

Sleigh riding on the Hudson.

The Long Island-born Pierson—who had served as district attorney in 1823, U.S. representative in 1830–34, and surrogate judge in 1835–40—was once a Jackson supporter. But by the early 1840s Pierson was finding common cause with men known as "Cotton Whigs,"[23] northern manufacturers and merchants who were careful of the views of slave-owning cotton-producers. Amos Briggs, who owned a large cotton mill on the Hoosic River at the southern end of Schaghticoke Village, definitely fell into the Cotton Whig group. And interestingly, Briggs was son-in-law to the largest landowner in the town, Bethel Mather, who had settled in Schaghticoke in the 1790s.[24] In 1827 Bethel Mather—another descendant of Timothy Mather, just like John C.—had joined with Yankee newcomers Briggs and Pierson to help found Schaghticoke's First Presbyterian Church.[25]

Given John C.'s later approaches to another Mather family in Albany,[26] the young newcomer to Rensselaer County surely introduced himself to his Schaghticoke relatives. The patriarch Bethel, fathered fourteen children and lived into his nineties, had a son, born in 1816, also named "John Cotton Mather." This second John C. Mather even had an interest in politics, writing letters for a local Whig committee—of the exact type 1813-born John C. Mather had worked for in Deposit—in the summer of 1840.[27]

As it turned out, John Cotton son of Bethel, left the Troy-Albany scene in 1844 when he migrated south to set up as a cotton planter.[28] On this occasion Whig leader and *Albany Evening Journal* editor Thurlow Weed wrote a warm letter of recommendation for the young "Agriculturist" of Schaghticoke.[29] Though Weed already opposed the cotton wing of his

party, he came through with this favor for the soft-on-slavery Mather. The slavery versus anti-slavery divide in New York State and national politics hadn't yet opened into the chasm of a few years later, but the link between Thurlow Weed and the Mathers of Schaghticoke, with pro-cotton Democrat Job Pierson hovering close by, is still interesting. It explains much about Deposit-born John C. Mather's future as a conservative Democrat with one leg in the Whig Party. This leg would be John C.'s brother Calvin, by the mid-1840s a Whig "stump speaker" and political operative of Weed's.

The letter for Bethel's son represents Thurlow Weed's first visible step into the life or neighborhood of John C. Mather of Troy. Weed—born poor in Catskill in 1797—had jumped to fame as a newspaper editor in Rochester in 1827. There, according to some, he cut the hair and beard of a corpse taken from the Niagara River to make it look like one William Morgan, a missing man believed murdered by local Masons. Weed's paper, *The Telegraph*, was then making political hay out of the Morgan case, using it to tar Democratic office-holders who were also Masons. Charges of political dirty tricks, particularly the fabricating of false evidence,[30] would follow Weed throughout life. In 1830 he launched the *Albany Evening Journal* and soon became a behind-the-scenes kingmaker—of senators, governors, and presidents—and legislative string-puller into the 1870s.

Who were the Whigs? In some ways they were like the Republicans of the Twentieth Century, very pro-business and tending against leveling measures such as the extension of voting rights. Whigs feared the mob and demagogues, seeing Presidents Andrew Jackson and Martin Van Buren as dangerous rabble-rousers and would-be dictators. The Whigs also backed state financing of canals and turned out to be very right about that.

The Democratic Party, shaped by Jackson, tended to support the interests of farmers and frontiersmen, and increasingly, of new immigrants. Thus, the party grew daily more important in Troy. In 1837 there had been a vicious riot in Troy on St. Patrick's Day, started by "natives" who hung Irishmen in effigy and then stoned and fired guns into Irish homes on Fifth Street south of Ferry, killing several people.[31] But Irish numbers grew so rapidly the group's size and political weight soon ruled out open attacks. Instead, from the early 1840s on, all the city's newspapers, even the Nativist-leaning *Troy Daily Whig*, printed respectful notices of St. Patrick's Day parades and other Irish events, often the doings of Father Peter Havermans, chief helper of the new immigrants.

Ethnic slurs which did make the pages of the Troy papers were on the subtle side,[32] like lists of police court defendants containing near 100% Irish names, and jokes: "An Irishman coming across a large turtle, with head and legs extended, retreated hallooing to his companion that he had found a box full of snakes" and "An Irishman being asked on a late trial for a certificate of his marriage, bared his head and exhibited a huge scar, which looked as though it might have been made with a fire-shovel."[33]

Given the rising tide of Democratic voters in Troy, Mather made a good decision to turn Democrat. It was definitely a good decision in the short term as another Democratic governor, Silas Wright, won election in November 1844 and reappointed Mather as a loan commissioner in January 1845.

By this date Mather had come far from the bookkeeper of 1840–41 working in his brother-in-law's business. After an 1842–43 listing as "merchant" at 271 River Street, he appears in the 1843–44 directory as proprietor of a "manufacturer's warehouse 221 River." He would keep this business listing through the spring of 1851 and an office at 221 River until he left the city permanently in 1855–56. By 1844 he and Aloa and three daughters—Emma, born 1838, Sarah, born 1841, and Sophrona, born 1843[34]—had moved into a new house at 17 Liberty Street.

From his manufacturer's warehouse Mather sold finished textiles for producers on commission, making "the usual advances on goods consigned to him." He also supplied machinery parts and materials to manufacturers:

> Satinet Warps; Jointless Wire Harness, with recent valuable improvements; Machine Cards; Revolving and Jaw Temples; Pickers of all sizes; Picker String Leathers; Belt d[itt]o; Calf Roller Skins; Sheep d[itt]o; Lacing; Roller Cloth; Broad and cassimer Shuttles; Satinet and cotton d[itt]o; Comb plate; Card Cleaners; Curling irons; Tenter Hooks; Card Tacks . . .[35]

On January 13, 1846, Aloa died "after a short illness." Her obituary writer (surely Mather) heaped tender praise on the young wife—praise which also tells of the writer's actively-capitalist mindset: ". . . she is already reaping the joyous fruits of *an interest* [modern italics] in the atoning blood of her gracious Redeemer."[36] The new widower sent his daughters to live with his parents, who relocated to Binghamton about this time.[37] He moved into "Mrs. Brewster's" boardinghouse on Second Street in Troy to live among other single men: merchants, lawyers, bookkeepers, clerks, druggists, and students.[38]

5

RISE

In the year of Aloa's death: ". . . he [Mather] was a member of the democratic state convention and took a prominent and active part in its deliberations."[1]

Mather's brother Calvin, a practicing lawyer since 1843, was already associated with Thurlow Weed and the Whig cause. On October 29, 1846, Calvin wrote familiarly to Weed from Binghamton: "Dear Weed, I am here. But can say no more just now. I shall be home Tuesday . . ." The letter goes on to describe Whig prospects in Broome County in the upcoming election ("but small hopes") and in Binghamton ("none") and requests letters from Weed to provide "Strengthening" for certain voters. A near final thought reads: "Strictly Confidential I think this District will be ballanced—on Gov."[2] (The last remark faintly foreshadows 1852–53 charges by some Democrats that John C. Mather was improperly *balancing* Whig and Democratic interests.)

Calvin probably still worked for Weed when he wrote to New York Whig Hamilton Fish on September 20, 1847 seeking aid, probably an office, for a Mr. Norton. His note followed a rebuffed attempt to see Fish the same day; Calvin promises to call the next day in Albany.[3] Years later, two Trojans remembered the lively and resilient Calvin:

> "You recollect Cal Mather,"
>
> "Yes," replied Uncle Will, "I certainly do. He was quite a character in his day . . . a lawyer and a political stump speaker in old Whig days."
>
> "Well," continued the other, "as I was passing along here one day in the spring, when the street was afloat with mud and crossing was quite an undertaking, I heard Mr. Paine [cashier of

Fishing Station: Sturgeon, Shad, Bass.

> the Bank of Troy] call out in so loud a voice from the opposite side of the street that everybody in the vicinity could hear him distinctly: 'Mr. Mather, Mr. Mather, there is a note of yours at the bank which has been protested, and the bank would like to have you call and pay it.' 'Mr. Paine, Mr. Paine,' replied Mather in an equally loud voice from the opposite side of the street, at the same time beckoning with his hand and taking out his pocketbook.
>
> "The cashier, thinking he meant to pay the note, came across the street through the mud, whereupon Mather put back his pocket-book into his pocket and then propounded to him this question. 'Mr. Paine, is the amount of that note $5.50 or $50.05? — — me if I have not forgotten which it is!' Mr. Paine did not reply and paddled back through the mud, evidently thinking that the amount of the note and the fact that he owed it did not trouble Mather, which it did not in the least."[4]

In this same year, 1847, Calvin's equally resilient brother, just "let go" from his loan commissioner poisition by incoming Whig Governor John Young, served as alderman from Troy's First Ward.[5] John C. would fill the same one-year position again in 1850. No doubt his status as a kind of closet Whig helped him in the First Ward, then home to many merchants and industrialists. A short 1868 biography of John C. Mather gives the man himself more credit: "Possessed of winning manners and unusual firmness of purpose, he soon won the confidence of the people, and was twice chosen a member of the Common Council of the city of Troy from a District largely Opposition, and at a time when no other Democrat on the same ticket succeeded."[6]

The year 1847 brought a bigger office within reach, too. In September the Democratic State Convention nominated Mather as a New York State canal commissioner. But the dramatic withdrawal of the "radical" wing of the party from the Syracuse convention doomed him in the general election. The issue causing the split was the Wilmot Proviso, a bill then before U. S. Congress which called for a ban on slavery in all territory won in the Mexican War of that year. New York State's conservative Democrats, by this time known as Hunkers—either from the old Dutch word for farmer, "junker," or from the faction's hankering or "hunkering" after offices—opposed Wilmot. Its supporters, the radical Democrats, from this point known as Barnburners, "being likened to the farmer who burned his barn to get rid of rats,"[7] gathered in their own "Free-soil" Democratic convention under the leadership of John Van Buren, son of Martin, and others.

Up until this point, the state's Democrats had mostly divided over canal funding with the Hunkers taking a Whiggish stand and wanting to plow canal tolls back into canal improvements, while the soon-to-be Barnburners favored using some toll money to pay down the state debt. John C. Mather and Job Pierson came down solidly on the Hunker side on both *canal* and *slavery* issues, and both supported the Hunker presidential candidate of 1848, Mexican War hero General Lewis Cass. "Mather adhered with unflinching energy and tenacity to the National or Cass section [of his party],"[8] and when the most unbending Hunkers became known as "Hards," Pierson "continued until the last, the hardest of the 'Hards.' "[9]

The Barnburners ran their own Free-soil candidates in 1848 and thus split the Democratic vote, allowing Whigs to triumph statewide and nationally. The defeat pushed New York's Democrats together again in 1849,[10] and the next year, the nation as a whole followed suit, papering over the slavery issue with the "Compromises of 1850," agreements in the tradition of the Missouri Compromise of 1820.[11] All this smoothed the way into office for John C. Mather:

For [Mather's] stand in behalf of the nationality of his party [in 1848] his political friends determined to present his name again to the people of the state, which they did in 1850, when he was a second time nominated for Canal Commissioner by an emphatic majority of the State convention, Gov. [Horatio] Seymour (in office 1853–54 and 1863–1864) and himself being the Hunker representatives on the ticket . . . Messrs. Seymour and Mather were subsequently endorsed by what was called the Union Party in the City of New York, which was composed of a large body of conservative Democrats and Whigs who were opposed to Northern sectionalism."[12]

Seymour lost the governorship to Whig Washington Hunt despite a split in Hunt's party mirroring the Democratic division of 1848. (New York's conservative Whigs had walked out of their September convention to protest a resolution praising anti-slavery champion William Seward.[13] The walk-outs became the "Silver Grays" after the silver-gray hair of conservative leader, Francis Granger.[14] The anti-slavery Whigs, led by Seward and Weed, became the "Woolly Heads" after the curly hair of their supposed African American clients.) Unlike Seymour, Mather won in 1850, and from January 1, 1851, gained the power and prestige of a canal commissioner. The great public works project of the Erie Canal (and also the Champlain Canal) was actually in process of being overtaken in both passenger- and freight-carrying capacity by the railroads, with 1855 marking the high point for canal tonnage and tolls. But the public still marveled over the amazing earthwork and over canal transport itself.

A traveller boarded a seventy-foot-long packet boat, "decked all over, with a row of curtained windows from stem to stern," and then settled back—inside the interior cabin or atop the deck—to watch the ever-changing panorama along the canal banks, while experiencing almost no sense of motion. Horses walking towpaths beside the canal drew the boats with long ropes. At night the packet's cabin provided shelf-like beds, "one above another," for twenty people, with a curtain to divide the women's sleeping area from the men's. At mealtimes a long table was run out in the center of the cabin. The absolute safety, dependability, and placidity of canalboat travel were its novel features, though the "navigation of an interminable mud puddle" could produce "an overpowering tedium."[15]

Travellers were often surprised by the look of the canal. Abolitionist Henry B. Stanton, husband of feminist Elizabeth Cady Stanton, had imagined "a pellucid stream" and was shocked to find the Erie "the muddiest ditch I ever saw." Nathaniel Hawthorne described it as "dark and turbid as if every kennel in the land paid contribution to it."[16] In 1852 a reporter for the *Lansingburgh Democrat* wrote of the canal terminus at West Troy: "In summer the air near the canal is a conglomeration of pestilential vapors . . ."[17] But along the dark, foul-smelling ditch, canalboats carried a wealth of goods,[18] making every canalport—in the November 1853 words of Hard Democrat and John C. Mather ally James E. Cooley—"like the gorgeous city of Venice into whose voluptuous lap once poured the golden commerce of the East."[19]

John C. Mather shared his very important job with two other canal commissioners. He was commissioner of the Eastern Division; Frederick Follett, a Genesee County Democrat, was Commissioner of the Western Division; and Charles Cook, a Chemung County Whig, oversaw a middle section. There was also a nine-member Canal Board—made up of the state's lieutenant governor, attorney general, auditor, comptroller, engineer, and surveyor, along with the three commissioners—which weighed in on all, or almost all, canal decisions.[20] But a majority of the Canal Board members were Democrats,[21] with only one Barnburner, Lieutenant Governor Sanford Church, among them. So Hunker John C. Mather, with his "unusual firmness of purpose" and useful Whig contacts, soon gained control of the board as revealed, or at least suggested, by his place in the spotlight when the board's actions came under fire.[22]

But in 1851 no clouds hung over Mather's enjoyment of office, outside some problems with his friend, Henrietta Robinson, to be touched on in her 1854 trial. In February John C. was an honored guest at an all-male Washington's Birthday dinner in Troy: ". . . two tiers of tables extended the entire length of the [Troy House] building and wing, east and west, one hundred and fifty feet. . . . The windows were darkened, and the bright gas lights shone with dazzling brilliancy. The hall was skirted with red and white bunting . . ."

The "smoking viands," cold dishes, and dessert "pyramids" of fruits and cakes adorned the tables from the outset of the dinner, which featured dish after dish of Hudson River oysters and fish (stewed, fried, in pies, with egg sauce, with wine sauce, etc.) and delicious-sounding game (wild pigeons, wild goose, wild duck, quails, prairie hens, partridges, venison) along with farm-raised veal, beef, pork, lamb, mutton, chicken, and "vegetables in season." After the feast, Governor Washington Hunt addressed the politician-filled gathering in a bi-partisan spirit, condemning the "demon of faction." Troy's Mexican War hero, General John Wool, then raised the demon by announcing to newspaper-reported "Sensation": ". . . there was but one subject which engrossed public attention at this time, and that, he was sorry to say, was a *black* [original italics] one."

A self-proclaimed "Union man," Wool warned against politicians' agitation (i. e., abolitionism), thus expressing Hunker and Silver Gray views.

Martin I. Townsend, future defense counsel for Henrietta Robinson and Barnburner Democrat, stood up for his abolitionist views in a post-speech toast to "Gen. Washington": "His patriotism was broad as his whole country. His philanthropy embraced the whole Human race. Let him whose sympathies are less expanded beware how he profanes that sacred name."

John G. Britton,[23] another lawyer and future Robinson-affair player, made two less high-minded toasts: to "The Wives of America, in War the Commander of our Home *Infant-ry*—in peace our *Companions-in-Arms*" and to "A Good Day's Brewing." The rest of the nearly two dozen toasts were of the general and high-minded type: "Our Glorious Union," "Trojan Enterprise," "The City of Troy," "The brave Kossuth [celebrated Hungarian patriot then visiting New York State]," etc. Except for John C. Mather's. He honored two only moderately famous New Yorkers: "Attorney General

Chatfield" and "Hon. Noble S. Elderkin . . . late Speaker of the Assembly." Chatfield was a Hunker Democrat who served on the Canal Board with Mather and through 1851 would generally vote with Mather on board decisions,[24] while Elderkin of St. Lawrence County, later identified as a "Freesoil Soft,"[25] came from the opposite end of the party. Thus Mather paid attention to the *present and practical* matter of helping along party unity.[26]

In July he returned to Broome County to give the Fourth of July speech in Binghamton. He must have been a good speaker, like his brother Calvin who would later be praised for "an eloquence that . . . captivated the multitude."[27] Fourth of July speeches then took the form of mini-histories, beginning with the Pilgrim Fathers and traveling forward. Mather followed the pattern, and at last, "touched discreetly on the distressing but stereotyped subject of slavery."[28] As at the Washington's Birthday dinner, so many people were trying to tiptoe round this elephant in the room!

In the same month Governor Washington Hunt, who had out-manoeuvred opposition Democrats by calling a special session of the Legislature in June, signed a new law which suddenly infused a lot of money into canal projects. From as early as the 1830s problems had arisen with the design of the Erie: traffic back-ups before locks, boats wedged against one another in the forty-foot-wide, four-foot-deep canal, and improperly-angled banks crumbling into the water. In 1836 work began to broaden and deepen the waters to seventy feet by seven feet,[29] until in 1842 the Legislature's fiscal conservatives, mainly the Democratic Radicals, passed the "Stop and Tax" law. This put things on a pay-as-you-go basis and brought the enlargement to a near-standstill.

But in July 1851 Hunt's new "Nine Million Act" reopened the funding tap by allowing the Canal Board to issue stock against future revenue. Great excitement followed among contractors and politicians—sometimes the same people—and their friends and supporters. The excitement would reach near-furor that December in the "Big Letting of 1851," when Mather and the other commissioners gave out the valuable contracts from their offices in Albany's white marble State Hall. Calvin acted partly as John C.'s agent at this time. In the later words of Albany lawyer John K. Porter, counsel for the New York State Assembly impeachment action against John C. Mather in September 1853:

> How happened it that General [Calvin's militia title] Mather, the brother of the respondent [John C.], the partner of Mr. Christye, the attorney of Mr. Law [canal contractor and shipping magnate George Law], the friend of Story, is in possession, during the session of the letting board, of matters which have not publicly transpired, and communicates to Mr. [Minor C.] Story what awards he was to receive before those awards were made?[30]

6

TROUBLE

The storm over the Big Letting began to break even before completion of the contract awards on the last days of December 1851. The December 26 *Troy Daily Times* warned: "The Buffalo Register says the canal lettings are to be 'parceled out among a set of personal and political favorites without regard to the interests of the state.' We shall see."

On January 12 and 15, the *Troy Daily Times* cited instances of higher, even highest, bids winning canal contracts,[1] and by the 20th, the newspaper reported on state Senate and Assembly resolutions for "a Joint Committee to look into the alleged Canal Frauds."[2] On this last day the Canal Board requested the state Court of Appeals to rule on the legality of the "Nine Million" law itself. Mather supported this move in an apparent attempt to take cover from the anger of his party's Barnburner wing.[3] Questions about the lettings bubbled along in the early spring of 1852 and then went underground, as far as newspapers were concerned, until the spring of 1853.

The charges against Mather—as eventually laid out in his trial of August and September 1853—condemned him for seizing the power of the larger Canal Board via the smaller Letting Board and then ignoring state law, which required the "awarding of contracts to the lowest responsible bidders of sufficient ability who offered adequate security."[4] As a result: ". . . the state was shorn of about $3,000,000 in that memorable week of 'the Golden Fleece.' "[5] Hard Democrat John H. Reynolds "on behalf of Commissioner Mather" would defend his client by asserting, a bit weakly, that the "sufficient ability" and "adequate security" terms of the state law gave Mather an absolute pass on his choice of contractors.

Reynolds would also point more convincingly to the political origins of the charges against Mather,[6] but not convincingly enough (for us) to hide the truth of much homely testimony cited by John K. Porter, "Counsel for the Managers on Behalf of the Assembly." For example: "Merritt Potter, a lumberman of West Troy, who has been in that business from his boyhood," stated along with four others, "that the hemlock lumber delivered at West Troy [for improvements to the West Troy Dock] was not worth more than $10 a thousand, and that the pine could have been procured at that point for $13 a thousand." A Mather underling had paid $18 per thousand for the hemlock and $31.50 per thousand for the pine.

John K. Porter's charges suggest Mather and others on the Letting Board profited from the contract awards through some form of rake-off. Letting Board members were Canal Commissioners Mather, Follett, and Cook plus State Engineer and Surveyor Hezekiah C. Seymour. Porter: "The lower bidders are discarded collectively; a democratic bidder receives a fat contract, as an encouragement from Messrs. Mather and Follett; another fat contract is allotted to a whig bidder, as an encouragement, from Messrs. Seymour & Cook. Thus the public treasury is made to pay one man a bonus for being a democrat, and another a bonus for not being a democrat; one man a bonus for being a friend of Mr. Mather, another for being the friend of Mr. Seymour."[7]

There is little doubt John C. Mather demanded some fat from the padded, winning contracts. At the very time of the first protests about the Big Letting, a letter from Governor Washington Hunt to Hamilton Fish, dated Albany, January 24, 1852, complained of attempts by "Mather" to wring personal profit from appointments planned by Hunt:

> Geer [either the "Judge (Walter) Geer (of Glens Falls)" referred to by Henrietta Robinson in early May of 1853 or his son, Asahel C. Geer of Troy] placed himself in the hands of those precious worthies Mather and Thayer [likely Francis S. Thayer, a state senator from Rensselaer County in 1868–71]. They got the control of his resignation. Then they managed to withdraw his bill and to prevent any charges being placed before me. They offered the resignation for sale and made a variety of efforts to control the appointment ["this Coroner's office"]. They offered it to Ives for $3000 but he refused to treat with them. Mather had the impudence to write me that Geer would resign if I would appoint their candidate, but would not if I intended to appoint Ives. I repelled their advances with indignant contempt and ordered an investigation into the charges made public by the Supervisors. They fought hard, but on being cornered sent forward the resignation, which letter he had carried for some weeks in his pocket.

New State Hall.

Though the "Mather" here may well be the Whig Calvin, there wasn't much "space" between the brothers and their political operations (as seen in Calvin's activities in December of 1851). Yet personal graft was not the disturbing issue of the Big Letting for critics. A March 1852 editorial in the *Troy Daily Times*—which claimed to be independent though in fact was Soft Democratic by 1853—pinpoints the real grievance:

> The canal-letting 'plug muss' has snarled up the politicians in a queer manner. For instance the *Argus* [Hunker] and *Journal* [Woolly Head Whig], at Albany, are as cozy as 'sucking doves,' going hand in hand in favor of the lettings, and arguing that there has been no fraud at all in the business. . . . Then, again, there are the other two organs of the two parties at Albany—the *Atlas* and *Register*—the one the radical organ of the democracy, the other the silver gray organ of the whig party—two antagonistic elements which we would suppose could no more mix than oil and water—they are agreed in denouncing the lettings as a fraudulent transaction! All hostility between them has ceased and they denounce the *Argus* and *Journal* as organs of the contractors, and the apologists of fraud! As it is reported that neither the barnburners or silver grays got any fat jobs, the consistency of their organs in this matter will at once be conceded . . .[8]

So the Hunkers and liberal or Woolly Head Whigs—the regular wings of their separate parties or the wings which had never seceded—were dividing the contract spoils between them and excluding the less-regular members of their own parties, a shocking act to contemporary party loyalists. The extent of cross-party cooperation was revealed in the mid-March testimony of Canal Commissioner Charles Cook before the legislative investigating committee formed that January. Cook told of Attorney General and Hunker Democrat Levi Chatfield approaching a cluster of Canal Board members, Cook included, with an offer "in which he proposed . . . to allot George Law contracts for work to the amount of $1,500,000 and allow Lieutenant Governor Church [the one Barnburner on the board] to take care of his friends in the west, and vote those two through the Board first, and divide the balance of the work between the two political parties equally . . ." Cook and the others, gathered in the house of Barnburner lawyer Peter Cagger, rejected this plan. Chatfield countered with the same scheme, but limiting Law to a $1,000,000 share. After another rejection, Hunker emissary Chatfield and all the men at Cagger's house agreed simply on "dividing the whole work equally between the two political parties."[9]

The Whig Cook's account smears both wings of the Democratic Party with its mention of proposed set-asides for Hunker-connected Law and for the Barnburner Church. Obviously there were bones thrown to Whigs which Cook doesn't comment on, but there's no reason to disbelieve him about Law. After all, George Law's attorney Calvin Mather was then hanging around the State Hall, carrying messages between Canal Board members and bid-seekers—at least carrying one message to bid-seeker Minor C. Story.

George Law, "the colossus of contractors, the mastodon of men . . . upwards of six feet in height, and of perfect proportions, with physical strength to match his Herculean frame,"[10] was a national figure by 1850. Born just north of Rensselaer County in Washington County, the farmboy Law had walked to Troy and worked as a hod-carrier there before becoming a stonemason on the Delaware and Hudson Canal. By 1829 he was a contractor on the D & H and in 1837–39 won contracts to build sections of New York City's Croton Aqueduct. In the 1840s, by then hugely rich, Law bought two New York State rail lines and also developed a steamship line to California via Panama. In 1852 his already-high profile mounted higher when he dared the Spanish in Cuba to fire on one of his ships, *Crescent City*—banned from Havana harbor through some snafu—and won the bluff to the pleasure of U. S. "jingos." Like another alleged Mather brothers' associate, Myron H. Clark,[11] George Law admired the anti-immigrant Know-Nothings. In 1855 some members of that party would put his name forward as candidate for President.[12]

Despite the simmering criticism over the Lettings (plus Mather's defeat in the sale of Geer's resignation), 1852 was not a bad year for either Mather brother. On the surface, John C.'s ventures in particular proceeded smoothly. That fall he launched the Manufacturer's Bank, capitalized at $200,000, in Troy. While just one of the bank's ten directors,[13] John C.'s ability to "place" canal toll money—the tolls rested in local banks for a time—made him a key figure.[14] In October the *Troy Daily Times* ran a friendly notice on the Manufacturer's Bank:

> The $1, $2 and $3 bills of this Bank have made their appearance. The designs are very pretty—emblematic of manufacturers, commerce, and the results of enlightened enterprise. They differ from most bills in the bold and heavy impressions made. This will 'take the eye' of some; others will not like it so well. To us, it appears very rich and beautiful . . . The bills correspond with the institution—having a substantial appearance and a sound, good look.[15]

But at just this time, the first inkling of a shifting and stiffening of party divisions—an ominous inkling for Mather—surfaced in the *Troy Daily Times*. This was an October 25 mention of "Hard-shells" (soon-to-be plain "Hards," and "Softs") in the state's Democratic Party.[16] Hards and Softs weren't quite the same as the old Hunkers and Barnburners. At the Democrats' national convention in June 1852 and again at their New York State convention in September, numbers of Hunkers—importantly former New York Governor (1833–1837) William Marcy and future New York Governor Horatio Seymour —compromised with and drew closer to the Barnburners.[17] These Hunkers, termed Softs, left behind the uncompromising Hunkers, termed Hards.[18] And soon the Soft name embraced the whole moderate to left wing of the Democratic Party including the old Barnburners. The Hards, with John C. Mather one of their stalwarts, were a smaller and angrier group than the old Hunkers. Events in the spring of 1853 only increased the Hards' fury.

From the opening of the new legislative session, some old Barnburners newly-allied with some old Hunkers as Softs revved up the effort to punish Letting Board members John C. Mather, Frederick Follett, and Hezekiah C. Seymour.[19] On March 17 the state assembly appointed "a select committee . . . to examine into the propriety and legality of the official conduct of state officers."[20] In the course of its less-than-month-long examination, the committee lost interest in Follett and Seymour, except as their actions aided or abetted the alleged misdeeds of Mather. Follett had turned into a Soft by this point,[21] plus the committee discovered most of the inflated 1851 contracts had been for work on Mather's eastern end.[22] And on April 13, Mather learned from "a friendly messenger": ". . . the committee had represented to the House that I [Mather] had committed 'high crimes

Canal boats on the North River, New York. 1852.

and misdemeanors' and that they had also introduced a resolution for my impeachment."[23] The assembly would battle over this resolution through the spring and early summer of 1853 until its passage in late June, leading to Mather's trial in the State Senate from July 27 through September 16.

As the move to impeach Mather was building, he and other Hards along with Softs lobbied the new Democratic administration in Washington for jobs. On March 9 the now-Soft *Troy Daily Times* disingenuously rebuked Mather for traveling to the Capital "when the canals are just being put in a navigable condition and require the closest attention of every officer . . ."[24] The *Times* writer, probably editor John M. Francis, needn't have worried. New President Franklin Pierce left New York patronage decisions to his Secretary of State, William Marcy, who favored Soft appointees.

The Hards' disappointments over the spring of 1853 became so well known, they gave rise to jokes, including a funny poem, "The Customs," in the *Troy Daily Whig* of May 30. The comic hero of this lampoon, an unsuccessful Hard office-seeker, had much in common with Mather's old mentor, George R. Davis, who traveled to Washington in May to seek the Postmaster's office in Troy. There Davis had a run-in with his former protégé which must have added to Mather's mental burden, despite Mather's surface composure: "A flare-up occurred in the Post Office Department on Saturday, between Davis and Mr. Mather, in consequence of Davis having discovered on the files of the office a very strong letter from Mather in opposition to his appointment. Davis denounced Mather in unmeasured terms, but Mather listened to his abuse with contemptuous nonchalance."[25] The *Troy Daily Whig* explained the situation: "it was "not that Mather loves Davis less, but that he loves Hunkerism [the terms Hunker and Barnburner were still current] more." This second Spring-of-1853 trip to Washington—Mather was in there in mid-April[26]—ended when he returned to Troy on the night of May 21 and then soon left for Albany. Did John C. Mather go to see Thurlow Weed at this time? Another of Calvin's notes to Weed, dated May 17 from New York City, points in this direction:

> My Dear Sir,
>
> I must go to Cincinnati tomorrow morning to be gone some weeks. In the matter of my brother all things will be ready. I hope on reflection your views will harmonize with ours for I have a great horror of a tedious examination that shall last all summer [just what happened!]. You know that in relation to the Vanderbilt matter the bill [part of Soft Gov. Seymour's initiative to resolve the canal funding crisis] is with the Judiciary Committee of the house.
>
> They ought not to report on it or certainly not in favor of it.
>
> I send 250 cegars [*sic*] of a choice Brand. I beg you to take a pull at them.
>
> I am truly,
>
> Calvin E. Mather
>
> John will be in Albany Thursday night.[27]

The "Dear Sir" is more formal than Calvin's earlier "Dear Weed," and the "I hope on reflection your views will harmonize with ours" suggests a rift. The negative publicity about the 1851 contracts had definitely put Calvin, along with John C., under a cloud. An *Albany Evening Atlas* editorial of May 10 named Calvin along with Weed allies Seth C. Hawley and ex-Governor Alvah Hunt as key players in the contracts affair.[28] The *Atlas* spotlighted the three Whigs in answer to an item in Weed's *Albany Evening Journal* about the "notorious democratic plunderers" of the lettings scandal.

Calvin was actually on his way to Cincinnati either in company with or to meet former State Engineer and Surveyor Hezekiah C. Seymour, another Whig, with both in pursuit of a "very extensive Railroad contract in the west."[29] Was this trip, which would end disastrously for both the younger Mather and for Seymour, partly a way for the two men to get out of town? Bolstering this idea we find Hawley was out west at this moment, too, and somehow involved with both Calvin and Seymour in the railroad venture.

Hawley wrote to Weed from St. Louis on May 10, the date of Calvin's New York City-mailed letter to Weed, claiming to be writing on behalf of Calvin who was "at this moment suffering of neuralgey in the right arm which makes an amanuensis necessary." Could Calvin have reached St. Louis in one day? Hopefully, Hawley wasn't trying to cut Calvin out of the deal in some way![30]

In yet another view of these western operations, three days earlier on May 7 Alvah Hunt had sent Weed a copy of an earlier Hawley letter—dated May 2 from Louisville, Kentucky, and originally sent to Hunt—which reported enthusiastically about work on a Louisville to Nashville rail line. ("Broke ground this morning at 6 o'clock in the City Depot grounds by 100 Irishmen") Hunt added his own enthusiastic comments to Weed, urging the Dictator to invest either "*privately* or otherwise." The ex-Governor closed his letter with a single-line paragraph: "A mutual friend of ours would like to live west for a time, I think; though terms to that effect have not been used—& after that turn Sailor or Traveller!"[31]

This last thought might refer to either Calvin Mather, Seymour, or Hawley—since all had been tarred by their activities in December of 1851, at least in the view of the *Albany Atlas*. But the desire for flight described by Hunt seems almost too strong to fit the situations of any of these men, and it's tempting to read the sentence as an allusion to John C. Mather. By May 7 he had been singled out as sole defendant in a probable impeachment trial (the Assembly still had to pass a resolution sending Mather to his Senate trial), and likely already known to Hunt and Weed, Mather was being menaced by an unhappy and violent mistress.

Henrietta Robinson had threatened Mather's life in April at her meeting with Edwin Brownell in his courthouse office.[32] Brownell, who had earlier broken away from his tête-à-tête with Robinson to relay her complaints to Troy Police Chief Amasa Copp, surely told Copp and perhaps others about the later threat.

PART THREE

PRETRIAL

JUNE 1853–APRIL 1854

Monumental statue of Emma Willard
Sage College, Troy, NY

7

CONTAGION

Towards the end of June 1853, as Henrietta Robinson was still recovering from the hallucinations or breakdown of her post-arrest period, John C. Mather reeled from a series of body blows. Within 48 hours of the church elders' decision to investigate his "moral and religious character," the State Assembly approved the impeachment resolution (June 22).[1] Almost incredibly, one day later Calvin Mather died at the house of Hezekiah Seymour in Cincinnati, with John C. likely learning of his brother's death by telegraph that day.

While an obituary in the *Broome County Republican* gave 34-year-old Calvin Mather's cause of death as "congestion of the lungs,"[2] a month later almost to the day (July 24, 1853) 42-year-old Hezekiah Seymour died as well.[3] The deaths of these two youngish men at the same address suggests infectious disease, and epidemics notoriously followed new railroad and canal works. Disease scourges of the era included water-borne typhoid fever and louse-borne typhus, known as "ship fever," as well as smallpox. But since 1832 the most lethal summer killer had been water-borne Asiatic Cholera. Cholera bacilli multiplied in the intestines of the infected, emitting showers of poisonous toxin which then passed into the bloodstream to cause violent nausea and diarrhea, and often, fatal shock. The stricken were sometimes well in the morning and dead by evening, though victims could also linger for weeks.

Nationwide epidemics of cholera occurred in 1832, 1849, and 1866, but between and around these years, post-1832, it was endemic. As the *Lansingburgh Democrat* noted in 1854: "The Cholera seems to have taken a permanent place among the diseases of the country . . . Now we look for it every summer."[4] In fact Troy experienced the second-worst cholera epidemic

of its history in the spring and summer of 1853.[5] It was so bad the city's newspapers—filled with anxious notices about street-cleaning, liming, and the readying of hospitals[6]—couldn't address the crisis directly. John Francis of the *Troy Daily Times* noted the danger of smallpox only on May 20 when he praised the Troy Hospital for its "apartments . . . separated with brick walls."[7] Four days later Francis wrote simply of "contagious diseases" when urging the city to set up a second hospital.[8] It wasn't till the summer of 1854 that the dreaded word surfaced in the newspapers. Then, the *Troy Daily Whig* figured the city's cholera cases at under 200 from June 8 through August 14.[9]

The one-year embargo on the word "cholera" had a lot to do with protecting the city's business interests, but also related to the shame of the disease in the mid-1800s. It was then distinctly disgraceful to die from cholera. While no one knew what caused the disease, up-to-date medical opinion rejected the idea of contagion. Most physicians held the "miasma" theory, that conditions of fog, light, and heat, maybe also involving foul gases rising from garbage dumps or sewers, caused the disease in susceptible persons.[10] Susceptibility was key. Clean-living, upright, morally strong persons were believed immune, while drunkards, prostitutes, other morally-damaged people, and those always surrounded by dirt and noxious fumes—the poor—were seen as natural victims.[11] Thus cholera deaths "among the respectable, *including even ladies* . . ." caused "an uncommon sensation" in New York City in 1849.[12]

The Asiatic cholera, which more likely than not killed both Calvin Mather and Hezekiah C. Seymour, would never appear as the cause of death in their obituaries. Other actors in the events swirling around Henrietta Robinson from 1853 to 1855 may have also succumbed to cholera; Mather's friend John G. Britton and defense attorney Job Pierson are possibilities. The cholera issue would even surface in Robinson's 1854 trial, suggested briefly as a cause for the deaths of Lanagan and Lubee.[13]

In the midst of the disease outbreak, two distinguished Trojans worried about another kind of contagion. Mrs. Emma Willard, revered founder of the Troy Female Seminary, and her son, Dr. John Willard, sent a sharp joint letter to the *Troy Daily Whig* to protest a story on the scandalous prisoner, Mrs. Henrietta Robinson. The two Willards wrote, not in answer to any *Whig* article, but to something that must have appeared in the liberal Whig *Troy Daily Post,* which would turn, with no change of politics, into the *Troy Daily Traveller* a year later.[14] The Willards' letter ran on July 9, 1853:

> To the Editor of the Troy Whig:
>
> By the falsehood of an impostor, the names of the ladies of a most interesting family, that of the late much lamented Mr. Wood of Quebec, formerly members of the Troy Seminary, have been mentioned in a connection highly derogatory. We allude to the report that one of these ladies is the Mrs. Robinson now in Troy jail for murder. It is said that Mrs. R. is beautiful and accomplished, and has asserted that she was formerly a pupil of the Troy Female Seminary, and a Miss Wood of Quebec. As the Misses Wood were well known to the first families in Troy, with whom this woman also pretends an acquaintance, the story hence originated, that the murderess was one of that family, although no human beings are less likely to have committed the crime for which she awaits the action of the law. This horrid report was in Troy circulated with the name of one of the younger of the Misses Wood, but it has now gone forth through the newspapers, connected with that of the eldest, one of the most gentle and feminine of her sex.
>
> Fearing that from the New York papers, this report will be copied into those of Great Britain, we feel it our duty to come forward at once with a denial, begging that it may be immediately denied also by those who have unwittingly aided to spread this injurious falsehood.
>
> We know that this Mrs. Robinson is not one of the Misses Wood, and we do not believe that she was ever a pupil of the

> Troy Female Seminary; because our kind feelings toward all our pupils are well known; and in her present extremity, if Mrs. R. had ever been our pupil, she would wish to see us, but this, on the contrary, she pertinaciously refuses.
>
> Of the four beautiful and amiable daughters of the late Mr. Wood, who were pupils of the Troy Female Seminary, every one married and is now living in Great Britain, and they are all allied to eminent families.
>
> Their brother, Mr. Wood of Quebec, is now in Troy, having come to sift this injurious report. Had its originator been a responsible person, he would have been prosecuted for a libel. After this denial its repetition would be not only false, but it would justly be regarded as libellous.
>
> Emma Willard,
> Former Principal of the Troy Female Seminary
> J. H. Willard
> Principal T. F. S.

As modern investigators, we happen to know the Willards protested with a clear conscience. We can travel into the nineteenth-century "future" and examine Wood daughter death notices and certificates plus other papers—letters, diaries, and legal documents—which firmly exclude all the Misses Wood as candidates for the "Henrietta Robinson" of 1850s' Troy (see Appendix I). But in 1854 and 1855, John Francis of the *Times* and others[15] would rightly point to the Willards' strained logic. As Francis wrote in March of 1855: "Most people regarded this in a different light from Mr. Willard—that the very fact of Mrs. Robinson refusing to see the Principal of the Seminary, under the circumstances, rather went to confirm than to disprove the rumor that she was one of the Wood family."[16]

Many voices[17] would also heap scorn on another odd claim by John Willard. In June of 1854, Dr. Willard described the only contact he and the brother, William Wood, managed to have with Henrietta Robinson in July of 1853: "When we reached her room the Sheriff opened her door, so as to give us an opportunity of seeing her as she lay upon her bed. She was so covered that we saw only the upper part of her face and her hand. From the size and appearance of the hand and wrist I was more fully confirmed in my opinion [that Robinson was not a Miss Wood], if possible, than I had been before. She, as usual—and as she had done two or three times by Mrs. Willard and myself—refused to see us."[18]

The hand and wrist evidence was sillier than the Willards' other ideas about the jailed woman. Why were they scrabbling after straws of proof in this way? Why were they so desperate?

A glance at the history of the Troy Female Seminary and at Emma Willard's own life offers some explanation. The seminary, founded in 1821, had been the first girls' school in the nation (and world) to offer systematic, high school- and college-level instruction in academic subjects. At the time of its founding and even into the 1850s, higher education for women battled strong disapproval. The public mind linked educated women with radical politics and sex scandals, partly as a result of the careers of free love-advocates: Aphra Behn, London playwright of the 1670s and 1680s; Mary Wollstonecraft, author *A Vindication of the Rights of Women* (1792); Fanny Wright, antebellum writer, feminist, and utopian activist; and others. Almost singlehandedly, Emma Willard was in the process of dispelling the sexy-disreputable air which hung about all efforts to give women more than elementary schooling.

It was a difficult struggle, requiring confidence, ability, and tact—since Willard chose to proceed in a soft, superficially conservative way. Her early life had perfectly formed her character for the task. Born in 1787 in Berlin, Connecticut, she was the much-loved daughter of an aging Revolutionary War veteran who encouraged her early love of learning. The pretty child grew into a statuesque, dark-haired, extremely attractive woman. She became a common or elementary schoolteacher and in 1810 married rich widower Dr. John Willard of Middlebury, Connecticut. The doctor showered his young wife with the same kind of love and encouragement she had received from her father and supported her wish for improved schooling for girls.

From the teens of the century, she argued, very non-threateningly, for their better education. She urged the patriotic good of creating better—more moral and knowledgeable—mothers to train the new republic's sons. She soothed male fears, addressing:

> . . . the absurd prejudice, that if women's minds were cultivated, they would forget their own sphere, and intrude themselves into that of men." [Woman's "sphere" concerned both male and female thinkers of the era. As work moved out of the household and into factory workplaces—thus upsetting old arrangements of social power and control—many grew anxious about women's roles. Male thinkers strove to seal women firmly within the household world; if rowdy young male clerks and factory workers now escaped the parental control of "masters," at least women ought to remain obediently at home!] And whence arises this? Not from a liberal and candid investigation of the female mind in general, but because a few individuals of masculine minds have forcibly broken through every impediment, and rivalled men even in their own department. These however, do not constitute the rule, but the exception.

> They might as well reason that because there is now and then a brawny woman who can lift a barrel of cider, her whole sex should be kept constantly within-doors and not allowed to exercise [in fact, an actual prescription of some mid-Victorian teachers of girls] lest, if they should attain the full perfection of their bodily strength, they would contest the prize upon the wrestling ground, or attempt to take the scythe and the hoe from the hands of men, and turn them into the kitchen.[19]

In 1819 Willard presented a "Plan for Improving Female Education" to the New York State Legislature: "Well-dressed, handsome, with the bearing of a queen, intelligent and yet womanly, she impressed them not as the much-scorned female politician, but as a noble woman inspired by a great ideal."[20]

Though the queenly Willard didn't manage to extract any money from the state, she opened her school in Waterford, just north of Troy, that year. And in 1821 Troy's Common Council came through with $4,000 and a leased lot on the city's Second Street. The investment paid immediate dividends. Just three years later the relocated seminary hosted Revolutionary War hero General Lafayette at an elegant reception that cast a high-toned glow over the city as a whole.

For its first two decades—before the founding of many other "seminaries"—the Troy Female Seminary drew students from Europe and Canada as well as from the American South and Midwest, though with Troy-Albany-area girls still making up one-third to one-half of the student body. The daughters of "Mr. Wood of Quebec City" were among the early foreign students. According to the school catalogues Georgiana, born in 1818, attended from September of 1832 through July of 1836; Emma, one year younger, attended from February 1835 through July of 1837; Charlotte, born in 1826, attended from February 1843 through July of 1845; and Harriet, born in 1828, attended from August of 1843 through July of 1845.[21]

During Georgiana and Emma's terms at the school, Mrs. Willard had sole charge of the Seminary (her elderly husband died soon after the move to Troy). In keeping with her "better wives and mothers" gloss on women's education, on Saturdays the students "rolled out piecrust for Sunday's dinner" as carefully as they studied "in the Latin and higher mathematics" on weekdays. The Sunday meal was always the same, "consist[ing] of cold boiled ham cut in thin slices, with delicious mashed potatoes, and pie—our pies." Through the eyes of this same student of 1833, Mrs. Willard's:

> . . . dress was always handsome, of black silk or black wool, with a fichu-like effect of white mull or lace. I never remember to

> have seen her without her turban, a large, imposing affair built of soft white stuff, which added greatly to the regal effect she produced with her high brow, side curls and strongly marked features. Her expression was one of kindly shrewdness . . . She was kind, but somewhat hasty in her judgements, and, like all persons of imperious temper and despotic rule, not always just. Some of the more shy and easily frightened of her pupils could have testified to this. But if feared by some of the girls, she was heartily admired by all of them, while her vivid, magnetic personality was undoubtedly the inspiration of the school . . . She laid great stress upon manners and was very particular about our personal appearance. Meeting a girl in the hall, she would stop to arrange the drapery of what was at that time invariably a low-necked gown, saying as she patted the bare, girlish shoulder: 'There, my dear, I think that is more becoming.[22]

While Georgiana and Emma Wood experienced the full force of Willard's personality, their two younger sisters did not—and for an interesting reason. Emma Willard had been lucky, for a woman of her time, in the characters of her father and first husband. But in 1838 she married a Dr. Christopher Yates "of Albany and New York."[23] A gossipy letter of Thurlow Weed's of this year rudely calls him "long bait Yates."[24] From the day of the wedding, Yates treated Willard badly, scoffing at her teaching and writing—she had already published successful textbooks—and doing his best to loot her estate.

Throughout her career Willard kept feminism at arm's length. In 1829 she had written to fellow educator and proto-feminist Catherine Beecher: ". . . the only natural government on earth is that of the family—the only natural sovereign, the husband and father. Other just governments are these sovereigns confederated . . ."[25] And in 1870, the year of Willard's death, her sister would write, ". . . she [Emma Willard] had no sympathy with the declaimers of women's rights."[26] Yet Dr. Yates's cruelty plunged her into a true feminist drama. Willard left Yates in June of 1839, returning to Connecticut where she petitioned that state's legislature for a divorce. The divorce took four years, and Willard only returned to Troy, and a new problem, in August 1844.

She had had the forethought to transfer all her rights in the seminary to her son, Dr. John Willard, before marrying Yates. But Dr. John had grown fond of his 1838-assumed position as principal of the school and apparently refused to reinstate his mother as head of her beloved creation.[27] With no real recourse, Emma Willard accepted her ouster and moved into a small brick house on the grounds of the school. Henceforward, she would play a lesser role in Seminary life, devoting herself mostly to writing. This personal scandal—for every divorce then rated as a scandal—and its unhappy aftermath only provided more reasons to firewall the "Miss Wood" rumors of 1853 and later.

Who were the Misses Wood exactly? Over the years the four daughters studied in Troy, their father, Robert Wood, ranked as one of Canada's wealthiest lumber merchants with a vast "timber cove" and fine home at Sillėry, a suburb of Quebec City. Wood and his wife Charlotte Gray, married since 1817, also kept a city house on "St. Lewis" Street, in one of the "Upper Town's" finest quarters. Inventories of Robert Wood's property, one made in 1827 and another after his and his wife's deaths in 1847, show how lavishly comfortable and cultured the Wood family homes were, with Brussels carpets, mahogany chairs, quantities of silver and china, plus a library containing works of English literature and history as well as ancient classics (Plutarch's *Lives*) and a few American books (a life of Benjamin Franklin and novels of James Fenimore Cooper).[28]

Robert Wood's or his wife's bookish bent maybe prompted the couple to send their daughters to the Troy Female Seminary. In other ways, the Wood girls resembled the upper-crust Canadian girls met by nineteenth-century visitors to Quebec: lively teenagers who went into society early and enjoyed a freesocial life by European standards.[29] "Canada," now Quebec Province, was then a social hothouse, given the presence of British regiments and their officers. Thus when "the four beautiful and amiable daughters" of Robert Wood arrived in Troy between 1832 and 1843, they made quite a splash, "mov[ing] in the best social circles of our city."[30] On top of the $150 per 22-week semester which Wood paid for each daughter's education, surviving school records for the younger girls, Charlotte and Harriet, show they spent $100 a semester, together, on dresses. The girls also bought shoes from shoemakers James Johnston, Caleb P. Kent, and Adolphus Hull, furs from furrier Anthony Seiler, and watches from watchmaker Dennis Fitch in Wards One and Two.[31]

The rich, socially experienced, and well-dressed Wood girls boasted an added glamour: they had or claimed to have a "royal" in their family tree. The *Dictionary of Canadian Biography*—after describing Robert Wood's career as "timber culler, timber merchant, and shipowner" and giving the value of his vast estate of £54,152, excluding Quebec City real estate, at his death in 1847—records:

> It is not, however, for his role as a prosperous timber merchant that Robert Wood is remembered. He is better known as one of the children said to have been born to Prince Edward Augustus [later Duke of Kent and the father of Queen Victoria] and Therese-Bernardine Montgenet, known as Mme. De

> Saint-Laurent. Family tradition states that he was given to the prince's former servant, to be raised as his son. That there is no record of Wood's birth or baptism in parish registers (the exact date is found in his mother's request for guardianship and on a memorial window placed in the Cathedral of the Holy Trinity, Quebec, by his children) was long considered an indication of royal descent . . .[32]

The *Dictionary* concludes:"The information surrounding the family tradition of Wood's origins has been proved inaccurate and recent scholarship has established that no children were born of the 27-year relationship between the prince and his companion."

Actually, "the family tradition" looks stronger than the "recent scholarship" on this point (see Appendix II). But there's no doubt about the Robert Wood/Duke of Kent rumor. On May 31, 1854, just after the close of Henrietta Robinson's trial, the *Troy Daily Budget* would note, slightly garbling the account: "The *Whig* is trying to make out that Mrs. Robinson 'is some pumpkins.' It says: 'A friend of ours, an Englishman, well posted in whatever relates to titles and blood, asserts that *Mrs. Robinson* is related to Queen Victoria, her father (Wood of Quebec) being a son of the Duke of York."

8

LONG HOT SUMMER INTO FALL

Soon after July 9, 1853 (the date of the Willards' first letter to the *Whig* about Robinson), William Frost Wood—the 28-year-old brother of Georgiana, Emma, Charlotte, and Harriet—in company with Dr. John Willard tried to see the prisoner, but only glimpsed her partly-veiled face as she refused the interview. Willard later admitted, as he and Wood stood at the open door of her cell, with Robinson lying semi-shrouded on her bed, "She recognized Mr. Wood [easy enough to do by process of elimination if Robinson knew Willard's appearance]."[1] Whether this encounter was painful for Henrietta Robinson or not, less than two weeks later, on July 23—according to identical reports in both the *Budget* and the *Whig* of Monday the 25th—she made "a deliberate attempt at self destruction."

> About 4 p.m., some one of the servants about the jail came down stairs and informed the Sheriff that Mrs. Robinson had been vomiting for some time and very freely, and that the contents of the stomach had a blueish appearance, resembling vitriol. Mr. Price immediately visited the woman and found the statement true. Mrs. Robinson stated to him that she had taken a considerable quantity of vitriol, enough she had supposed to put an end to her life, of which, she said she was heartily tired. She remarked that she had "seen trouble enough."
>
> Drs. Brinsmade and Adams were called at once and administered correctives. She suffered greatly during the night of Saturday, and doubts were entertained of her recovery. Yesterday she was better, though very weak.
>
> By what means she became possessed of the poison is a mystery. It is supposed however that she brought it to the jail

> with her, carefully concealed in some portion of her superabundant wardrobe.[2]

She was very sick. Deputy Sheriff William Hegeman later spoke of this time: "I think it was in July or August that it was supposed she would die in jail."[3] In a cascade of events, two days after Robinson's suicide attempt, the Court of Impeachments met in the Senate Chamber in Albany to finally deal with the charges against Mather. Two fellow Hards, John H. Reynolds and James T. Brady, defended him while Soft or Barnburner legislators prosecuted. Arphaxad Loomis of Herkimer was a key prosecutor, pursuing the defendant via every motion and rule of order possible. Herkimer County was then a Barnburner-Soft stronghold. Loomis, himself, owned mills on or near the canal-way at Herkimer Falls,[4] and it's a good bet he hadn't benefited from any of the canal contracts in 1851.

Mather's trial marched on through August, covered in detail by Troy and Albany papers, as Henrietta Robinson recovered once more in her second-floor cell. By August 31 she had so regained her health, the *Lansingburgh Democrat* reported: "Mrs. Robinson, the alleged murderess, now confined in Rensselaer County Jail . . . appears to be in good spirits and is not in so much of a hurry to have her existence terminated as she manifested some weeks ago. She is quite cheerful and declares herself prepared for any fate."

Her enforced drying-out in jail—she had "no intoxicating drinks in jail to my [Hegeman's] knowledge for the first 3 or 4 months she was there"[5]—surely had a lot to do with this. In October, Job Pierson in a court appearance "for the prisoner" would object to a fall of 1853 trial: "The woman's mind had been so deranged that he [Pierson] had been unable until quite recently to converse with her."[6]

Though this view jibes with some later comments on Robinson's lingering, post-summer of 1853 mental confusion, Pierson was then doing all possible to delay the trial, as proven by his later calls for postponements. Anyway, by October of 1853 Robinson appeared outwardly well, with the *Troy Daily Times* almost gushing over her first court appearance on the 11th :

> The woman Robinson was richly dressed in Court this morning. She was veiled, so that we could not get a view of her countenance. She wore a low-neck, splendid black silk dress, with rich lace under-sleeves, a blue silk velvet mantilla—a very rich and costly article—a dashing display of jewelry, &c. Her "outfit" must have cost from $200 to $300!
>
> On being remanded to jail, she walked off accompanied by the Sheriff with firm and elastic step, and in a manner indicating that the pride of the woman is still there.

To backtrack a step or two into August and the first weeks of September 1853, Mather was attending his Senate Chamber trial at this time.[7] But in off-hours he must have worked to muster political support, buttonholing every stray Whig or Democrat in or about the white marble Capitol building and nearby State Hall. By the second week in September, he knew everything was going to come out all right for him, in the short term anyway. Two things were happening at the same time: his Senate trial, which wouldn't end until September 16, and a series of political caucuses leading up to and including the Democratic State Convention, which opened in Syracuse on September 12. On September 6, Mather received cheering news when Hards—or as they were sometimes called, "Adamantines"—carried most of Troy's wards in the elections for convention delegates, with "three cheers for Mather" raised in the First Ward party meeting.[8]

Then, on the second day of the Syracuse convention (September 13) to great sensation, the Hards walked out after losing control of the platform. They lost hold of the *literal platform*, the planks on which Hard Chairman of the State Committee, Minor C. Story, was standing, when—in the later words of a Hard journalist—"a delegation of the bruisers, pugilists, and 'short boys' of New York City . . . furnished with free tickets and well primed with liquor . . . [and] come up by the railroad the night before" drove Story from it.[9,10] The next day, the Hards made their walk-out permanent. They "bolted" to convene their own separate convention in "the ladies' parlor of the Globe Hotel," as the *Albany Evening Atlas* expressed things.[11] The *Atlas* was truly a "Freesoil" paper at this time, more solidly abolitionist and more opposed to canal expenditures than the simply "Soft" *Troy Daily Times*,[12] for instance. The *Atlas* also published a comment on the seceding Hards as "the Law and Seward troops,"[13] pointing up the strange bedfellow-ship of the liberal, Woolly-Head wing of the Whig party (Thurlow Weed, William H. Seward) with Know-Nothing-sympathizers (George Law) and with Hard, pro-slavery Democrats (Mather, Pierson, et al.)

Anyway, the Hard convention rallied round Mather, nominating him for another term as Canal Commissioner on September 13. Three days later, with these favorable tides running, the Senate cleared Mather of all charges. The Hards hailed the "triumphal acquittal"[14] with bonfires and cannon-firings in Troy and Watervliet as well as other "fired salutes"[15] in Rochester and New York City. But Soft and Barnburner-Freesoil papers were quick to point to the votes which went against Mather. Senators actually voted 18 to 14 against him on the charge he "did knowingly, negligently, and corruptly make . . . a wasteful and extravagant contract for the materials [for the West Troy Dock],"[16] a tally just shy of the two-thirds majority needed for conviction.

The *Atlas* also charged "whitewash"[17] in the impeachment affair and condemned the Hard ticket, "the chief components of which are men thoroughly steeped in corruption."[18] But all this was on the mild side compared to what Hard orators—like Hard nominee for New York State Comptroller James Cooley, "one of [Mather's] most violent partizans"[19]—would soon fire back at *Atlas*-supported candidates. For Mather and the rest—Hards, Softs, and Whigs alike—now went into campaign mode.

Campaigning in the 1850s meant "[*gun*]powder, liquor, and music,"[20] parades, open-air speeches, and more. A Whig procession once featured a hickory sapling with live raccoon, a party symbol, clinging within its branches, and both parties regularly put up "liberty poles" as signposts for free-flowing kegs.[21] Such rowdy street politics made it extra shocking to many when women began to take a few small steps into the political world at about this time. Some campaign speeches of the 1850s almost qualify as "X-rated," by twenty-first-century standards due to their violent imagery. On the eve of the November 1853 elections, James Cooley denounced New York Soft leader John Van Buren and Soft President Franklin Pierce:

> Bronson's [Greene C. Bronson, fallen Hard office-holder] head in a basket" says this itinerant polluted speech filter of Short-boy obscenity [J. V. B.] as he swings his listless length from one barnburner squad to another . . . [like] another profligate prostitute of ancient times who was seen with a very good man's head in a charger, which to gratify a base passion had been severed by order of a drunken Governor at Judea, at a bacchanalian banquet given at the 'White House' or bestial mansion of that wicked prince near Jerusalem . . .

> [F. P.] went into the Presidency on the popular sentiment pervading all classes of our people, contained in the compromise measures [of 1850], which recemented the north and the south, and healed up the lacerated wounds infected by rabid secessionists and frantic free-soilers, sealing with the indelible impression of infamy, those disorganizing, unprincipled desperadoes, whom to the dishonor and disturbance of the country, and to the lasting disgrace of the President, he has treacherously raised up from the tomb of political pollution and taken to his bosom as his confidential councellors [sic] and advisers [sic]. These, and their minions, everywhere placed in positions of power throughout the land, revelling in official rewards, like poisonous and deleterious exhalations arising from a slough of stagnant putrefaction and death, stroll through the country from one end of it to the other, armed with slung shots, bowieknives, brickbats and bludgeons . . .[22]

Despite the all-out language the Hards didn't win, but they succeeded as spoilers. And according to the regular Democratic ticket-supporting *Budget*, just before the election Hard candidate for Attorney General, James T. Brady—one of Mather's lawyers during the impeachment trial—"virtually came out at the Hard meeting in New York . . . in favor of the Whig candidate [Ogden Hoffman]."[23] So Mather faced his early November election defeat with some preparedness. Still, this must have been a sad time for him. Once spoken of as a candidate for Governor (in 1852[24]) he had now failed to win re-election to a lesser office. Did he lie low during the rest of the winter of 1853–54? While he went to two last Canal Board meetings in Albany in December,[25] he kept up "a continued absence from this city [Troy]"[26] through November and December of 1853, when the Clerk of the Sessions of the Second Street Presbyterian Church was attempting to serve a kind of summons on Mather. He would not appear before the church elders to confess "the truth of the charges" against him until July 17, 1854.[27]

9

LIMBO TIME

Mather remains largely out of sight of the newspapers through the spring of 1854. On February 17, Editor Francis or another writer of the *Troy Daily Times* rather contemptuously commented in the course of a story on a Buffalo libel suit: "By the way, what has become of that suit of Mather's against the *Albany Atlas*? [Had he sued over the 'men thoroughly steeped in corruption' comment?] There's a dark spot there that needs rubbing out . . ."[1]

Mather hadn't *yet* become just a footnote in the political history of New York State. A *Budget* notice of June 13, 1854—appearing after Henrietta Robinson's May 22–29 trial with its mentions of Mather—names him as a chief Hard leader.[2] Plus, Mather's future success in New York City in 1857 reinforces the idea of ongoing political clout.

But as he enjoyed a vacation at least from public scrutiny, a sea change was underway which would *eventually* doom the old, under-the-table Hard Democrat and Liberal Whig alliance. In December 1853, Illinois Senator Stephen A. Douglas had introduced a bill into U. S. Congress, the "Kansas-Nebraska Act," which called for elections in the two territories to decide whether they would enter the Union, separately, as free or slave states. Douglas claimed the recent Compromises of 1850 had nullified provisions of the Missouri Compromise which forbade slavery north of latitude 36° 30' in old Louisiana Purchase territory; this would have mandated Kansas as free. His move almost had an air of "gotcha!" and sparked a lot of instant opposition in the North. Then, during the long congressional battle over the act from January 1854 until its passage on May 30, many middle-of-the-road Northerners stopped believing abolition was a dangerous, radical-fringe cause and took up strong anti-slavery positions.[3] Slavery, already a key issue in the dance of New York State's party factions, became even more

important, stressing what relationship remained between Thurlow Weed's Woolly-Heads and Mather's Hards.

The two groups' cooperation had already dwindled by the close of the summer of 1853 as Mather and his Hard faction moved into the welcoming arms of the Silver Grays. When Mather had withdrawn Canal Commissioner's advertisements from the *Budget* in the summer of 1853, he had given them to the *Troy Daily Whig*, the conservative or Silver-Gray Whig organ.[4] Ideologically, an alliance with the Silver Grays made better sense for the Hards than the alliance with the Woolly Heads, since both conservative groups wanted to appease the South and both showed a sympathy for the

Know-Nothings. (The *Whig* functioned as apologist and best friend of the Know-Nothing movement in Troy.) And we remember here Mather's links to fairly open Know-Nothing George Law, through Calvin, and his alleged links to Know-Nothing-tinged Whig Myron H. Clark.

In October of 1853 the *Troy Daily Times* had commented on Mather's relationships with Troy's two Whig papers: "The Softs gave us some advertising when they got up their meeting. The Hards don't furnish us any. For the purpose of helping stir up a little fun, however, we have notified the public of their contemplated gathering this evening. The pay, of course, like the Commissioner's official notices, will go mostly to the *Whig*, with a little dribble to the Post [precursor of the *Traveller*] just to prevent its growling."[5]

In June of 1854, the *Budget* would refer to the Silver Gray *Whig* as "the Hard Court Journal."[6]

Yet a thin thread or "dribble" of mutual interest continued to run between Woolly Heads and Hards and would even survive into the summer of 1855, when liberal Whig newspapers would cover the Robinson affair in a way far kinder to John C. Mather than Soft Democratic organs.[7] Also, wary politician Thurlow Weed would back alleged-Mather-friend Myron H. Clark,[8] mainly known as an anti-liquor man, as Whig candidate for Governor in the fall of 1854—over strong abolitionist William Seward. This was the confusing political situation at the time of Robinson's trial of May 22 to May 29, 1854. It was an odd, teetery-tottery time of rising passions in conflict with old "friendships," yet with some old connections holding firm, especially within the Robinson trial arena.

During the spring of 1854 a handful of newspaper notices followed Henrietta Robinson's progress towards her days in court. On or about February 23, the *Albany Atlas* informed: "Mrs. Robinson's trial for murder by poisoning takes place in Troy, on Monday next. Able lawyers are employed in behalf of the accused." The *Troy Daily Times* quickly contradicted the *Atlas*: "No, she will not be tried at the coming term. Hereafter we may explain the reasons for the farther procrastination that we understand is predetermined upon. In the mean time, the accused keeps up a miniature Bedlam in jail; she is a perfect 'fire-cat;' and will neither keep quiet herself, not allow any rest to other prisoners within the sound of her vociferations."[9]

On February 29, though "the counsel for Mrs. Robinson stated that they were ready for trial," District Attorney Anson Bingham called for a new postponement, citing vague problems with the prosecution case; it was "defective in some material points" and required "new indictments."[10] In early March, Soft or still-further-Left newspapers complained of the delay. Both the *Albany Evening Atlas* ("Freesoil") and the *Troy Daily Budget* (Soft) reprinted an article from the *Utica Observer* (Soft): ". . . the *Troy Times* [Soft] in relation to Mrs. Robinson's trial says: 'We hope that this virago and courtesan will soon meet her deserts. She has already been too long shielded from the law. It is becoming notorious that her trial was once put off because another trial was under way.' Will the *Times* explain the reason for the *past* as well as the 'farther procrastination' of this matter. It is a subject that deeply concerns the public. The *Times* promises to comply with the *Observer*'s request."

But in April, Robinson's trial was delayed again[11] at the prosecution's request: "there was an important witness absent in Illinois . . ."[12]

During this limbo time, the Wood family stepped into the picture once more. In February or March, a Wood family friend, William H. Jeffery, visited Troy and tried to meet with the imprisoned woman. Jeffery was a relative of the Woods by marriage, specifically the marriage of Charlotte Maria Wood to William Francis Augustus Eliott. Sir William Francis Augustus Eliott's uncle, Admiral George Augustus Eliott (b. 1799), had married in 1837 "Alicia Anne, only daughter of the Hon. Thos. N. Jeffery, Collector of the Customs at Halifax, Nova.Scotia."[13] On April 8, 1854,[14] William H. Jeffery wrote from Quebec to George M. Tibbits, the head of one of Troy's leading merchant families:

> Dear Sir,
>
> I received yesterday a Communication from Mr. [Job] Pierson that perfectly bewildered me especially as I had an interview with Mr. [William] Wood the day previous, however this Letter perfectly staggers me how to come to a conclusion of who this Woman really is. You have no doubt heard from Mr. Pierson the nature of the interview after Mrs. R. received my card, she scolded him because he did not bring me to see her, saying she would have been pleased to see me, and went into particulars respecting my history and connections with her Father (that is, Mr. [Robert] Wood that nobody could know unless you or Mr. Pierson mentioned it to her, or she is the person who I really fear she is. I am really sorry that I did not wait a few days to see her, but still I am doubtful whether if I had remained she would have seen me, but merely said so Knowing that I had left the City.
>
> Mr. Wood has shewn me Letters from all his sisters, portions of which I have read which would certainly lead you to believe that they were all in England & Scotland, but the circumstantial Evidence that is brot. to bear against that is equally as strong, and it really puzzles me to come to a conclusion what to think of the matter & the further I go into it, the more mystery appears to envelope it.

Her Uncle [probably William Petry of Quebec] that is the Uncle of Mr. [William] Wood who married his Mother's sister (I write under the impression you will see in my mind there is no doubt) says if the Navigation was open he would immediately start & settle the question beyond a doubt, but he is rather feeble in health & not at all able to make a journey of that kind.

I would like to go again and try further in seeing this Mysterious Woman. I hope she may get off, without reference to who she is, she is someone knowing the family well, if not Miss Wood.

Let me know if you hear of anything, especially if she's brot. to her trial & it is ascertained who she is, or Tel: *[telegraph]* me if she proves to be a Miss Wood, & let them collect the payment here. Waiting anxiously to hear some further information.

I remain Dear Sir,
Yours Truly, W. H. Jeffery[15]

Jeffery's surprisingly open remarks—particularly his "or she is the person who I really fear she is" and "you will see in my mind there is no doubt"—boosted the "Miss Wood" rumors in Troy, for Tibbits didn't keep the information to himself. John Willard would refer to the April letter in a letter of his own to the *Whig* written after the close of Robinson's trial.[16]

In the last week of April, the prisoner herself freshly astonished the citizens of Troy. As the *Troy Daily Times* told the story:

> As usual, the Grand Jury at the close of their session to-day, visited the Jail for the purpose of seeing its inmates. They visited the different apartments, and found everything clean and in good order.—Finally, the Jailor, Mr. Hegeman, offered to conduct them to the room of Mrs. Robinson in compliance with their particular request, as each one of them was very anxious to see her. The door was opened, and the Jury with much dignity walked in. They surrounded a large rocking chair in which (as they supposed) they beheld her sitting closely veiled. Some of them very politely asked her to withdraw her veil. She made no response whatsoever, but sat perfectly motionless. Their anxiety was so great, they requested the Jailor to remove her veil, which he declined to do. At last a person stepped up and removed it, when to their very great surprise they found no Mrs. Robinson there, but on the contrary a silk dress very neatly stuffed, equal to the latest Paris fashions! The bird had flown—where? The Jailor was asked if she had escaped. A general search was instantly

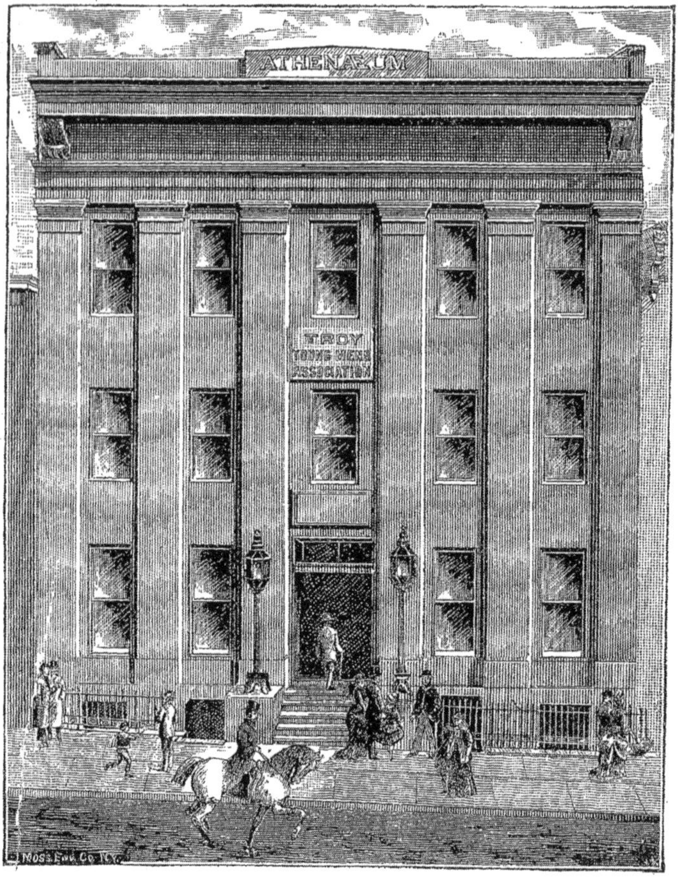

Athenæum Building.

made. A slight 'twitter' was heard proceeding from under the bed. The curtain was raised, and there she lay so full of laughter she could hardly contain herself. There is considerable method in this woman's insanity, surely.[17]

PART FOUR

TRIAL

MAY 1854

Martin I. Townsend
(Courtesy of New York State Library)

10

DAY ONE—OFFICERS OF THE COURT

At noon[1] on May 22, 1854, exactly one year less three days from Henrietta Robinson's fatal visit to the Lanagan bar, Judge Ira Harris of the Rensselaer County Court of Oyer and Terminer gaveled the woman's trial to order in Troy. It took place in the courthouse which stood—and still stands in rebuilt form—on the southeast corner of Second and Congress Streets.

Robinson had already been inside the building on the spring evening in 1853 when she found Poormaster Brownell in his basement office and complained to him of Mather's neglect and community attacks. In a curious geographic concentration, the Second Street Presbyterian Church, scene of meetings on John C. Mather's moral fall, stood just south of the courthouse on the same side of Second. And only two dozen paces or so south from there was Mather's boardinghouse, on the far side of east-west-running Ferry Street. The Troy Female Seminary buildings—including Emma Willard's small home—lay on the opposite side of Second, at the southern end of Congress Park, but within clear view of both "Mrs. Brewster's" and the courthouse, which fronted the northern and open end of the park.

The 1836-built courthouse, with its Greek Revival façade of six Doric columns and architrave cut from soft, white Sing Sing marble, was a grand palace of justice and a worthy expression of the wealth, pride, and idealism of many Troy citizens. Its classical grandeur now supplied the backdrop for the sensational trial, though failing to tone down any of the quirky, lively proceedings about to unroll.

These began without the defendant, as defense counsels Job Pierson and Martin I. Townsend asked Judge Harris to order the jury drawn from "the country towns" rather than the City of Troy—an effort to limit the damage of the past year's articles on Robinson in Troy papers. Harris found

Court House.

he "had no right to give such an order," but then, in a mild and equable way, promised to suggest the plan to the sheriff.[2]

Given Robinson's link to prominent Hard Democrat John C. Mather,[3] the politics of trial participants are important—even if, in the end, the factions represented *cooperated* more than *conflicted*. The first thing we notice is the absence of Mather's overt political enemies, the Soft Democrats, from the officers of the court, with one exception: defense counsel Martin I. Townsend—about whom more shortly. It was a Whig- and Hard Democrat-heavy court and so a friendly one for Mather.

The 52-year-old Judge Ira Harris, a Union College graduate and long-time Albany resident, was a liberal Whig of the Thurlow Weed stamp.[4] After terms in the State Assembly and State Senate in the mid-1840s, he had won election to the New York State Supreme Court in 1847 and since then gained fame for anti-rent decisions.[5] The handsome, heavy-faced Harris—he looked like the popular idea of a noble Roman Senator—would go on to run successfully for the U. S. Senate in 1860 as a candidate of Thurlow Weed's newly-created Republican Party.[6]

County District Attorney Anson Bingham was a Whig of some stripe,[7] assisted by his brother-in-law, Henry Hogeboom, of unknown political views, and by George Van Santvoord, who was certainly a Hard Democrat. Dark-haired, sensitive-looking Van Santvoord was junior partner of Troy lawyer and politico David L. Seymour, identified as a Hard Democrat by June of 1854.[8] Both Hogeboom and Van Santvoord came from Columbia County, just south of Rensselaer. Hogeboom sprang from the river port of Hudson and likely still lived there in the spring and summer of 1854.[9] Van Santvoord had served as an assemblyman from Columbia County as recently as 1852,[10] and at the time of Robinson's trial lived in the Village of Schodack at the very southern end of Rensselaer County.[11] It almost looks as though Bingham chose out-of-towners to help him with the politically-delicate Troy City prosecution.

The most senior defense counsel, grey-headed Job Pierson, one of the "hardest of the Hard" Democrats, brought his current partners, William A. Beach and Levi Smith. These younger men—Beach was 45 and Smith 31—had only recently arrived in Troy.[12] Smith soon disappeared from the Robinson trial, but Beach, who would play a sizable role, must have been another Hard Democrat given his partnership with the ultra-Hard Pierson.[13] Beach would gain national fame in the near future. After quitting Troy for New York City in 1870, Beach acted as plaintiff's counsel in the sensational Beecher-Tilton trial of 1875, in which wealthy Brooklynite Theodore Tilton charged Henry Ward Beecher, high-profile minister of Brooklyn's First Presbyterian Church, with seducing Mrs. Tilton. Beach cut a dashing figure: "He was of ordinary height, strong physique and imposing appearance. His voice was wonderfully winning and under perfect control . . . Of an austere and melancholy caste, much of a recluse, and always dressed in black, he was the Hamlet of the American bar . . . He was not a great examiner, being too domineering and methodical. A poor student of human nature, he treated all witnesses alike, and was slow to trim sale [*sic*] for shifting winds . . . but his courage, manners and powers were lion-like and overwhelming, beyond all comparison."[14]

Ranged alongside the Pierson firm at the defense table were men from three other Troy law offices. One eminent lawyer was 46-year-old A. B. (Abram Baldwin) Olin of the "Olin & Geer" partnership. The Vermont-born A. B. was a Whig[15] and a liberal-leaning one, since in 1856, he—like Harris a year or so later—would run as a Republican for the U. S. House of Representatives and proceed to carve out a career in Washington.[16] The "Geer" of his Troy partnership was none other than A. C. (Asahel Clarke) Geer, son of the "Judge [Walter] Geer" referred to by Henrietta Robinson during her late April or early May meeting with Edwin Brownell. Either A. C. or his father, Judge Walter—both Whigs—had been the "Geer" who connived in the 1852 "Mather" scheme to sell Geer's resignation.[17]

Samuel Stover represented the Stover and Jennyss partnership at the defense table. Neither he nor partner Richard Jennyss—who tried to retrieve John C. Mather's letters from Robinson after her arrest—would have big careers like Beach, Olin, or even A. C. Geer who served as a federal Internal Revenue officer in the 1860s. Stover and Jennyss, both men in their thirties, were Hards, closely associated with Mather.[18]

The one man in the defense lineup who was politically out of place was Martin I. Townsend of "Townsend & Kellogg."[19] The Williamstown, Massachusetts-born Townsend was a Soft Democrat of very Barnburner-y, Freesoil-type views. A member of the "New Light" First Presbyterian Church of Troy and an early abolitionist,[20] his views resembled those of the *Albany Evening Atlas* more than those of either the *Troy Daily Budget* (regular Democrat-Soft) or the *Troy Daily Times* (Independent-Soft).[21] In May of 1854, Townsend was the only clear Mather political opponent among the officers of the court.

Long active in Troy's Democratic Party, Townsend was a "strong, robust gentleman"[22] of 44 in 1854. He had an agreeable, bulldog-ish face but not a handsome one by nineteenth-century standards. He was no "Hamlet" like Beach. Years after the Henrietta Robinson trial:

> . . . Martin I. Townsend and Beach were pitted against each other in arguing a case before the court [in Troy]. Beach at that time dyed his hair and beard, and Townsend's hair was white, although the ages of the two men did not differ much. Beach, in addressing the court, when alluding to Townsend, spoke of him as his venerable friend, and this he kept up repeating until the old Roman, who then as now, hated shams of all kinds, became wearied and annoyed with the frequent use of the name which Beach applied to him. When replying to the court Townsend remarked that he was no more venerable so far as years could make a man so than Mr. Beach, and that, although there was a difference, the court could readily understand that it was one of appearances and merely a colorable one. Beach, who at times was petulant, took offense at Townsend's remark, and for quite a while did not speak to him when meeting in the street.[23]

Townsend comes off far better in this story than Beach, and as well as having been early and right (to all modern minds) in his abolitionism, Townsend was a cultivated man. Library records of the Troy Young Men's Association show he was a voracious reader of novels and history. In contrast, Mather borrowed few books, mostly collections of political speeches.[24] Late in life Townsend would write two books of his own: one on the newly-discovered Mayan pyramids and another on his family history.[25] He had also traveled to Europe in 1850, sending letters—much occupied with condemning European aristocrats—to the *Troy Daily Budget* during his journey.[26]

Why was the sophisticated liberal, Martin I. Townsend, on the defense team among the friends of John C. Mather, and who was paying him? In 1898 the long-lived defense attorney explained in an article written for or given to the *Troy Northern Budget*: "When the trial came on there appeared for the defense as counsel Hon. Job Pierson, Hon. W. A. Beach, Hon. A. B. Olin and the undersigned, Martin I. Townsend. [The undistinguished Stover is forgotten.] We counselors understood among ourselves that Pierson, Beach and Olin were retained by Mrs. Robinson's friend [left tactfully unnamed], under whose protection she had been living. Townsend alone was retained by Mrs. Robinson."[27]

There's no compelling reason to disbelieve Townsend about this claim. Robinson had the funds to hire a lawyer, given the description of silver and jewelry found at 627 River Street. It's also possible the Barnburner lawyer inserted himself into the case *pro bono* to get in shots at Hard Democrat Mather—which he would definitely do. By most accounts, Robinson's mental state was in good enough order by the fall of 1853 as well, though she continued to avoid saying anything about May 25 and the deaths of Lanagan and Lubee. She also kept mum about her own past life. Townsend, who would defend her with an insanity plea, naturally stressed the abnormality of these two silences:

> In my conversations with Mrs. Robinson in preparing for the trial I could obtain from her no fact bearing on the case, and I could obtain from her no fact as to who she was or what she was or how and why the affair had happened at Lanigan's any more than if she had been the most complete imbecile, and everything which I ever learned about the case had to be learned in the courthouse, from the police officers who arrested her at the time she appeared in the streets as related, and from Mrs. Lanigan's testimony at the trial, and I came to the conclusion that Mrs. Robinson had not been educated among persons of intelligence and was a person of a very low order of intellect, although her manners and conversation, as far they went, indicated that she was a lady who esteemed a correct personal carriage beyond all price.
>
> I am now inclined to the opinion that the shock she sustained when her companion abandoned her [with the alleged intent] to form a lawful marriage completely destroyed the balance of her mind and that she has never recovered . . .[28]

But already, from uncovering Robinson's real grievance against the Lanagans—their house had become a center of community anger against her—we doubt if the "balance of her mind" was so "completely destroyed," and thus have small reason to believe someone else, some third party (neither Robinson nor Mather) hired Townsend. Contemporaries talked of hidden hands behind Robinson's lawyers, though, and one suspicion, printed by the *Albany Evening Atlas* soon after the trial's close, may have related to Townsend: "A gentleman whose name may be found upon the list of lawyers in Troy, asserted in this city, that he had been retained by the family of Mr. Wood to defend the prisoner." Though with its next sentence the *Atlas* disparaged the idea: "If retained at all, it was probably by the paramour of the degraded woman . . ."[29]

At 3:00 P.M. on May 22, the teams of lawyers, all young to middle-aged men except the sixtyish Pierson, sat at their respective tables when Sheriff Price led Henrietta Robinson into the courtroom:

> A large number of spectators were present, and Mrs. R attracted all eyes. She was richly and fashionably appareled, wearing an elegant black silk dress, white hat trimmed with artificials, and spotless white kids, which betrayed a very pretty and delicate hand. Her face was shrouded with a blue veil from the time she entered the court room until she left it. In person Mrs. R. is not above the medium height, is very erect and sprightly, and has a fine figure. We should say, also, judging from her disposition to converse with her counsel, that she has a talent for talking. She manifested considerable interest in the proceedings which were going on.[30]

Both the *Whig* and the *Budget* ran this paragraph in identical stories. The two politically opposed papers probably reprinted coverage from the evening *Troy Daily Traveller* of the day before, despite the fact the Silver-Gray *Whig* and the Soft Democratic *Budget* were each at odds with the liberal Whig *Traveller*. (The *Traveller*'s lavish coverage of Robinson in 1855 hints its now-lost coverage from the spring and summer of 1854[31] was lavish, too, forming a "well" from which other journals drew.) The *Times* relied on an independent report, thus giving a few more details:

> Prisoner . . . took her seat inside the bar near her counsel. She was closely veiled and remained so during her stay in Court. She was richly dressed in black silk, a finely worked collar and undersleeves, wearing a white shirred bonnet, ornamented with artificial flowers, (overhung with a heavy blue veil,) white kid gloves, black silk long shawl, lined with white satin. Her whole apparel was of that "fashionable" description adapted to exhibit her form to the best advantage.
>
> She manifested considerable uneasiness at times, during the empaneling of the Jury, and particularly during the opening of the case by District Attorney Bingham.[32]

The *Whig* and *Budget*'s picture of a "sprightly" and "talkative" defendant contrasts with the *Times*'s picture of Robinson's "uneasiness." David Wilson gives a variation of the *Times*'s view in his *Henrietta Robinson* of 1855: "She at first manifested considerable uneasiness, but in a short time assumed an air of the utmost composure, remaining in her seat, motionless as a vailed [*sic*] statue."[33] The papers covered the jury questioning, revealing that many antebellum New Yorkers opposed capital punishment. The 1850s were an optimistic, reforming time; by early 1852 at least two states, Michigan and Rhode Island, had banned the death penalty.[34] But Bingham and his co-counsels easily found men enough with "no conscientious scruples against hanging." The first prospective juror called, John Cline of Pittstown, declared, "Life for life is scripture, and that is what I go for." The forthright answer went down well with both defense and prosecution for Cline was "Sworn," as were most of the prospective jurors.[35]

While several Troy City men had been among the jury pool, none were chosen to serve, with this an early success for the defense. Actually, one juror, Alanson Cook of Brunswick, a town east of Troy, was hardly an unread or uninformed country person. A former Trojan, he had had a long career as a newspaper editor and part-owner of the Democratic *Troy Daily Budget* in the 1830s and 1840s. As a winner of state contracts for printing in the 1840s, he had owned a press in Albany as well. He had even competed successfully for national printing contracts from the U.S. Post Office before bad health led him to "settle on a farm in Brunswick at the edge of the city." During his retirement, this highly political former editor, a Hard Democrat by 1854,[36] "was repeatedly drawn upon for juries and served as foreman with marked ability and acknowledged impartiality."[37] Trojans of the 1850s saw nothing wrong with semi-professional jurors, and Cook would play his usual role as jury foreman in the Robinson trial.

District Attorney Bingham opened his case: "Gentlemen, the prisoner at the bar, Henrietta Robinson, has been heretofore arraigned, charged with the murder of Timothy Lanagan, in this city, on the 25th day of May, 1853. She is now here for trial. The crime of murder is well understood. It has but one meaning . . ."[38]

He then confirmed the early newspaper reports about Robinson's arrival on River Street—"It will appear that the prisoner, on the 25th of May last, resided in the extreme north part of the city, and had resided there previously, a year or more, keeping house"[39]—before declaring the question of her identity off-limits: "What her antecedents have been, it is not necessary to inquire, nor do we know."[40]

In his account of Timothy Lanagan's and Catharine Lubee's deaths, Bingham told of the two pre-poisoning instances when the Lanagans had driven Mrs. Robinson from the grocery-bar: the night of the early spring dance and the "forenoon" of May 25. He went no further into Robinson's relations with the Lanagans or the neighborhood as a whole, or what might have prompted these bad relations. His opening dealt mainly with Mrs. Lanagan's account of May 25, with the promised testimony of druggist William Ostrom about his sale of arsenic to Robinson, and with the Night Police's discovery of arsenic at 627 River Street after Robinson's arrest. Bingham closed "near 6 o'clock," when Judge Harris adjourned the court until the next morning.[41]

11

DAY TWO—THE DOCTORS

"The prisoner came into Court this morning dressed in a light plaid silk, veiled as before. There were but few spectators in the Court at the opening."[1] But the thinly-populated courtroom soon filled "during the afternoon with a full representation of ladies."

The prosecution's first witness, Dr. Henry Adams was the self-described "family physician" of the Lanagans "before his [Timothy's] death."[2] Adams, who practiced from North Fourth Street (five short blocks east of River) knew Robinson as well.

Mr. Hogeboom asked the Court if it was not proper for the prisoner to remove her veil, so as [to allow Adams] to identify her. The court stated that there would probably be no objections. It was removed by the prisoner for an instant.

"That is the lady," said Adams. "I knew her some three months previous to this occurrence; she lived nearly opposite Lannagan's on River street, farther north . . ." Here Hogeboom produced a "diagram" of the streets, pored over and "pronounced correct by the witness." This had little to do with the rest of Adams's testimony. He was present to tell the story of Timothy Lanagan's last hours and supply the cause of death. Adams's descriptions of his patient's "vomiting," "severe evacuations," and "burning pain," were graphic and sad, but the Fourth Street doctor hardly rated as a good witness. Hogeboom had to drag the answers he needed from Adams. Adams: "I do not know what he died of; I suppose it was from the effects of poison administered. It is my impression that he died from the effects of poison administered; this is my decided belief. I could not exactly tell by the symptoms as to the nature of the poison; the symptoms would correspond with the effects of arsenic."

Normal School Building (Albany).

Adams failed Hogeboom in another area, too. He had heard a deathbed statement by Timothy Lanagan, which he remembered this way: "The expression was that the villain had destroyed him and he *[Lanagan]* should not recover." But on "cross," Beach drew out that Adams had tried to cheer his patient with hopes of recovery, and this, in Judge Harris's view, ruled out the extra weight then given "the dying declaration of a party who was about to die, and who could not have any motive but to tell the truth." Harris: "If these physicians had informed him that he must die, and there was no chance of recovery, it would have been different. On the contrary, the physicians told him he might recover."

Dr. Adams held his own against Beach on one issue. This was Beach's suggestion—obvious from Adams's responses—that Lanagan had simply fallen victim to the cholera epidemic then present in the city. While Adams offered, "I do not think he [Lanagan] was a man of vigorous constitution"—the weak were viewed as prone to cholera—Adams cleared Lanagan of other supposed predisposing factors: "I believe his habits were regular; he was a temperate man as far as I knew." The family doctor also discussed "evacuations" at length, judging Lanagan's had not been of choleraic type, before Hogeboom on re-cross led the hesitant Adams to say: "I think I could pronounce with confidence that he *[Lanagan]* did not die of cholera."

Dr. Avery J. Skilton, who had also attended Lanagan but unlike Adams had been present at the autopsy as well, next took the witness stand. The 52-year-old Skilton was a neighborhood man, too, with home and office on North Fourth not far from Adams's. But as current president of the Rensselaer County Medical Society,[3] he seems to have been a more high-powered doctor. He was definitely more confident: "I have no doubt as to the cause of death being produced from mineral poison; as a professional man I fully believe the poison administered was arsenic . . . In medicine these symptoms are so sure as to leave the physician no chance to doubt. I do not admit that I could be mistaken."

But Henrietta Robinson's lawyers were high-powered, too. And one of them, probably Beach, cited *Beck's Medical Jurisprudence* and Beck's ruling that "it is not safe in case of poison to have the fact determined except by applying chemical tests to the matter found in the stomach." Skilton agreed that "the most prominent authors on the subject of poisons, medical men, are Guy, Christison, Beck, and Orfelia,"[4] but wriggled out of the spot where Beck placed him: "I assign as a reason why Beck took the position he does, was that the [coroner's] jury [of Beck's experience] were not physicians."

Then despite the fact Dr. Francis Dakin of the State Normal School at Albany *had* performed a chemical test on Lanagan's stomach and intestines in May of 1853, Skilton bumblingly said: "I am not certain that there was a chemical analysis of the subject. The stomach and intestines were taken out at the post mortem examination; they were taken charge of by Dr. Bontecou." [So at least, he, Skilton, hadn't misplaced them or forgot to test them!]

On May 22 the *Troy Daily Times* had lamented "that Prof. Daiken [*sic*], of Albany, an important witness who analyzed the stomachs of the persons murdered, is very ill, and will not be able to attend Court." But the defense questioning of Skilton now speeded Dakin's recovery. He would appear at the close of the next day to confirm his finding of arsenic.

In the meantime 29-year-old Dr. William Seymour, a future president of the Rensselaer County Medical Society who had assisted at the Lanagan autopsy, said more about the "white powder" and "inflammation," though under Beach's Hamlet-like gaze Seymour conceded: "The inflammation of the stomach was not necessarily made by poison." George Van Santvoord ushered in Seymour's last gruesome bit of testimony: "I saw no other evidence of disease, except that exhibited by the stomach; the powder was entangled in a thick mucus; the Doctor scraped it up with a knife, and put it on paper; I do not think there was a teaspoon visible."[5]

The medical questioning took its toll on Ann Lanagan: "[Next] Mrs. Lannagan, the wife of the murdered man, was called as a witness. She appeared very much enfeebled and had nearly fainted away in her seat at an early part of the day. Some time elapsed before she became collected enough to answer the questions propounded by the counsel."[6]

After describing her own arrival in the neighborhood and meeting with Henrietta Robinson—"I was two months living there before I became acquainted with her"—Ann Lanagan told the story of May 25, 1853. A midday dinner break interrupted her tale, along with defense objections, mainly efforts to keep mentions of Catharine Lubee's sufferings and death out of the proceedings. At the close of direct testimony about May 25: "[Prosecution] Counsel renewed the offer to prove the dying declarations of Mr. Lannagan. [But] Court: Do not think it will answer."[7]

Judge Harris wasn't leaning toward the prosecution in his rulings, but neither was he leaning toward the defense in any obvious way. As the prosecution began to lead the widow through the story of the trouble at the March 1853 dance, the defense objected and was overruled: "The Court thought it was proper here to show any unkindness of feeling between them even at this time. He [Harris] did not see any other way than to let the matter come out."[8]

It came out, complete with description of Robinson's drawn pistol and threat to bar-patron David Smith to "blow his brains out." On cross-examination of the widow, Job Pierson tried for admissions that, despite the March incident, *no* "unkindness of feeling" had existed between the Lanagan family and Robinson. On the surface, Pierson got what he wanted. Ann Lanagan said, "I did not feel unfriendly towards her at the time I told her to go home [on the night of the dance]." The witness also agreed she "Did swear on the Coroner's inquest that there was no cause of enmity between myself and husband and Mrs. Robinson." But Lanagan's complete replies to Pierson—filled with homely details about money, food, beds, borrowings, and visitings—showed the tension, anger, and fear bouncing episodically between Nos. 622 and 627 River in the spring of 1853. At the close of his cross-examination, Pierson drew from Ann Lanagan her knowledge of an illness claimed by Robinson late in the day of the poisonings: "I can't tell you from whom I heard that Mrs. Robinson was sick. I think I heard of it the day following my husband's death—can't be certain Haley did not say she was sick when he came over [surely on his unsuccessful mission to bring Ann Lanagan back to No. 627 River after the poisonings, not on his earlier errand about the loan]. Knew that Mrs. Robinson was in jail the day following the death, but heard she was taken sick before going to jail."[9]

This "illness"—so slight it didn't keep Robinson from walking downtown where she was arrested the same evening—seems more damning than guilt-clearing. It looks like something invented to allay suspicion, and maybe even part of a last-ditch ploy to lure Mrs. Lanagan to Robinson's cottage to do away with her there.

Druggist William Ostrom, a key prosecution witness, next mounted the witness stand: "I did know a Mrs. Robinson at that time [May 1853]. Should know her now, if she would raise her veil."

> Mr. Hogeboom: I submit, your honor, that we shall be obliged to try that veil experiment once more. [Laughter and excitement in the room, during which the officer commanded order.]
>
> Mrs. Robinson made no motion to raise her veil; she was conversing with Mr. Beach.
>
> The Court said: If the witness prefers it, she may step forward to where the witness is, and unveil herself to him alone. [Mrs. Robinson came forward to the witness, and ascending the platform, raised her veil in the face of the witness.]
>
> That is the lady, sir; she was in my store several times in the month of May, 1853.[10]

Ostrom then gave his important nugget—". . . in that month she purchased arsenic at my store; it was between the 10th and the 25th of May; she bought as near as I can recollect two ounces"—before discussing the woman's different visits to his store.[11] His portrait of her on a Saturday evening prior to the 25th—either the 14th or the 21st:

> She was very much excited at the second time she called . . . judging from her appearance, flushed countenance and excited manner, I have no doubt she was in liquor . . . On the Saturday I speak of, her excitement and mode of dress, her flushed countenance and language, led me to believe she was intoxicated. Her language was not as polished, not as good as formerly. Having a revolver was another reason why I thought she was intoxicated. [Then in obvious concession to queries by Beach] She made no use of vulgarity that I recollect of. The excited state of her mind, and the flush in the face, might have been produced by other causes than liquor. They might have proceeded from a deranged mind connected with a diseased state of the person. . . . She was of rather florid complexion usually.[12]

As the jury absorbed these images, Hogeboom recalled Skilton to describe Catharine Lubee's symptoms, with Abram Olin objecting, unsuccessfully, for the defense. But Olin kept up the defense's line of attack on Skilton by pounding away at the missing chemical analysis.

The next day, the *Troy Daily Times* would inform its readers: "The prisoner generally walks from the Court House to the jail, accompanied by the officers. Her desire to have them follow a long distance behind is not gratified. Last evening, Ferry street, from Franklin street to the Jail, was crowded with spectators to get a sight of the prisoner. She appears much disturbed and irritable. She has fallen away very much in flesh since her imprisonment."

12

DAY THREE—THE VEIL

The *Troy Daily Times*:

> The prisoner was brought into court richly dressed and veiled as usual.
>
> Judge Harris said, we have thus far proceeded in the trial of this case, with the prisoner masked. We are now trying a person without the Court or the Jury ever seeing her. It is but a ceremony. The Jury are required to look upon the prisoner, and the Prisoner to look upon the Jury. I feel a repugnance to try a person whom I never saw and cannot see. I am unwilling to proceed farther without the prisoner being unmasked. I believe it is the duty of the Court to require her to unveil her face. I regret the necessity, but I deem it my duty to impose this upon the Prisoner. She ought to know that it is a just demand, and to obey voluntarily. I shall not raise any unreasonable coercion in the case.
>
> The prisoner was then requested to remove the veil from her face.[1]
>
> Mrs. Robinson rose from her chair, and, raising her vail, said, "I am here to undergo a most painful and important trial. I do not wish to be gazed at."[2]
>
> [She] immediately replaced the vail, and resumed her seat . . . The Prisoner continued to sit vailed. There was a slight pause—a dead silence for a minute or two—during which time all eyes were turned toward the masked figure, when the judge ordered the counsel to proceed.[3]

Night Policeman Charles Burns testified about Robinson's arrest and the search of her house, including his finding of the arsenic under the carpet. Unfortunately for the defense, William Beach's "cross" of the Night Policeman only pulled out more lurid damaging-to-Robinson details, like Burns's comment about the paper of Spanish flies and his description of Robinson's staging of her entry into the jail to avoid the jeers of street loungers. At one point, after mention of the locket found in Robinson's cache of jewelry under the carpet at No. 627: "Mrs. Robinson bent forward and whispered to her counsel. Mr. Beach, addressing the witness, said, 'The prisoner is anxious to know what has become of that locket.' "[4]

The implication Burns had pilfered the item was the defense's only score with this witness. And Beach had no questions for the next prosecution witness, wholesale provison dealer Burr Lord, who told of Lanagan's ghastly appearance and complaints of illness on the afternoon of May 25, 1853.

With Dr. Reed Bontecou, Troy's coroner in 1853, the defense had more to work with—though only as far as the second part of Bontecou's testimony, drawn from him on cross by Job Pierson, went. Bontecou's first, direct testimony obliterated the possibility of a natural death for Lanagan:

> I was associated with Dr. Dakin in making an analysis of the contents of the stomach; I took the stomach from the body myself; I analyzed the contents of the stomach in latter part of June last; the analysis continued two or three weeks.
>
> I applied chemical tests with a view of ascertaining the substances which the stomach contained. We found arsenic in the stomach. We applied several different tests; they resulted in showing arsenic. In Mr. Lannegan's intestines we found 40 grains; there was enough to produce death; he died in consequence of the poison, which I can state professionally.[5]

After pointing out Bontecou's junior position to Dakin in the chemical analysis, Pierson moved on to Robinson's manner after arrest, when Bontecou had patted her down for weapons and then visited her several times a week for a few weeks. Pierson had barely launched into this line, when Judge Harris, alert to the defense's planned direction[6] ". . . stated that if the defence were to rely upon facts relative to the sanity of her mind, he would request the prisoner to remove her veil. He said he would give such an order to the Sheriff—that the veil would be removed. He regarded it as an imperative duty, that the veil should be removed, if the defence were to set up the plea of insanity."[7]

The *Troy Daily Budget*: "Mr. Beach here removed the veil from her face. She was seen smiling and keeping her hand and kerchief up to her face." The *Albany Evening Atlas*: "After some little time Mrs. Robinson raised her veil, but concealed her face from the jury by her fan. Under an intimation that this would not be allowed, she finally removed her veil and remained entirely unveiled, a short time, when she again partially drew it over her face."[8] The *Troy Daily Times*: "After removing her veil, the prisoner kept her face concealed most of the time with a white handkerchief. Her face was flushed, and appeared to have been painted."[9]

Bontecou, prompted in turn by Pierson and Beach, described Robinson's "wild" and "unnatural" behavior on the evening of the 25th and during her first weeks in jail. The prosecution made no objections and offered no re-cross to challenge these opinions from its own witness. Bingham just produced Dr. Dakin at last to confirm all Seymour and Bontecou had said about the autopsy samples. Dakin even brought along an extract from Lanagan's stomach to show the jury: ". . . the result of the analysis—the compositions obtained—are in that jar [produced in Court]."[10]

Dakin didn't explain the new (1840) forensic techniques which allowed arsenic identification.[11] But it was a good thing antebellum scientists had these tests, as there was no United States' federal or state law similar to Britain's "Arsenic Act" of 1851, which required druggists to add soot or indigo to the deadly white powder—thus giving potential poisoning victims a better chance of avoiding spiked foods and drinks. And antebellum newspapers actually convey the idea arsenic poisonings were *rife* throughout the society.[12]

On the close of Dakin's brief testimony—we imagine him still pale from his illness—the prosecution rested, and this caught the defense off-guard. After a request "for a few minutes consultation with counsel"[13] which then ran into the long dinner break, Job Pierson launched the defense case with a *more* or *less* false disclaimer: "We, as counsel, have nothing to expect from this unfortunate woman. In the language of the grand juror's oath, we act neither for reward or the hope of reward. This prisoner I never saw or heard of until this offence."[14] Pierson joined with District Attorney Bingham in putting the defendant's past off limits: "I do not know the antecedents of this woman; what her life and character have been she utterly refuses to disclose to anyone. So of her family and connexions. All we know of her is that she is a lady of unusual intelligence and highly polished manners."[15]

With these issues out of the way, he argued for an acquittal mainly on the grounds of insanity:

> I was told by the officers of the prison that she was insane. I felt it my duty—perhaps it was not—to go and see her. I did

> so. I found her a perfect maniac; her mind was tottering, and reason was dethroned. It was weeks and weeks before I could get anything from her at all satisfactory . . . what I say will be substantiated by others . . .
>
> Indeed, gentlemen, her conduct in court shows you that she is not right in her mind. I do not say or believe, she is insane, but her mind has lost its balance in a degree. That she was insane, in every sense, both before and after the death of Lanagan, the evidence will be sufficient to convince you beyond all doubt.[16]

He named his upcoming witnesses to Robinson's strange acts, synopsizing their evidence, before launching his second back-up argument:

> There is not a particle of evidence that she put arsenic in the beer. True, she had arsenic in her house. There are hundreds of houses in Troy in which arsenic is kept. And gentlemen . . . What motive was there in this case? No motive under Heaven. To be sure there was the disturbance at the dance, but that was all made up, and they were as good friends as ever again, visiting each other, she trading with the Lanagans up to the very morning of the alleged murder.

> . . . there is no human being to give color to the suspicion that Mrs. R. put poison in the beer, except Mrs. Lannagan . . .
>
> I do not wish to attack the character of any human being; but we must look at things as they are. Who was Miss Lubee? An unmarried woman; and who was Mrs. Robinson? A woman residing in the neighborhood spending much of her time at the house of Lannagan, and a pretty woman to say the least. Jealousy, gentlemen, sometimes goes a great ways. Certain it is that Mrs. Lannagan did not drink of the beer; and I am justified in saying that she did at no time intend to drink it. I cast no aspersions . . .[17]

Pierson's casting of the aspersion—despite his denial—closed his speech, and here Judge Harris tried to de-veil Robinson once more: "Mrs. Robinson, after some hesitation, threw her veil partially over her bonnet, and as if sobbing, bent forward her head, burying her face pretty much wholly in her handkerchief. She was much affected, apparently, throughout the afternoon, and succeeded in partially concealing her face from view. The Court room was crowded during the afternoon."[18]

The defense began their slate of witnesses with William Hegeman, sometime-deputy and sometime-physician at the Ferry Street Jail. He told of her outbursts, oddly-timed laughter, and fits of paranoia, drawing a convincing picture of instability beyond mere alcohol abuse. But then as now, legal insanity was a hard bar to reach. American courts followed—and most still follow—the British "McNaughton Rules," established in 1843 after the unpopular acquittal of one Daniel McNaughton who, while delusional, had murdered Tory Prime Minister Robert Peel's secretary. Key McNaughton rules hold that juries, not doctors, are the final judges of defendants' sanity and defendants must be totally unable to tell right from wrong to qualify as legally insane.

And prosecution cross-examination of Hegeman often uncovered method behind the defendant's strange acts. It was, after all, winter when she broke apart some of her furniture and burned it in the stove of her cell. And perhaps the single wineglass full of brandy which Hegeman prescribed for Robinson—"seven or eight times in all"—to combat "diarrhea, head ache, sleepless nights" had resulted in drunkenness on occasion?

Robinson's young neighbor, Mary Jane Dillon, turned into the courtroom crowd-pleaser of the afternoon. In Judge Harris's opinion a very pretty girl,[19] Dillon artlessly recited story after story of Robinson's doings and sayings as the woman grew more frantic and vengeful across the spring of 1853. One story especially shocked contemporaries because of the bold, vigorous, "masculine" Robinson it revealed:[20]

> She *[Robinson]* said she could jump into the river and swim until she got tired, and then she had a cork which she could put between her teeth, and rest in the water and not sink. I was on the bank of the river with her near her house, which was near the bank of the River; before she went on the bank of the river, she saw a boat coming down; she said that Oliver Boutwell had stopped the navigation, and the boat couldn't pass. While on the bank of the river, she began to hoot at the hands on the boat, but they did not hear her. She had a revolver in her hand, and began to climb up the rocks. She got about half way up, and turned to me and said, "Mary Jane, wouldn't I make a good soldier?"[21]

Dillon's "vastly entertaining"[22] testimony also included a glimpse of antics more alarming to Dillon: ". . . she frightened me; she took hold of me the same as she said she did hold of the man [Patrick Galvin, when according to Robinson 'he was going to lay violent hands upon her']; but she laughed and seemed so pleasant about it that I thought little of it afterwards; when she saw I was frightened she laughed; I was not frightened by her much afterwards."[23]

In Dillon's eyes, Robinson was never drunk. "I never knew Mrs. R. to drink anything stronger than peppermint cordial," claimed the young seamstress, just before the six o'clock close of "the third day of this extraordinary trial."[24]

13

DAY FOUR—BOMBSHELL

When the trial reopened on Thursday morning, a strange bombshell had fallen or was on the point of falling outside the courtroom, which would affect the day's legal actions and the whole rest of the proceeding. This bombshell was an accusation—probably far more specific than the June 1853 charge which had drawn Emma Willard's letter of denial to the Whig—pointing to "Henrietta Robinson" as the second eldest of Robert Wood of Quebec's daughters, Emma Cecilia, though it did not specifically name this Miss Wood. The accusation, within the page two editorial of the Thursday morning *Troy Daily Whig*, had likely reached readers by the court's opening at 8:30 A.M. It definitely reached them by mid-morning:

> It may not be improper to say that the current belief is—not to use a stronger term—that Mrs! [*sic*] Robinson, the Prisoner, formerly—some twenty years ago—resided in this city, as a pupil at the seminary; that her maiden name was Wood; that her family was one of wealth, standing and respectability—and resided somewhere near Quebec; that while here she moved in the best social circles of our city, as did three sisters who also attended the Seminary at different times; that she subsequently married an army officer in Canada, who died; that she then married a surgeon in the army, in the Provinces, from whom she separated; and that she is now here the Veiled Prisoner at the Bar, charged with the crime of murder.[1]

Was the *Whig* reporting the reaction to its own May 25, 1854, editorial when it noted a day later that "usual attendance" at court on Thurs-

The Elm-tree Corner. (Albany)

day morning swelled late in the morning, and: "Mrs. Robinson was more cheerful . . . and was less tenacious about the veil—partially disclosing her face most of the time, and readily unveiling (but for an instant only) when witnesses intimated that they could not identify her without?"[2]

Robinson's ease *after* publication of the item about her connection to the Wood family is interesting. What could it mean? Some fragments of trial testimony plus one brief newspaper notice would soon hint at an answer. But for now, let's look at Day Four of the trial alone.

It began, probably according to long-set defense plans, with butcher Anthony Goodspeed who told of Robinson's behavior in his shop one day in March 1853. She had repeatedly asked for game—out of season—talked of "people abusing her at the dam," of her own swearing out of warrants against her neighbors, and then, immodestly, she had placed her foot on "a stairs there" and requested Goodspeed to tie the fastening of her gaiter. Prosecutor Hogeboom challenged this proffered evidence of mental imbalance in a curious way. After drawing from Goodspeed the fact Robinson's gaiter laces *had* been untied—and therefore the woman's request was rational, if unusual—Hogeboom plunged into a line of questioning bent on drawing John C. Mather's name into the trial record. The Town of Nassau lawyer queried Goodspeed in such a way the butcher replied: ". . . she [Robinson] did not say anything about getting men discharged at the state dam; I think she meant the state dam; I do not know who had charge of the state dam." [It was Mather, of course, as New York State Canal Commissioner in charge of the "Eastern District.][3]

What was happening to the gentlemen's agreement between prosecution and defense, openly endorsed by both Bingham and Pierson, not to dig into Robinson's past or "connexions"? It looks as though with publication of that morning's editorial in the *Whig*, all deals were off. Interestingly, both prosecution and defense teams, friendly from the outset, began to take the same tack, each bringing Mather to the fore though with the defense doing so most dramatically. But the prosecution led the way in this.

Mary Jane Dillon returned to the stand, after Goodspeed, for cross-examination by George Van Santvoord. As with Job Pierson's cross of prosecution witness Charles Burns, there tumbled out more on Henrietta Robinson's odd doings, though whether *more* or *less* helpful to the questioner's case, it was hard to say. But Prosecutor Van Santvoord ended with a clear attempt, or at least threat, to establish Robinson's most important recent "connexion." Dillon could only provide partial answers: "I do not recollect who I have seen there. I have seen Mrs. Lanagan's sister there, just coming to the door and returning again; my father came in to work in the garden. I saw another man there one day; I do not know who he was; had a slight glimpse of his face; was a middle-aged man . . ."[4]

Following Dillon: ". . . the counsel rested some fifteen or twenty minutes, during which Mrs. R. and her counsel commenced conversing freely together. At times she was noticed apparently crying, and at others showing her usual cheerful and smiling aspect; after a while she drew the veil over her face, and seemed to be speaking very positively for much of the time of something; making many gestures with her head and hands, etc."[5]

Robinson's emotion was explained by Martin I. Townsend two days later in open court:

Mr. Townsend alluded to an article in the *Whig* of this morning, which spoke of a change in tactics of the defence [*sic*], after the case had proceeded some length, which resulted in bringing out prominently the name of Mr. Mather, as having relations with this woman some time prior to the commission of the deed. He said that there had been no change in tactics . . . It had been suggested that this evidence had been brought out, through a change in tactics, at the desire of the prisoner. On the contrary the prisoner had, when a conference of the Counsel took place, insisted that this evidence should not be brought out . . .[6]

Years later, in his 1898 interview with the *Budget*, Townsend would say this about the defense "tactics":

"I had expected to occupy an entirely secondary position upon the trial until the testimony for the people closed, when the counsel for the prisoner held a consultation. The three counselors for the politician said: 'What can we do? We are employed by this gentleman. We are here in his service. We do not feel ourselves at liberty to expose his name and his relations to this woman when we are here in his service and on his behalf.' And from that moment the whole burden of the case was left to rest upon me."[7]

If Townsend correctly reported the words or at least the feelings of his fellow defense team members, Pierson and the other Mather-allied defense lawyers agreed to the attacks on Mather. Anyway, they *agreed enough* not to jump up in court and object to Townsend's charges. It really looks as though *all* the Robinson trial lawyers thought Mather was responsible for the Wood- and Willard-damaging editorial in that morning's *Whig*, and *even* his Hard friends judged Mather had gone too far. The lawyers had good reasons for believing Mather had "placed" the article. First, it appeared in the *Whig*, a paper that would be labeled "the Hard Court Journal" only a few weeks into the future.[8] Second, the Troy men may have remembered the liberal Whig *Post* had published the first allegation about the Wood family in late June or early July of 1853,[9] at a time when Mather's relations with the liberal wing of the Whig party were more solid than his relations with the Silver Grays.[10]

If Mather had launched the *Whig* article in a second attempt to shift the scandal from his shoulders onto those of the Woods and Willards, the move was a mistake for him. It resulted in an avalanche of comments on his role in Robinson's life over the coming days. But if the new Wood allegation had been thrown out, even in part, to lead the public's eyes away from a certain recent part of the life of the woman now on trial (about which, more shortly) the move was successful in this area.

The assault on Mather, beginning halfway through Day Four, highlights the cooperation between the prosecution and defense—actually the cooperation between *all* parties, prosecution, defense, and judge, involved in the trial for most of its course. Why would so many of Troy's legal men come together (though with Mather's Hard allies at the defense table sitting mute) to attack Mather? One answer may be the Woods had important friends in Troy aside from the Willards, specifically the merchant George M. Tibbits, recipient of Jeffery's letter of April 8, 1854. The son of "the richest man in Troy,"[11] Tibbits was the nearest thing to leader of the city's old elite of commercial wealth. In January of 1853, his own son's loss of the presidency of Troy's Young Men's Association to a son of one of the new iron-manufacturing families, the Warrens, sparked enough bitterness to show what a watershed event for Troy's upper crust this was.[12]

Plus the hometown Willards may have commanded wide loyalties. Emma Willard was more than just a member of Troy's establishment by this date. She was one of its jewels, a source of immense community pride because of her national and international fame.[13]

Now, with some form of permission from Pierson though over the objections of Robinson, Townsend laid bare the accused's relationship with Mather, aided by two fellow Democrats, local politicos and probably both Softs: Edwin Brownell, the former poormaster, and Moses Warren, sometime Rensselaer County sheriff.[14] Brownell told of Robinson's claim of marriage to Mather, of her threats, and of his own (Brownell's) visit to No. 627 River when "Mather was not there . . ." Warren established Mather's whereabouts for the evening of May 21, the night when Robinson walked to the boardinghouse. Then the young druggist, John H. Knickerbocker, drove home the point that Robinson was seeking Mather's lodgings during her late-night quest.

After the midday break, Townsend recalled Dr. Hegeman, querying him first about Mather crony Richard Jennyss's visits to the jail. Having established that Jennyss visited "the next morning that she said she had heard people at her door to destroy her [*sic*]," Hegeman described Robinson's hallucinations once more, with Townsend drawing as much insanity-mileage as possible out of this. The prosecution hadn't cross-examined Brownell or Warren or Knickerbocker, but Hogeboom now rose to ask Hegeman more about Jennyss and also about Stover. He repeatedly asked the doctor-jailor about the two lawyers' visits to the jail. Was Hogeboom implying the two had either coached Robinson in her "craziness" or they had influenced Hegeman into seeing her behavior as crazy? Partly, it seems. But it also appears Hogeboom acted just to get the lawyers' names out there and link them with Mather. While Hegeman failed to pronounce the wanted name—"I do not know by whose request they [Jennyss and Stover] came"—he provided other gifts to the prosecution. On the destroyed furniture: "About the time she burnt the chairs, she complained we had not given her firewood enough." And Hegeman also told of Robinson's low and unladylike tobacco habit: "I used to procure for her sometimes 2 or 3 lbs. snuff at a time—sometimes once a month, sometimes once in two months."

Townsend next called Jennyss himself to the witness stand, not to hector him about Mather, but just to corroborate Hegeman's account of Robinson's hallucinations. Prosecutor Hogeboom took up the slack on the Mather references. As he had done with Hegeman, Hogeboom's re-cross focused on Jennyss's links to Robinson's ex-lover, pulling out the nugget about Mather's letters to Robinson as well as the interesting fact that Robinson had told Jennyss "she could not write her name." At this point William Beach reminded everyone of the main thrust of the defense case—announcing the defense plan to use "medical works touching on insanity" in their final arguments—and "stated that the evidence for the defense had now closed."

The prosecution resumed with short testimonies from four witnesses. The first, John Upton, couldn't have been in the witness seat for more than a minute or two before defense objection, supported by Judge Harris, swept him from it. Upton's remarks, reported in the *Troy Daily Times* were: "Lives in Albany; lived there 20 years; I do know the prisoner, but not by the name of Mrs. Robinson; I have seen her without her veil; she once resided in Albany; she resided there in March, '51. Know John C. Mather."

Only this much had escaped Upton, when Hogeboom asked, "Did you see her in company with Mr. Mather in that month?" and the defense axe fell. Why was the defense so opposed to this line of questioning? Townsend had already raised Mather's name several times, after all. Two short notices in two separate Albany papers—the *Albany Evening Atlas* and the *Albany Evening Journal*—of this very day, May 25, 1854, suggest an answer. The *Atlas*: "Justice Parsons of this city has been called to Troy as a witness in the case of Mrs. Robinson."

And Thurlow Weed's *Journal*: "The Murder Case in Troy. Witnesses from here have been summoned to attend in the case of Mrs. Robinson, now on trial at Troy for poisoning Lanagan. It appears that Mrs. R. lived in this city some years since, and was a source of annoyance to her neighbors, one of whom was determined to see who were her visitors. For this purpose he made a close inspection of a man coming from Mrs. R's house, upon which Mrs. R. drew a pistol and threatened to shoot him. For this she was arrested and brought before the police magistrates."

A City of Albany directory for 1851 confirms Parsons served as one of the city's two Police Court or Justice Court judges and Upton served as one of its constables. Clearly, the two men were prepared to describe some run-in Robinson had had with the law when living under a different name in Albany. Intriguingly, during the Big Letting in December of 1851, Mather had given a $12,000 canal contract to a "Jno. Upton & Co." for construction of a "Feeder, Bulkhead, Bridges, etc. at Rome," and Constable John Upton had not resumed his police job in 1852. Also, despite Upton's claim to Albany residence at the 1854 trial, that city's directories no longer list him after 1851, suggesting he had relocated to Rome, site of the planned feeder, bulkhead, and bridges.[15] Mather could well have given Upton one of the fat contracts as payback for smoothing over some Robinson-created trouble in Albany from earlier in 1851 under her other name. Though admittedly, if Mather *had* done so, ex-Constable Upton didn't remain very

Mansion of Hon. George Tibbits. (From a painting by Cornelia A. King, August, 1819.)

loyal to ex-Canal Commissioner Mather three years after the fact. For in arguing, unsuccessfully, for more testimony from John Upton, Prosecutor Hogeboom made it clear Upton was prepared to talk about Mather as well as Robinson: "We propose to show by the witness on the stand that Mr. Mather was at this woman's house in Albany in March, 1851, and was seen sitting at her table."[16] But of course, any person, willing or unwilling, may be subpoenaed as a witness.[17]

Hogeboom also told the assembled court he needed Upton—found so alarming by the defense—because otherwise: ". . . the Jury will be told that while this woman claimed to be very intimately and personally acquainted with Mr. Mather, there was not a particle of evidence that she ever saw him."

Hogeboom may have believed this, since none of the questioning so far had produced any eyewitness sightings of John C. Mather together with Henrietta Robinson (Mary Jane Dillon's glimpse of the unnamed "middle-aged man" at No. 627 obviously doesn't count). But it's almost certain Hogeboom was wrong here. Townsend's 1898 reminiscence of the trial convinces us he had formed his defense strategy, based on the reality of Robinson's relationship with Mather, from early on the 25th and before the Soft lawyer rose to examine any witnesses. Judge Harris believed this. In sustaining the defense objection, he: ". . . intimat[ed] that it seemed unecessary to establish the point contended for by counsel; it was not likely it would be controverted." Harris held out a further friendly hand to ex-Commissioner Mather: "Offers to prove similar intimacies between the same parties at Troy, at a later period, were made by counsel for the prosecution, but declined by the Court."[18]

With Upton now banished, the prosecution hurried its three remaining witnesses onto the stand. Robinson's next-door neighbor Oliver Boutwell added his mite to the intoxication versus insanity debate ("I used to often see her . . . when I thought she was the worse for liquor.") The flourmill-owner also provided a completely rational explanation of Robinson's comment to Dillon about his (Boutwell's) having stopped navigation on the river: ". . . there is a lock on the east side of the river, through which boats pass; the boatmen complained that the water from my mill made a difficulty in their passing up and down; it was their complaint that my race had the effect to throw the boats onto the other side . . . onto a rock in the vicinity . . ."[19]

Bar-owner Peter Cox testified to Robinson's alcohol intake during her boycott of the Lanagans' after the dance incident. Her apparently daily consumption was ample, if not outrageously large: "Sometimes she would buy half a pint of brandy, and at others a quart of beer; sometimes not so much." And finally, Constable Franklin Bowman stressed Robinson's rationality at the time of her arrest, when she had asked for clothes and her gold watch to be brought from No. 627 River Street to the jail: "I don't know that there was anything strange in the manner of her asking for them . . . [though] her appearance and manner in jail was somewhat excited." With these final licks in for the prosecution, "both parties rested" in preparation for the long closing speeches of the next day.

14

DAY FIVE—SOME ANTEBELLUM LORE

The court met a quarter of an hour early, at 8:15 rather than 8:30, on Friday morning due to an expected but rare event. As if the drama of Robinson's trial was not enough, a total eclipse of the sun would occur that afternoon, briefly plunging the courtroom into darkness so deep Prosecutor Van Santvoord, then speaking, fell silent and sat down, while the whole of "the large and densely crowded room" kept "perfect silence."[1] The vivid testimony of the day before, but more important, the Miss Wood allegation first appearing in the Thursday morning *Troy Daily Whig* had packed Friday's proceedings.

Did Robinson find some pleasure in her starring role before this full house? *The Troy Daily Times*: "The prisoner appeared in Court, dressed as usual in black silk, and veiled. She appeared quite at ease and less agitated than on previous occasions."

Defense Attorney Martin I. Townsend spoke first, opening with delicate references to the politically-fraught nature of the trial:

> His associates . . . had desired him to address the Jury upon the law and the facts, because he stood in a different position from some of them. He should remark fearlessly upon the testimony; he should do his duty as pertains to this case, without regard to consequences. He spoke with great embarrassment . . .
>
> My position, from the very nature of the case, is an embarrassing one . . .

Townsend next referred to the difficulty of any insanity plea, announced as the defense line from the first. There had been only a single successful insanity plea, he told jurors, in the last two decades of Rensselaer County history: the case of Patrick Conway, murderer of Mrs. Groesbeck, "whose infirmity while he was yet in jail, became so palpable and apparent, that he was finally discharged by common consent."[2] But Townsend also mentioned a case of greater and more long-lasting fame, that of William Freeman, who murdered a whole family near Auburn, Cayuga County:

In that case, Governor Seward [he had served as Freeman's lawyer after his years as Governor in 1838–42] against unanimous public opinion, and the furious clamor of the populace contended that he [Freeman] was a lunatic. The trial occupied a month, and he was convicted. It was a most horrid murder, and the perpetrator was a poor, ignorant negro. Governor Seward was dissatisfied with the conviction, and appealed from the prejudiced verdict of the jury; but before the case could be brought to argument in a higher tribunal, the negro died in jail, an evident and universally acknowledged idiot.[3]

Townsend did *not* bring up the successful insanity pleas of two celebrated New York State capital case defendants whose life situations had been much more like Robinson's. Amelia Norman, mentioned earlier, and Margaret Garrity were "fallen women" in desperate straits, though, unlike Robinson, both had committed their crimes on the bodies of their seducers. Norman had attempted to kill the father of her illegitimate child, and Garrity had killed her former lover. All-male New York City juries had listened to Norman's and Garrity's tragic stories and found the two women—in 1844 and 1851, respectively—temporarily insane on commission of their crimes. Their acquittals had been popular ones, accepted by the public at large. Townsend surely shied away from mentioning these verdicts through fear of highlighting key differences—damaging ones to his client—between the New York City women's acts and those of Robinson.[4] Without doubt, if Robinson had killed Mather, and Mather alone, her attorneys would have had an easier sell to 1850s-era jurors. Also both Norman and Garrity had stabbed their victims, assaults that didn't carry the same aura of premeditation as the use of poison.

Townsend did, apparently, raise the case of Adeline Phelps at this time.[5] In the summer of 1852, Adeline Phelps, a penniless and unmarried woman of forty living with her parents in Northfield, Massachusetts, learned that her 83-year-old father, Elihu, had deeded "the little property on which he lived, worth one or two hundred dollars, to the town of Northfield."[6] Adeline then confided to a neighbor, ". . . he [Elihu] had no right to deed the place away, and she would be willing to go to hell to see him burning in it."[7] A short time later Elihu died with symptoms retroactively diagnosed as poisoning from "a mercurial preparation."[8] Like Henrietta Robinson, Adeline had made some odd remarks before the fatal events leading to her trial. At different times she had said water and milk from nearby farms was poisoned and the Phelps' farmhouse cellar held dead men's bones. Also, Phelps had actually spent several months in the Brattleboro Lunatic Asylum on two different occasions, in 1844–45 and in 1847, before her father's death. So her acquittal on an insanity plea—devised by her lawyers against her own wishes, as in the Robinson case—had more than strange remarks to stand on. Townsend approved it and would go on to read from the Phelps' trial record in his closing argument. Strict application of the "McNaughton Rules" probably should have convicted Phelps. But antebellum juries, like twenty-first-century ones, must have often unconsciously assessed a murder's justification, granting insanity loopholes to the killers of cruel people, though never or rarely to the killers of innocents.

Among the just acquittals which Townsend held up to the jury, he talked of two unjust ones. In both these cases defendants of high status had walked free after murdering victims of lower status, to later public scandal. In 1836 New York City clerk Richard P. Robinson had escaped conviction after much circumstantial evidence pointed to him as the axe-murderer of high-class prostitute Helen Jewett. Robinson's father was a large landowner in Connecticut, and the son also benefited from then-current notions about the evil influence of cities' fallen women on pure young men from the countryside. Influenced by these ideas, the jurors refused to believe the other prostitutes living at the murder site. In 1853 an educated cotton planter, Matthew Ward, killed a Kentucky schoolmaster who had whipped Ward's younger brother and also called the boy a liar.[9] Ward went free, "escap[ing] on the same grounds that acquitted Phelps" according to David Wilson's

The "Powell" off the Storm King Valley.

rendering of Townsend's speech.[10] While Townsend undoubtedly brought up the Richard Robinson and Matthew Ward cases to neutralize any jury hostility to their verdicts—and by extension hostility to an acquittal for Henrietta Robinson—the status issue was important in the Troy trial, too. The defense repeatedly stressed Robinson's social standing as a "lady," even if a fallen one.

Townsend returned to the theme of just acquittal by praising the verdict in the case of British subject Alexander McLeod who had boasted in a Buffalo barroom of taking part in the firing of an American steamboat, *Caroline*, on the Niagara River in 1837. More than a dozen men may have died on board the *Caroline* when she was sent aflame over Niagara Falls by a party of British raiders. Then again, it was possible only one man had died, with his death occurring in the initial attack on the docked vessel; authorities never had a proper list of the crew. The second possibility lessened the horror of the event, but still left McLeod subject to a charge of murder in a Utica court. The British party had burned the *Caroline* because the steamboat had been ferrying supplies to a Canadian rebel group based on two Niagara River islands. This group, headed by William Lyon Mackenzie, a former Toronto mayor, was then waging a mini-War of Independence against the colonial government of Canada, with the support of some U. S. citizens. Mackenzie's Rebellion would come to its unsuccessful end the next year. But the *Caroline* affair lived on as a troubling international incident. How lucky then for the U. S. government, which was just bettering relations with Britain, when the Utica jury of 1841 accepted McLeod's lawyers' argument that the man was only a foolish boaster who had had nothing to do with the incident. Anyway, Townsend championed the McLeod acquittal as an example of cool deliberation winning out over popular prejudice—tossing it into his argument as one more brick in his everything-but-the-kitchen-sink defense of Robinson.

From this tour of legal battles, Townsend moved to restate Job Pierson's opening argument. Like Pierson, Townsend stressed the defendant's incompetence—"It is shown that this woman was totally insane and irresponsible for her acts"—before replaying the defense's back-up position: "Mrs. L[anagan] had a young husband and he was visited by a young woman [Robinson], and he [Townsend] would sooner believe that she (Mrs. L.) committed the crime, than that Mrs. R. is guilty." In begging the jury to turn aside prejudices "in regard to the postponements of the trial," the defendant's veil, and Robinson's lifestyle, Townsend laid out Robinson's uneasy social position: "We find her living alone; calling herself by the name of Robinson; yet with circumstances showing that she was living secretly, clandestinely as husband and wife with Mr. Mather, and she claims to be his lawful wife."[11]

From this point on, with a few brief detours, Townsend told a compelling story of insanity caused by sexual and social ruin, with Mather front and center as villain of the tale. Townsend drew on newish psychiatric theory about insanity and particularly female insanity to bolster his story. He spoke of "monomania," first named by French physician Jean-Etienne-Dominique Esquirol. Esquirol's definition of "Homicidal monomania, mania without delirium" comes close to a description of Robinson on May 25, 1853:

> . . . [in this state] the insane attempt to take the lives of their fellow-beings. Some, having become exceedingly susceptible, as well as very irritable, in a fit of anger, smite, and slay those who resist them, or by whom they think themselves opposed. They destroy persons whom they regard, rightfully or otherwise, as their enemies; from whom they deem it necessary to defend themselves, or on whom they must take vengeance . . . These maniacs perceive, compare and judge correctly; but they are drawn aside, from the slightest cause, and even without an object, to the commission of acts of violence and fury . . . whilst they abandon themselves to the commission of acts the most reprehensible . . .
>
> But does a form of mania really exist, in which those who are affected by it, preserve the integrity of their reason? . . . I think it is [*sic*].[12]

Esquirol's homicidal monomaniacs would eventually turn into the psychopaths of mid-twentieth-century psychiatry and then into the sociopaths of late twentieth-century and early twenty-first-century medico-legal theory. Of course, the McNaughton Rules and the statutes they had inspired in New York State and other states rejected a defense based on monomania, but, as the Norman, Garrity, Phelps, and Ward cases showed, Esquirolian arguments were worth a try with antebellum juries. Other writer-physicians had popularized and added to Esquirol's ideas. James Prichard, Britain's "Commissioner in Lunacy" of 1844–48, came up with the term "moral insanity" to describe "a morbid perversion of the feelings, affections, and active powers, without any illusion or erroneous conviction impressed upon the understanding . . ." Prichard's category neatly dovetailed with ideas of moral corruption leading on to insanity.

And women were seen as particularly fragile, mental health-wise. Esquirol: ". . . physical causes act more frequently upon them than men; they become more frequently insane before the age of twenty years; are more subject to dementia; and their delirium is religious or erotic. Almost all their insanity is complicated with hysteria."[13]

Townsend preached directly from case studies of Esquirol:[14]

> Insanity is likely to ensue in females from love—the more clandestinely, the more fatal are the visions of happiness that fill her mind: the beloved object stands in the foreground—everything is concentrated in one individual. Desertion by and by comes, and what a black scene of horror. There is more in it than fancy and caprice—a woman's fortune is comprised in her affections . . .
>
> With women, honor, existence, everything centres in the man on whom she places her affections. If passion has led her beyond that, you can imagine her fate. If the lover deserts her what in Heaven's name is there left to comfort the heart of the wretched woman. This woman had maintained an intimacy in one direction. She expected to be married—he had been absent for some time—she heard that he was to be married to another lady—she felt that she had been deserted. She was of a respectable family—and though she had led a somewhat irregular life, she had hoped that marriage would restore her to position. All her hopes centered in one man and that man deserted her. Is there a woman that God ever made that would not have become insane under the circumstances? The apprehension of desertion had been entertained for some time, and it was probably from the first suspicion that her irregularities of conduct commenced. As the suspicions were strengthened her derangement of mind increased. If there was not here full and adequate cause for her insanity, then where can it be found?[15]

Only Robinson's derangement, according to Townsend, had resulted in the crime against "the Lanagan family" as stand-ins for Mather: ". . . you can and will imagine upon whom she would have wreaked her vengeance, had *he* been near her at the time. The revolver would have been called into requisition, you can well imagine upon whom."[16] Townsend ended his five-hour address by denying Robinson had been drunk rather than crazy on the day of the murders, by briefly and implausibly reviving the "aspersion" against Ann Lanagan, and finally by offering a kind of apology to Mather: "It had been an unpleasant duty to present the name of a personal friend (though political opponent of his, Mr. T's) in this cause, but it was necessary to a full discharge of duty."[17]

According to David Wilson's 1855 account, Henrietta Robinson, who had sat like stone during Townsend's long argument, now whispered: "A very able speech, Mr. Townsend, but you might have said all that was necessary in fifteen minutes. The idea of my insanity is absurd."[18]

After the midday break, George Van Santvoord shouldered the main burden of the prosecution's closing argument before the jam-packed courtroom. He refuted the lack-of-motive issue, pointing to the trouble at the barroom dance and the loan rejection of about the same time, and saying rather insightfully: "She [Robinson] seems to have been remarkably susceptible to insult . . . This woman is of a reckless and depraved nature, of violent temper, and quarrelsome disposition, and it is unnecessary to show further motive . . ."[19]

He continued ". . . there never was an adequate motive for murder in any case," citing Troy's most notorious poisoning murder *excepting* the Henrietta Robinson affair, the case of young Henry Green who, in 1845, had fed arsenic to his beautiful, actress bride. Green's only motive had been a vague hope of marrying a wealthy former girlfriend. The prosecutor would also mention, near the end of his four-and-one-half hour speech, two other notoriously guilty murderers, "Mrs. Whipple" and Polly Bodine. He offered them up as just two among "numerous other instances where females have been guilty of the horrid crime of murder."[20]

Unlike Green, neither Whipple nor Bodine had been punished for their crimes. Albany's Elsie Whipple had conspired with her lover, Jesse Strange, to kill Mr. Whipple in 1828, but Strange went to the gallows and Elsie went free, thanks mostly to nineteenth-century society's reluctance to view a middle-class wife and mother as a potential assassin.[21] Equally, Bodine had surely murdered her sister-in-law and infant niece on Staten Island in 1843 (and—like Richard Robinson—Bodine had tried unsuccessfully to burn the remains) but due to family loyalties (Polly's brother supported her) and to jury sentiments like those in the Whipple case, three separate trials between 1843 and 1846 failed to convict the woman. Was there a hint in Van Santvoord's mention of the two that it was necessary to expose a guilty woman, but not, in the end, to hang her or send her to prison?

Van Santvoord brought up Robinson's suggested insanity in a "loaded" way: "There is an impenetrable mystery, he [Van Santvoord] said, surrounding the history and character of this woman. If the defense had seriously intended to sustain their plea of insanity, they should have dispelled this mystery, and given the court and jury some clue to her antecedents. *They have not intimated she belonged to a family in which the misfortune of insanity was hereditary* [modern italics] . . . Her past career, her character, her face, have been assiduously concealed from observation. In no sense has the veil been raised . . ."[22]

Now it was known in Troy the Woods of Quebec either claimed descent from royal madman, George III, or that some at least linked them with the mad king.[23] Van Santvoord almost seemed to chide the defense for not acknowledging the "Miss Wood" rumors as true so as to properly defend their client. But since they hadn't, he also seemed to say, they had little

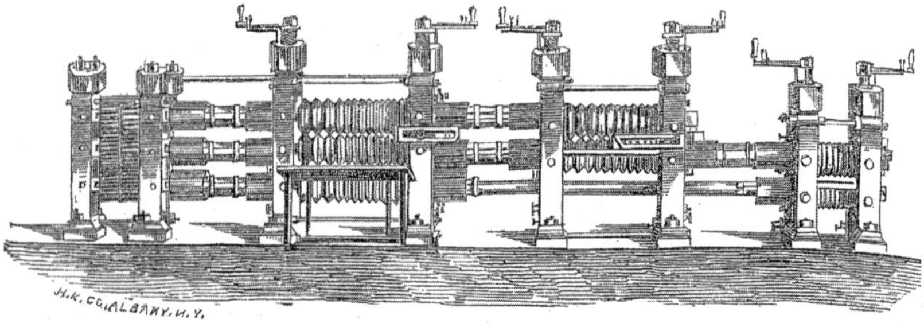

Iron Rolling Mill.

grounds for painting a portrait of the defendant as a delicately-organized lady, driven mad by the actions of Mather: "She is represented, he [Van Santvoord] said, as the crazed Ophelia, but I tell you, gentleman [*sic*], that this woman who carries pistols in her bosom and drinks bad brandy, who indulges in profane and obscene language, as she did in the presence of Mary Dillon, would not be likely to go mad through love for ——— [Mather], or any man. Up to the first of April, at least, she must have been sane, because it is demanding too much of our credulity to believe that he [Mather] would have lived with a crazy woman."[24] Not surprisingly, Van Santvoord named drunkenness as the cause of Robinson's unusual behavior. Intoxication then offered no shield to a lawbreaker, as Van Santvoord and later Judge Harris made clear to the jurymen.[25]

Van Santvoord knew his Esquirol and Pritchard as well as Townsend[26] and held forth about "monomania" and "moral insanity" with ease. But Van Santvoord deplored: ". . . the novel doctrine that a person, insane on one topic, should be relieved from [legal] responsibility . . . This theory was from the French school, and was not recognized, in this country, as of itself sufficient to shield the murderer from punishment."[27]

He acknowledged one United States court decision had trended in the Esquirolian direction, but damned the judge in the case, one Edmonds, who "has since become an advocate of spiritualism . . . who wanders about the country discussing that absurd delusion."[28]

Van Santvoord, also like Townsend, spun a novelish narrative to explain Robinson's acts. Townsend had told the "vile seducer" story of much antebellum fiction[29] and non-fiction (i. e., the newspaper accounts of the Norman and Garrity trials). Van Santvoord's storyline meshed with Townsend's as he explored the fallen woman's side of the tale in a way quite sympathetic to Robinson:

> During the day which Mary Dillon spent with her, her conversation generally was rational and agreeable, and these stories [of Irish and French lords, castles, stepmothers], instead of indicating insanity, I regard as the occasional breaking out of her natural propensity to lie. But there might have been some truth, he [Van Santvoord] said, in the story of her mother's death. The tears she shed over the picture, let us trust, gentlemen, were honest tears. I do not believe there ever was a nature so entirely depraved but it still retained some hallowed recollections—some lingering affection for home and kindred. But then she laughed and danced, and for this reason you are told the prisoner was insane. On the contrary, how natural, how like womanhood it was. The picture of her dead mother recalled the scenes of her childhood—the happy days of her innocence. No wonder the woman wept. The recollections of the past brought with them nothing but a sense of misery. And the frantic dancing and laughter, what were they but the strivings of a wicked heart to throw off the painful memories that oppressed it?[30]

The scholarly Van Santvoord, whose eight-volume *Lives of the Chief Justices of the United States* would be published later that year, sprinkled his argument with direct literary references, too. Along with the writings of Pascal and Newton, he quoted Shakespeare—Lady MacBeth's "Out, damned spot!" speech—and George Moore's *Lalla Rookh: An Oriental Romance*, first published in 1817 and still popular in the 1850s. *Lalla Rookh*, a lush, exotic narrative poem, contains several stories. Van Santvoord drew from "The Veiled Prophet of Khorassan," whose title character is a wicked and deformed Muslim holyman. Van Santvoord may have cited the electrifying: "He rais'd his veil—the Maid turn'd slowly round; Look'd at him—shriek'd—and sunk upon the ground!"[31] But whatever passage, it surely presented the jury with an image of evil behind a veil.

Van Santvoord dropped the Moore lines on the heels of his remark about the defense's failure to "raise the veil" and right after negative comments on Robinson: "Those who have caught a glimpse of her countenance have alleged that it exhibits evidences of beauty. But relying on the testimony of Mrs. Lanagan, and the girl, Dillon, I feel justified in venturing the conjecture, that if that countenance was examined closely, there would also be found lurking there, the features of violence, profanity, and murder."[32]

According to the Wilson account of the trial, Robinson turned to her counsel at the Moore quote, asking "in a low tone, but quite eagerly, 'What is that?' It was repeated to her. 'O yes,' she said, 'now I remember; Lalla Rookh; that's admirable; that's apropos.' "[33]

Van Santvoord's speech closed with a postscript sympathetic to the prisoner: "It sometimes happens . . . that the jury bring in, with their verdict of guilty, a recommendation to mercy. I have no objections to your pursuing a like course in this case, if you think proper. The court, likewise, may possibly join in a request to the governor for a commutation of punishment. If she receives this favor, *which is probable* [modern italics], she may deem herself most fortunate."[34]

And while Wilson's 1855 account makes no mention of this, the *Troy Daily Times* of Saturday, May 27, 1854, shows Van Santvoord sympathizing with Mather as well: "Counsel regretted that Mr. Mather's name had been brought into this court in the manner it has been. There was nothing to show that he had any association with her, whatever. He believed it did not strengthen the Defence [*sic*]. Nobody doubts that this woman uttered a falsehood, when she told Mr. Brownell that she was the wife of John C. Mather."[35]

Like Townsend, Van Santvoord now appeared to edge away from all earlier thrusts at Troy's still-powerful Democrat. He spoke until the close of the day's session at 7:30 P.M.[36]

15

DAY SIX—VERDICT

The court re-convened at half past eight o'clock Saturday morning. Mrs. Robinson came into court accompanied by Sheriff Price, dressed much as on the preceding days, and veiled so as to defy the gaze of the crowd assembled to get a glimpse of her. The court room was filled, and a large number of ladies were present.[1]

Within the wood-paneled courtroom with its high-sided jury box and towering, pulpit-like judge's bench, Job Pierson picked up the defense's final argument. He beat over the same ground as Townsend for three hours while introducing just a few new points. One of these had to do with Timothy Lanagan's dying statement "the *villain* had destroyed him" (as reported by Dr. Adams). Pierson: "Who ever heard such an epithet applied to a woman!"

Townsend followed Pierson to protest, unconvincingly, the *Whig*'s sharp-eyed analysis of the defense team's attack on Mather on May 25. Since the *Whig* had touched off the attack with their "Miss Wood" bombshell, Mr. Brigham's daily was apparently keenly alert to all that followed.

At last Hogeboom rose for the prosecution summation which, with the dinner break, lasted from 11:00 A.M. until 5:00 P.M. The *Whig*: ". . . it can only be said it was a powerful forensic effort, and told with marked and visible effect against the prisoner . . . during the whole time [of the speech] he [Hogeboom] enchained and irresistibly charmed the attention of a densely crowded and we may say brilliant audience, for it was made up in a very great degree of the intelligence, beauty and fashion of the city. Quite one half of those seated in the room were ladies."[2]

Hogeboom, like Pierson, mostly re-trod old ground. But unlike fellow prosecutor Van Santvoord, Hogeboom now openly agreed with the defense picture of Robinson as a fallen lady. He called her "this vile-tempered woman, who had drunk a quart of beer before eleven o'clock"[3] and "a person of desperate and depraved character" and "a passionate, resentful woman,"[4] but he also mused: "Doubtless, as she mingled with the uncongenial company at the Irish dance, the recollections and associations of a more refined life crowded upon her mind, and left something of the spirit of the high-born woman lingering about her still."[5] And: "No matter how delicate the sex or *how high the origin* [modern italics] of the accused, if she is guilty, she should be so declared . . . We have had some melancholy instances elsewhere of *social distinction and wealth* [modern italics] securing immunity for crime . . ."[6]

Hogeboom contributed one unconsciously funny moment by reading lines from Shakespeare's *Twelfth Night*, and then contrasting the lady described in them with Robinson:

> . . . [She] never told her love,
> But let concealment like a worm i' the bud
> Feed on her damask cheek. Who pined in thought:
> And, with a green and sickly melancholy,
> Sat like Patience on a monument,
> Smiling at Grief.

He hardly had to spell out "She [Robinson] is unlike the lady described by Shakespeare."[7] Though whether any of the male jurymen laughed, inwardly or outwardly, at the contrast we don't know. Maybe the whole issue of women's behavior and true natures, even one woman's behavior and true nature, was then too disturbing to laugh about. But more about all this later.

Yet light moments definitely surfaced in the courtroom that day, and Robinson, engaged and upbeat, shared in them: "During the whole day, though at times much excited, she often conversed earnestly with her counsel and the Sheriff, and whenever Judge Hogeboom [prosecution counsel] indulged in a keen stroke of satire or a sally of wit, the prisoner was among the loudest and heartiest of those who laughed.—We heard her laugh repeatedly."[8]

The newspapers covering the Saturday session gave most space to Judge Ira Harris's final-hour charge to the jury. Harris, the liberal Whig, summed up in favor of conviction. He demolished or cast doubt on the main defense arguments, rejecting the hints against Ann Lanagan and supporting the drunkeness evidence while belittling the insanity evidence. And he said: ". . . it is never indispensable to a conviction that a motive for the commission of a crime should appear."

The trial testimony provided ample reason for Harris's "guilty" charge, without any other motives necessary. Yet it's interesting the liberal Whig ruled this way. Just as the liberal Whig *Traveller* would take the hardest line against Robinson—though not any kind of line against Mather—of all the

Troy papers in their 1855 coverage, Harris now viewed the defendant in an almost harsher way than Prosecutor Van Santvoord, the Hard Democrat. Admittedly, Harris gave a gentle, three-sentence nod to the defense: "Deal justly with this poor unhappy woman whose destiny is now committed to your hands. Deal mercifully with her too. This is your privilege. The law allows every well-grounded doubt to avail for her acquittal."[9]

Harris commented on the defendant's former status in a way that suggests there was little disagreement about the issue among the officers of the court, probably even Van Santvoord: "If it be true, as has been assumed throughout the trial, that the accused is of gentle birth and has once moved in a higher and more refined walks of life, what a painful illustration she presents of the rapid descent which a woman makes to the lowest depths of degradation and vice, when she once consents to take leave of virtue and innocence."[10]

At 6:15 P.M. the jury withdrew, with no question of holding over deliberations till the next working day. New Yorkers of the 1850s expected juries to decide verdicts promptly, for in adjourning, Judge Harris announced a special 8:00 P.M. session to hear the verdict. The jury wrangled and didn't come in until 9:00 P.M., to a courtroom then so crowded Robinson, with Sheriff Price's wife and daughter, had to come in a back way.

The Whipple and Bodine cases as well as the Norman, Garrity, and Phelps ones show nineteenth-century juries shrank from convicting women of hanging offenses. Killers of victims who could be portrayed as wicked seducers were in the best position, but even women like Whipple, Bodine, and Phelps benefited, with youth and attractiveness an extra plus for the female defendant.[11] On the whole, Robinson stood well in the balance of such unconscious calculations, being both "seduced and abandoned" and extremely good-looking—despite the difficulty over her choice of victims. But there was another factor in play, too, referred to glancingly in a single description of "bareheaded Irishwomen" who surrounded Robinson's carriage to "curse, ridicule, and upbraid"[12] the woman following her sentencing in the summer of 1855. The large Irish minority in the city surely agitated for Robinson's conviction in 1854 as well. In 1899, one of the trial jurors, then in his eighties, told of his experience: "I remember being on the streets after the woman had been convicted, and heard people saying that it would not have been safe for the jurors to have walked the streets of Troy had not a verdict of guilty been rendered against the woman. The public sentiment against her was very strong. I shall never forget the trial, and can certainly say that I never want to serve on another such jury."[13]

While ex-juror William Abbott spoke only of "public sentiment," there are reasons to read between the lines. As mentioned, the Irish had been a power in the city from the 1840s. And though just beginning to fill the very lowest positions in city government, they probably already controlled the streets of Troy to some extent, with gatherings—like the crowds surging in and around the courthouse during the last week of May 1854—filled with Irish. William Abbott and the other jurors, all out-of-towners, had chances to encounter the "Irish street" away from the courthouse, too: "We used to go out nights in pairs or singly . . . always accompanied by an officer."[14]

Irish anger toward Robinson sprang from solidarity with the two Irish victims, but there were extra spurs to that anger. Mather belonged to a church particularly hostile to the new Roman Catholic immigrants of Troy. Father Augustus Thébaud, who lived in Troy in the 1850s, later explained this, beginning with an account of the Roman Catholic-friendly element of Troy's establishment:

> . . . in my time [in Troy] the men of Dutch origin were not numerous; the most respectable families of the city were originally New Englanders from Massachusetts and Vermont, and I must say that the chief among them could not be called Puritans. They were most of them Episcopalians . . .
>
> The Episcopalians of Troy and also of Lansingburg [*sic*], adjoining it, were always very friendly to Catholics, and in the difficulties I experienced during the Know-Nothing excitement of 1857, I always found my chief support among them . . .
>
> . . . They were found in banks, manufacturing establishments, and great commercial houses. At home their life was distinguished by true refinement of manners and well-bred simplicity. Whenever I met any of them I imagined I was again among the Knickerbocker families I had known in New York. In both cases very little was heard of politics, in which they took little interest; but often travel and foreign countries were the subject of conversation.[15]

The old money! George M. Tibbits, recipient of the W. H. Jeffery letter, was one of this group. An Episcopalian, he gave money to Catholic charities in Troy and would travel to the Paris Exposition in 1866.[16] John C. Mather belonged to the "new money" group: "In Troy there was a very *respectable* [Thebaud's italics] body of New England Presbyterians, whom I will not accuse of carrying their intolerance as far as their ancestors had done. Three or four congregations under their pastors formed, as it were, the aristocracy of the city. The wealthiest among them were manufacturers, bankers, speculators, and wholesale merchants. Though they were not as refined in manners as the Episcopalians . . . they were far prouder and formed a little circle of their own. Some few among them were taking their first steps in the humanizing process . . ."[17]

Thébaud condemns "the sway" the Rev. N. S. S. Beman of the First Presbyterian Church—the New Light one which Aloa Porter Mather had left in 1843 and to which Martin I. Townsend still belonged the 1850s—held over all the Presbyterian congregations in the city. Every year, Beman gave a Thanksgiving Day sermon described by Thébaud as a "concoction of the coarsest abuse of the Pope, the papists, the foreigners in general, and the Irish in particular."[18] The fact Beman, an abolitionist, had no sympathy for Irish immigrants was not unusual in the world of antebellum reform.[19] Individual reformers or politicians often championed one or the other of the two groups then at the bottom of the social pile, but not both.[20] Thurlow Weed and William Seward were exceptions to this rule.

Along with Beman, Thébaud condemned, in a veiled way, the chief founder of Mather's own church, the "Old Light" Second Street Presbyterian Church. This was Henry Burden, then with Emma Willard, General John Wool, and Reverend Beman Troy's most famed citizens. Burden was an immigrant himself, a poor boy from Scotland, who had arrived in Troy about 1820. Within fifteen years he had invented "a horse shoe machine" and acquired a half interest in the Troy Iron and Nail Works which produced

The Reverend N. S. S. Beman's First Presbyterian Church of Troy.

the shoes according to the new process. By 1840 he owned "the entire interest" in the company that now boasted a water wheel sixty feet in diameter at its Wynantskill works at Troy's south end. Burden's "Nail Factory" was one of the chief sights in Troy. Visitors—including the schoolgirls Charlotte and Harriet Wood, as their 1843–44 school accounts reveal[21]—made special trips to see the giant wheel and the strange, new machinery which spat out railroad spikes and horseshoes. On Burden himself: "An accomplished mechanic, he could make a better piece of work than any man he could find in his shops; he could deal a heavier blow with the sledge than any of his strikers at the forge."[22]

Thébaud meant the Burden family when he referred to "a wealthy Scotch Presbyterian family" who owned a "large manufacturing establishment," and then Burden himself when the Roman Catholic cleric described the "head of the same great manufacturing establishment . . . [who] having built a church for his family, saw with pleasure the gentlemen employed by him attend this church on Sundays with their families; but he never would consent to give a seat to any low Irishman . . ." While a strange criticism for Thébaud to make (he couldn't have wanted to swell Presbyterian congregations, after all) it shows his animus towards the Burdens, as does his account of an accident at the Burden factory just months before Lanagan's and Lubee's murders:

> I vividly remember the cruel death of three young Irishmen lately landed. One of them was ordered to transport in an iron wagon a load of red-hot embers from the mill and throw it into an angle of the building. Two others were to help him. Snow had fallen during the night, and they were not warned of the danger of pouring out burning fire on the snow. They were supposed to know it. The sudden expansion of the vapor from the snow enveloped the poor boys, half-clad as they were. Their bodies were fearfully scalded and burned; and worse still, they all swallowed some of the steam. One of them died the same day. The others soon followed him. As usual a collection was taken up among the workmen for the bereaved families, and the employers did nothing . . .[23]

In addition to his religion, Mather, though a Democrat, had already given hints of beliefs opposed by the Irish of Troy. This refers to his friendship or alliance—mentioned by Robinson in 1855[24]—with Myron H. Clark, who was known *first* for his anti-alcohol stance, *second* for his Nativist opinions, and probably *third*, for anti-slavery views. Mather would remain a "National Democrat" or a Hard or pro-slavery man till the bitter end, the outbreak of Civil War, but Robinson naturally referred to a Mather-Clark bond which existed *before* her imprisonment.[25] After Mather left Troy and won a safe Hard Democratic seat in the New York State Senate from District No. 4 in Lower Manhattan (serving in 1858–60), he would make at least one damning comment about "rum drinking":

> I have sometimes witnessed scenes upon the line of the canal, when officiating as Commissioner, on the occasion of a brief suspension of navigation upon the Sabbath, caused by a break, which would almost defy description.
>
> Crowds of boatmen could be seen together in groups—some indulging in boisterous mirth, and others in the various games and sports which human ingenuity has devised for the idle and the vicious. Profanity, gambling and rum drinking ruled the hour . . .[26]

(What had he thought of Henrietta Robinson's beer and brandy drinking? But maybe she abstained in his company.)

So here was a woman linked with a Presbyterian politician who showed signs of flirting with Nativism and Temperance and was associated with a Troy industrialist who had a bad name among the Irish, and this woman had slain two apparently unoffending Irish immigrants. Irish fury probably tipped the balance in favor of Robinson's conviction.

Interestingly, the jurymen, all native-born Protestants, were "teetotalers" to a man, and this may have worked against the generous- to heavy-drinking Robinson, too.[27]

The jury revealed their emotional struggle when they re-entered the courtroom:

They sat with their heads inclined and the foreman sighed deeply and repeatedly.[28]

> "Some of them were in tears and all of them appeared to be oppressed . . ."[29]
>
> [The defendant] was not commanded to stand up and "look upon the jury," nor were the jury asked to "look upon the prisoner," but the verdict was pronounced while the prisoner sat vailed, within the bar . . . The silence was deep and the sensation intense.[30]

At last Foreman Alanson Cook uttered the word, "Guilty," followed by a polling of the jurors. Then, as Job Pierson tried to address Judge Harris, his client: ". . . under great excitement, and evidently in a very angry mood, exclaimed—'Shame on you Judge! There is corruption in the Court!' "

As Pierson struggled on in his attempt to get a postponement of sentencing, Robinson stood and in a "voice . . . firm, clear and musical, and pitched to a high key" called out once more: "There is corruption in the District Attorney! Some of the jurors are corrupt!" And after Pierson audibly tried to quiet her: "I will speak!"

At this point, Judge Harris granted Pierson's request, moving the sentencing to Monday morning, and adjourned court. "The vast crowd—one-third of which was composed of females—then slowly dispersed, and the prisoner, with a firm quick step, passed out with the Sheriff and his family, and drove off to the jail . . . On the way to the jail Mrs. Robinson laughed and joked about the scene that she had just passed through . . ."[31]

PART FIVE

THE VEILED MURDERESS

JUNE 1854–AUGUST 1855

Elizabeth Oakes Smith.
(Courtesy Schlesinger Library, Harvard University)

16

SETTLED BUT NOT SETTLED

The prisoner's spirits and courage remained high on Sunday:

> Yesterday [Sunday] she was found dressed throughout in a costume of spotless white, arranged with scrupulous care and neatness. She walked her room very much, and was repeatedly heard to say, with great energy and determination, though not directing her remarks to any person—"He shall never pronounce sentence against me! No, never!"
>
> When Dr. Hegeman, the Deputy Sheriff, visited her yesterday morning, she said to him, laughing—"You'll have a nice ["nice" meaning "hard"] time putting the rope around my neck, old boy!"[1]

Monday, in a way the seventh day of trial, drew the largest crowd of any day. The *Troy Daily Times*:

> We repaired to the Court House a little after 7 o'clock. There was at this time a large assemblage about the building, and the entrances both front and rear were quite choked up with people, a large majority ladies . . .
>
> By 7 ½ o'clock A.M., the Court room was more than half filled—the great majority present being ladies. Hundreds were pressing forward to the front and rear entrances for admission.
>
> At a few minutes before 8 o'clock, the front doors were opened, and a great multitude passed in, almost instantly filling every portion of the large room.

> The officers though vigilant and active, yet found it difficult to preserve order or seat and quiet the crowd . . .
>
> In disposing the people many amusing scenes occurred, illustrative of the obstinacy, the perseverance, the peculiarities, and the remarkable deafness and obtuseness of "some folks." All wanted the best seat—all wanted to get in front—and all asserted "certain inalienable rights," among which was, to sit or stand in such a position as to get a glimpse of the veiled Prisoner.
>
> Of all the crowd, numbering full 1500, more than one half were females. In strength of purpose and determination to enter the room at all hazards, they showed quite as much perseverance, activity, and tact, as did any of the "lords of creation."
>
> The gallery was crowded to suffocation; yet one lone woman wedged herself through the mass of people in it, and took up a post of observation in a front seat.

On the appearance of Robinson:

> The sensation at this moment throughout the Court room was very great. Every eye was turned upon the mysterious figure enveloped in the impenetrable blue veil. She walked to her seat with a faltering and uncertain step, and was evidently much excited and nervous. This, however, she soon mastered, and presently entered into active conversation with the Sheriff, her counsel, and the ladies who accompanied her (Mrs. and Miss Price).
>
> The morbid curiosity to see her was unabating and intense. It was almost impossible to induce the females to sit down. They persisted in standing upon the benches, and women who had little children with them, held them up in their arms to enable them to catch a glimpse of the culprit.

As soon as Judge Harris called for "perfect order and quiet," a violent knocking on the door from more would-be onlookers echoed through the courtroom. "An officer was dispatched to attend that door, and prevent further disturbance," and Harris called for order again. What followed was sheer anti-climax. William Beach picked up Pierson's argument of Saturday and called for further postponement of sentencing—for a grab bag of not very compelling-sounding reasons.[2] And though Henry Hogeboom argued "at considerable length" for immediate sentencing, Judge Harris "was inclined to yield to the request of [the defense] counsel, without intimating an opinion as to the points raised."[3] Thus Harris favored delay—and a possible softening?—of the woman's near-mandatory death sentence. Just as Henrietta

Robinson had received special consideration over her jail accommodations, she now received special consideration in the last phase of her trial. Actually, this postponement and later ones in 1854 and 1855 would almost exactly mirror the year's worth of postponements preceding the May of 1854 trial.

On Harris's ruling: "Mrs. Robinson appeared highly elated, and conversed in a lively spirit with her counsel and attendants. She evidently expects to meet a better fate than either hanging or life confinement in State Prison."[4] Some onlookers were less elated: "A woman who was among the first to get a front seat in the court room on the morning of Mrs. Robinson's expected sentence of death, and who successfully resisted all tendencies to fainting incident to the weather and the crowd, was as mad as a 'setting hen' because the sentence was postponed."[5]

But despite the still-open issue of her fate, Troy opinion-makers were ready to stamp "Case Closed" on the saga of Henrietta Robinson. The trial had determined her guilt and most newspaper writers and their readers had apparently "bought" the *Whig*'s charge about Robinson's true identity. The

The Albany Y. M. A.

Times editorial column of May 29: "It is now fully confirmed, we believe, that Mrs. Robinson was formerly a Miss Wood, and was educated many years ago at the Troy Female Seminary. She was recognized to-day by one of her former school-mates, who had some conversation with her." [The "Miss Wood" rumor, launched almost a full year earlier, was doing its work well since Robinson's veil-covered bonnet created a literal tent over her head, save for the moments when she raised the veil. Then, only those directly before her—Judge Harris and the witnesses—had a clear view of Robinson's face.][6]

Newspapers which had not already done so reprinted the *Whig*'s May 25 piece with its statement on long-term public opinion in Troy: "These, we believe, are the outlines of the narrative [allegations that Robinson was "Miss Wood"] generally credited—we may say not doubted, from the first—by very many. For what reason her identity has been attempted to be disguised, we know not.—Shortly after the prisoner was arrested, a gentleman from Quebec or vicinity, came here; and a statement was put forth to the effect that the prisoner was some other person; but it is now to be presumed that the representation is not sustained in the public belief."[7]

And the *Whig* chose this moment—May 29 or 30—to amplify the Wood allegation by running the item, quoted earlier, on the Wood family's wrong-side-of-the-blanket relationship with Queen Victoria.[8] The *Budget* breathed a sigh of relief and looked forward to a less frenzied news period: "Having got through with the Robinson trial, we will now be able to devote more attention to general news matters. Advertisers, whose privileges were encroached upon by the daily reports, will henceforth have no reason to complain."[9]

But Troy's editors and others were wrong if they expected a quiet summer on the Robinson front. The Woods and the Willards were poised to counter-attack, with a true news deluge about to descend.

17

BREAKING OF THE STORM

On June 3, William Wood wrote from Quebec City to the *Whig* as well as to Canadian newspapers which had picked up the Miss Wood story:

> . . . I feel myself impelled to deny that this Henrietta Robinson is in any way whatever connected with my family. I had four sisters, pupils at Mr. Willard's Troy Seminary, all of whom are now residing in Great Britain.—One of them [Emma, the target of the May 25 *Whig* piece] married an officer of the British army in Canada, and after his death married in Quebec Doctor Mackintosh of the Royal Artillery, with whom she is now living at Assynt House, Granton, Ross-shire, Scotland.
>
> *[Signed]* W. F. Wood
>
> Papers which have published an account of the trial of Henrietta Robinson will oblige by giving the above insertion.[1]

Wood's denial reached Troy papers on June 8 via Dr. John Willard, who enclosed it with his own letter to Editor Brigham of the *Whig*. After morning publication in the *Whig*, the two letters broke into the *Times* and *Budget* that afternoon. Willard's launched one defense, obviously supplied by William Wood, that would soon come back to haunt the Wood-Willard camp:

> . . . From some circumstances . . . I suppose her [Robinson] to be a Mrs. Campbell, (this I think is the name though I am not

Eaton, Gilbert & Co.'s Factories, 1850.

> positive) who was a native of Quebec, from a respectable family there, and who resided in the vicinity of Mr. Wood at the time his daughters were in Troy; and who knew of their being here. She married, but soon lost her husband. She not long after went to Mr. Wood to ask for assistance to go to Scotland to visit her husband's relatives. Mr. Wood gave her nearly fifty dollars, which sum she expended in Quebec . . . She afterwards went again to Mr. W. for money, which he not being satisfied with the disposition made of the first, declined giving. She very soon after set up a drinking house in the suburbs of the city, and while there pursuaded [*sic*] a young man of respectable connections in Quebec to elope with her to N. York. This is the last that is known of her. The young man was said to have been seen there as a cab driver. Now if Mrs. Robinson is this Mrs. Campbell, it is not at all difficult to see how she obtained the knowledge of many of the circumstances of which she has made use in persuading those who have been about her, that she was a member of the Wood family. Her knowledge of the persons of those belonging to families in which she professed to have visited could very readily have been acquired during the several months residence in this city previous to her arrest [and certain people claimed Robinson had lived in Troy as early as 1849—prior to her residence in Albany (See note 6 of Chap. 26)] . . . This supposition will easily account for her recognition of a lady whom she addressed in court by her family name, the lady having been married for several years.

More undoubtedly candid but weak-sounding arguments flowed from the Seminary principal:

Among other circumstances tending to show conclusively that Mrs. Robinson is not one of the Woods, is a remark made to me by Mr. Beach, one of her counsel, very soon after his first interview with her. 'I expected,' said he, 'to have found at least traces of education and refinement in her, but in a conversation of half an hour I found neither.'

Mr. Jeffreys, the gentleman from Quebec, whose testimony is so much relied upon as proving the identity of Mrs. Robinson with Miss Wood, did not even see her, while he was in Troy, and has recently written to a gentleman of this city, stating that he has since his return seen letters from all of the daughters of Mr. Wood, written within a short time past. [This was a bit dishonest since Jeffrey's remark about the letters appeared in the same communication which expressed his (Jeffrey's) fear that Robinson might be a Miss Wood.]

Another strong point is the fact that William C. Heart, who was in my office as book-keeper, during all the time that the Misses Wood were members of the Seminary, and who was necessarily perfectly familiar with their appearance, saw Mrs. Robinson repeatedly in the Bank, of which he is teller, and in the street, and though very much impressed by her English or Canadian look, still never thought, and is now quite certain from his recollection, that she cannot be either of them; and finally we have the word of a gentleman, Mr. W. F. Wood, whose character is unimpeached and unimpeachable, against that of a woman who has for years been leading a life of shameless profligacy . . .

Willard just couldn't stop, and a final outpouring included the foolish "hand and wrist" idea, not repeated here:

It is said that Mr. Wood might be influenced by a desire to cover the disgrace to his family, from the conduct of an unworthy member, and therefore would be led to make false statements with regard to it . . .

[At the time of his and Wood's jail visit] She [Robinson] said then, very much as she had done when I had called before to see her, that she had no brother, and she was not the person we supposed, meaning evidently she was not Miss Wood—and refusing what would have been a certain means of identifying herself if she were what she professed to be.

I should have made these statements before, but was in Virginia during the trial . . .[2]

None of the Troy papers which printed the two letters or excerpts from them—the *Whig*, the *Times*, and the *Budget*—were quite prepared to turn on a dime on the Robinson identity question. The fickle *Whig* came closest:

> Mr. Wood accounts clearly and satisfactorily for the present whereabouts of all the Misses Wood. Testimony could not be more direct or satisfactory, though it will be regarded as not a little remarkable that it should have been withheld from the public so long. How the impression started and gained so extensive credence we are not aware. The belief that Mrs. Robinson is Miss Wood . . . has been the prevailing one ever since Mrs. Robinson was arrested. Therefore, until the testimony now laid before the public is impeached, we must conclude that Mrs. Robinson is somebody else than Miss Wood.

The "until" of the last sentence expresses some doubt about the new claims, as does the title of the *Whig*'s June 8 article (largely made up of the two letters): "Is Mrs. Robinson Miss Wood?"

The *Times* went much further in doubting Wood's and Willard's claims. Editor John Francis commented in "The Veiled Murderess" (the first use of the term): "It appears to be shown by the statements of Mr. Willard and Mr. Wood, republished on our first page from the *Whig*, that Mrs. Robinson, the murderess, is NOT Miss Wood, any more than she is Mrs. Robinson; but the probability is that she is or was a Mrs. Campbell . . . We say this on the supposition that the statements referred to are correct; but we are in possession of several communications from sources entitled to confidence . . . showing different conclusions from Mr. Willard's."

In the same edition, the *Times* printed one of the "communications," signed "One who has seen both Mrs. Robinson and Emma Wood," high on their page two, under the headline "Mrs. Robinson;—Who Is She?" This column hung Dr. Willard out to dry for: any involvement in the affair ("He cannot guarantee the perpetual good conduct of all of his pupils."); misrepresenting Robinson's actions ("It is but justice to her to say that she not only does not pretend to be Emma Wood, but that she makes every possible effort to induce the Sheriff and jailor, as well as her counsel, to believe that she is not a member of the Wood family, and that if she were a member of that family she cannot be Emma."); and making his hand and wrist identification. The "One who has seen both Mrs. Robinson and Emma Wood"—maybe Francis himself—further held "A hundred persons who had known Emma Wood . . . did not come to the same conclusion as Mr. Willard did" about the woman's identity.

The *Budget*'s "Mrs. Robinson, the Woods, and the Willards" of June 8 attacked Willard over the same issues, and while the *Budget* summarized Wood's letter without direct comment, it indirectly challenged his statement:

> . . . [since June of 1853] the impression that Mrs. Robinson was a Miss Wood has been growing stronger. This was not owing to anything that Mrs. R. had said, but to facts within the knowledge of families in which the Misses W. visited during their residence here, and of their associates at school.
>
> . . . the Montreal Pilot and other Canadian papers, published full reports of the trial, including the lengthy charge of Judge Harris to the Jury, with the statements of the Troy papers relative to her supposed family connections, without contradicting any thing said here in respect to her origin.

By Saturday morning, June 10, William Wood and relation William H. Jeffery had arrived in Troy. Late in life, Martin I. Townsend would recall "a daughter of Mr. [Robert] Wood" had traveled down from Quebec at this time, too, but there is no contemporary news about this sister.[3] On June 10, 1854, Wood, Jeffery, Dr. Willard, along with "one or more of Mrs. Robinson's counsel" and "Mr. John B. Townsend"[4] visited the *Whig* office, bearing documents to bolster the Wood family position.

The *Budget* would soon complain of the funneling of all Robinson-Wood newsbreaks to the *Whig*: "Neither do we understand why the statements and proofs were furnished to only one of the papers of this city."[5] Both Emma and John Willard had addressed their initial "card" of June 1853 about Robinson to the *Whig*, and all later appeals from Dr. John Willard and William Wood had been sent to the *Whig*. The *Budget* writers professed not to understand the favoring of the *Whig*, but we understand rather easily. Conservative Whigs clustered at the upper end of the social and economic scale even more densely than Whigs as a whole, and so Troy's conservative Whig organ tended to be the newspaper of the city's most established citizens, like the Willards, mother and son, who subscribed to the *Troy Daily Whig* and the *Courier and Enquirer*, an Albany Whig paper.[6]

Thus it was an elite group that visited Mr. Brigham of the *Whig*, containing Wood and Jeffery from the pinnacle of Quebec City's social world, Dr. John Willard from the pinnacle of Troy's—at least in prestige—and John B. Townsend, Troy's "City Marshall."[7] And even if not there in body, the name and influence of George M. Tibbits, the "son of Troy's richest man," and confidant of Jeffery, surely went with the party. The visit brought results.

On Monday, June 12, the "Hard Court Journal," as the *Budget* was naming the *Whig* at just this time,[8] continued its new stance on the Robinson-Wood situation. This was pro-Wood though with a tiny chink in all statements through which some doubt might pass: "On Saturday we had a personal interview with Mr. W. who exhibited such evidences as would in connection with his previous statement under almost any state of circumstances be conclusive. He exhibited to us letters from all of his sisters, written within the last fifteen months, down to within a month—and several from Mrs. McIntosh (Emma Wood) . . ."

Along with mention of these letters "of a business and social character, bearing foreign postage marks and other evidences of their genuineness," the *Whig* printed the whole of a deposition by Montreal Justice of the Peace W. H. A. Davies who swore he had acted "for some years past" as attorney for "the said Mrs. MacIntosh," was in communication with her, "having to remit her money every few months," and knew she was in Overton, Scotland. The *Whig* itself opined:

> . . . there is a remarkable pertinacity in the public mind to believe still that Mrs. Robinson is a Wood. If there is any testimony, to prove this beyond vague surmises, unsustained assertions, and mere opinions, it has not been placed before the public. Whether those pretending to have such testimony, and who profess to hold to the belief that Mrs. Robinson is a Wood, will, by refusing to make such testimony public, subject themselves to the imputation of getting up and keeping up a delusion for sinister purposes, to the great injustice of the Wood family, or by placing before the public the reasons for such a belief, exculpate themselves from such a charge . . . remains to be seen.

The *Budget* actually charged *Whig* editor Charles Brigham with receiving "[cash] considerations" to change his position, though it's easy to imagine Willard-Tibbits clout combined with the new documents (beginning with Wood's letter dated June 3) were enough to re-orient the *Whig*'s coverage. If John C. Mather *had* planted the Wood daughter story in the *Whig* edition of May 25, as contemporaries seemed to think, Editor Brigham wasn't prepared to continue in this vein in the face of counter pressure from the Willards and Woods. Plus Mather, himself—whatever his involvement in the launching of the story—could now reasonably have wished to damp it down. His political enemy Martin I. Townsend had gone to town with the account of the ex-canal commissioner as wicked seducer of a formerly pure, high-born young woman, clearly the "Miss Wood" of the *Whig* reports though never so-named by Townsend. Townsend's scenario cast Mather in a far worse light, according to antebellum mores, than the prosecution's implied scenario of Mather as lover or client of a long-degraded courtesan.[9]

The fact Mather's political enemies on the Soft *Budget* and *Times* picked up the Wood story "ball" as soon as the *Whig* dropped or began to back-pedal it confirms Mather or Mather's friends didn't drive the Miss Wood allegations post-trial. Throughout June and July of 1854 the *Budget* and the *Times* would be far more doubtful about the Wood family's counter-story than the *Whig*. There was also an anti-John Willard slant to the *Budget* and *Times* coverages, with Dr. Willard, not William Wood, the one most often attacked. John M. Francis of the *Times* had already zinged Willard over a petty issue from the eve of the 1853 murders: the doctor's refusal to allow a public concert in Seminary Park on May 24, 1853.[10] Willard wasn't a politician, but was a Whig, maybe enough reason for Troy Soft Democrats to target the Seminary principal, though they never expressed the least criticism of Emma.

The *Times* had enough scorn for William Wood, too. On June 12: "And now I insist, that when Mr. Wood knows his sisters are all in Great Britain, has seen them there so recently, has received letters from all of them within fifteen months, and we know Mrs. R. has been here so long; and still he comes down here to convince the community that she is not his sister; and to make sure, goes to the jail, and there sees her eyes and upper part of her face, and "knows at once it is not his sister," the community ought to be satisfied!"[11]

After disparaging the Wood and Willard arguments, Francis's paper tacked on without comment, as though to brush the item aside, an anonymous letter received by the paper dated "Green Island, June 9, 1854." This claimed Robinson's true name was "Robertson" and she was the daughter of "Dr. Robertson of Montreal who died in the Lunatic Asylum at Hudson, N. Y., about nine years ago," a plausible-sounding charge which, nonetheless, lived and died in this issue of this newspaper.

The June 12 article labeled William H. Jeffery "the agent of the Woods," rather than "friend," his usual description in Troy papers. If Francis had only known Jeffery was, in fact, a relative of Charlotte Wood Eliott's husband, his sarcasm would have been more biting still!

Of surviving area newspapers, only Mather's deep-dyed enemy, the *Albany Evening Atlas*, still had the ex-canal commissioner directly in its sights. On or about June 14, it published the item, partly quoted earlier, which suggested "the paramour of the degraded woman" had paid for her defense and then instigated "this conspiracy against the purity of . . . [the Wood] family name."[12] Others had the Woods and Willards on the front burner, with the *Lansingburgh Democrat* printing a new rumor on June 15: ". . . we propose a simple test by which the whole controversy may be settled. We are informed by a lady who was a boarding pupil at the Troy Female Seminary at the time Miss Wood of Quebec was there, and knew her well, that . . . [there was] a peculiarity in the formation of her right hand, *the little finger being turned inward, and across the two adjoining fingers* [original italics]. We believe this fact is no secret in Troy, and why it has not been alluded to before is somewhat singular. That Mrs. Robinson's finger is in the condition described, we believe has been fully ascertained . . ."[13]

On this very day, June 15, Mrs. Robinson at last received William Wood, who had been "with his friend Jeffrey, for several days past, seeking an interview."[14] Years later Wood wrote of the encounter: "When I saw her some 39 years ago, after a good deal of persuasion, I induced her to remove a thick blue veil she wore & on my unmasking I cd. not understand why she shd. be considered like a Sister of mine as I cd. not see any likeness whatever. She said she was very sorry indeed I shd. have been subjected to such an annoyance as she had never tried to pass herself off as a member of my family which I believe was a gross falsehood, however, as the woman was supposed to be insane, I can't understand why my word as to her false impersonation shd. be doubted against her's."[15]

Robinson's inadequate "very sorry indeed" plus William Wood's real bitterness over her "gross falsehood" and others' "doubt" ring true—to us. But the jail visit just added fuel to the fire of the "Miss Wood" story. The *Budget* offered up a very suspicious view:

> Mrs. Robinson who had been besought by her counsel to grant an interview to these gentlemen [William Wood and W. H. Jeffery], finally consented to see them one at a time, and she said she "*would see William* (Wood) *first* [original italics]." Accordingly Mr. Wood was ushered into her cell, Mrs. Robinson wearing the impenetrable veil, and all persons being excluded from sight or hearing of what passed between them. This interview lasted about *one hour and a half* [original italics], during which time Mrs. Robinson unveiled herself, and the two conversed face to face. Mr. Wood is understood to state as a result of this interview that the prisoner is not a member of his family, that he never saw her before, and that he is of the opinion that she has never been a resident of Quebec . . . After the interview [and after Robinson reneged on her agreement to see Jeffery] Mr. Wood again saw several of her counsel . . . [Wood] called to see her this morning [June 16], accompanied by one of her counsel, but she declined seeing them, and we understand Mr. Wood, after again seeing some of her counsel, was to take his

> departure for home today. It is understood that the prisoner was more cheerful after seeing "*William*," as she termed Mr. Wood, and it is said that she denies being one of the Woods, and seems gratified with the expressed opinion of a portion of her counsel and others that she is not one of the Wood family.[16]

Along with the sarcasm, The *Budget* served up direct arguments:

> Some two years since Mrs. Robinson stated to John G. Britton, and to others, without any apparent object, that she was a member of the Wood family. Before the commission of the crime of which the veiled incognito has been convicted, as well as during the progress of the trial, many of our citizens who knew the Wood girls when they were students at the Troy Female Seminary were of the opinion that Mrs. Robinson was a member of that family . . . Nearly all of our citizens who had an opportunity to see the features of Mrs. Robinson and Mr. Wood have been struck with the wonderful and marked similarity of appearance which existed between the prisoner and Mr. Wood.[17]

We have already met John G. Britton. He went to Troy's 1851 Washington's Birthday dinner with John C. Mather and other Troy VIPs. Lawyer Britton was a big buyer and seller of property in Troy. In 1844 he had purchased City Lot 61 from Oliver Boutwell, the lot then occupied at the north end by the house which would become No. 627 River Street, and, at the south end, by the brick house which would become No. 625 River or maybe by a vacant area where Boutwell's mansion would rise.[18] In September 1849 Britton resold the south half of the lot to Boutwell, but held onto the north half.[19] Britton's ownership of the house where Robinson lived might suggest Britton was a client of Robinson's. It certainly suggests Britton arranged for Robinson to live in the out-of-the-way cottage, even if this was just done as a favor for John C. Mather. Anyway, Britton was intimate enough with Robinson so he was a *reported* confidant: "Mrs. Robinson stated to John G. Britton, and to others . . ."

By June of 1854 no one wanted his or her name linked with Robinson's. Who better to report a statement of Robinson's than someone who was safely dead?[20] And even without Britton's double-entendre toast about "Companions-in-Arms"—at an event where no one else was making "wine, women, and song"-type toasts—there are hints Britton was a less than upright citizen (see note).[21]

On June 16, the day scornful accounts of William Wood's jail visit appeared in the *Budget* and *Times*,[22] Wood swore out another deposition, this time before Judge William B. Wright of the New York State Supreme

Court. Wood then forwarded the affadavit to the *Whig* where it appeared the next day and, like the other *Whig* scoops, was soon reprinted in full or commented on by the other Troy papers. The new Wood salvo highlighted the family's impossible position:

> . . . [I, William Wood] became very anxious to confront the woman face to face, in the presence of any or all of her counsel, knowing that she could not answer one out of a half a dozen questions I would put to her, which it would be readily seen a sister of mine could not fail to do,—supposing that I could thus readily dispel the delusion that she was a member of my family, I was also solicitous to see her and if possible ascertain whether she had actually any knowledge or acquaintance with our family, as what she was reported to have said seemed to prove.

But:

> After repeated attempts to obtain a sight of this woman since my arrival in this city, I only succeeded yesterday afternoon; and I now declare that never to my knowledge have I seen this woman before I saw her in the jail in this city nor have I now the slightest knowledge or suspicion who she is or where she came from.
>
> I have endeavored . . . to procure an interview with this woman in the presence of her counsel or of any person who knew my sisters, formerly residing in this city, but have not been able to do so. She promised yesterday and professed to be anxious to see me this morning in the presence of Mr. Pierson . . . but when we called there this morning I was informed at the jail that she was willing to see me alone or Mr. Pierson alone, but that she wholly refused to see me in the presence of Mr. Pierson or anybody else . . .
>
> It had seemed to me when the respectability and position of my family were thus assailed, that common justice required that I should be afforded every facility to vindicate both. It has resulted otherwise . . .

His explanation and plea finally touched the flinty, journalistic hearts of the *Budget* editor and *Times* editor or else intimidated the two men. After June 17, they and other area editors would almost completely abandon the "Wood" topic and the whole Robinson story for nine months, until March 1855 when the *Times* relaunched the business in a new form. But the *Budget*'s June 17 edition, the last to deal directly with the affair for many months, couldn't resist highlighting an apparent awkwardness in the Wood family defense: "It seems hardly probable, if Mrs. Robinson was Mrs. Campbell as stated, that the son of Mr. Wood should not have been cognizant of . . . [these] facts . . . and still less probable that he should have stated the belief [reported in *Budget* of June 16] that she [Robinson] never was a resident of Quebec."[23] The guess about Mrs. Campbell was foolish, but the woman was real enough, as would soon be revealed, and thus the story underlines William Wood's essential honesty in his response to the scandal.

The *Times* of the same date touched glancingly on the same issue, getting in another swipe at Dr. Willard: "Mr. Wood has more reason to invoke protection from his friends, than to censure this community for the doubt and distrust induced by the officious intermeddling of those friends."[24]

As if to mark the last flowering of the controversy in print—and one sign of how far it had entered public consciousness—*Times* advertiser, "Messrs. Fry & Hatch, the classical hatters," piggy-backed on the affair on June 17: "Who is Mrs. Robinson?—This question which has been agitated in the newspapers for some time past remains as mysterious as ever. Yet it cannot be at all doubted, that if those who display the least anxiety to obtain a knowledge of the secret of appearing in the best manner in propria persona, can, by calling on Messrs. Fry & Hatch . . . Their Rocky Mountain Beavers are all the go now . . ."

July brought the postscript about Dr. Willard's "Mrs. Campbell." On the sixth the *Troy Daily Times* printed a scoop of its own. As the *Whig* had acted as news conduit from the Willards and Woods, the *Times* now received and printed an affidavit from one Rose Renssley which destroyed what remained of the Campbell theory. Renssley:

> . . . on the 4th day of July, 1854, I called at the Rensselaer County Jail, State of New York, for the purpose of seeing Mrs. Robinson, and with her consent, was permitted to do so [Renssley's easy access to the prisoner is telling—in contrast to the trouble Robinson gave William Wood and William H. Jeffery]. I have a sister who married a man by the name of Campbell, was left a widow, and who also kept a hotel in Quebec.—Not hearing of her whereabouts for a period of about eight years, and seeing rumors in the public papers to the effect that possibly Mrs. Robinson might be Mrs. Campbell, and therefore my sister, I called upon her for the purpose of ascertaining if it were really so. I am happy to say that she is not my sister, whose maiden name was Sophia Andrews, and therefore she cannot be the Mrs. Campbell referred to.[25]

No other papers picked up the item, and only a violent incident in the Ferry Street Jail a few days later supplied more news of Robinson that summer. On July 9, she attacked Sheriff Price.[26] As the story was told years later:

> When the veiled murderess occupied an apartment at the county jail she professed an unbounded admiration of Mrs. Price and got along with her very well. She did not however have any sort of use for the keeper. Mr. Price was an agreeable man and presumably did everything for the comfort of his prisoner that he consistently could, but that made no difference in her attitude toward him, and one night, when he had carried up her supper to her and had placed his lantern upon the floor, she crept around like a cat, picked up the lantern and struck Mr. Price a blow upon the head which rendered him totally unconscious. This blow was not for liberty but was manifestly an act of spite.[27]

The Trojan writer of the account loyally cast the city's onetime public servants, the Prices, in a rosy light. It's hard to imagine Robinson was fond of either half of the couple. Trial testimony had told of the prisoner's complaints about lack of coal and firewood during the winter, and: "Keeper Price's wife was a thrifty woman. She knew how to manage not only to make the pennies but to save them. She had no idea of allowing much money to go out of her hands and she kept but one girl. Between this girl and herself not only was all the work of the family done, but that for the prisoners also. The prisoners food was cooked and their clothing was washed by Catherine Price and her one maid, and neither the keeper nor his good wife thought shame of the matter . . ."[28]

Catherine Price's penny-pinching plus the July heat of the second-floor cell—with its view of the jail's central hall, equipped with "gibbet" where all hangings took place—must have been hard on Robinson. But how many prisoners would deal their keepers a blow without any attempt at escape? What was wrong with Henrietta Robinson? Though she had failed to win an insanity acquittal, she was *not* behaving in an entirely normal way.

18

MORE MATHER

The Hard versus Soft division in the Democratic Party continued through 1854, with the Hards holding their own separate convention on July 12 in Syracuse. There, they voted to support "Nebraska"—a pro- or at least not anti-slavery position—and to condemn Governor Seymour's veto of the anti-liquor "Maine law" which Myron H. Clark and others had managed to get through the state legislature in 1853. So, many Hards—and not Mather alone—were anti-drink. The ex-canal commissioner was surely present in Syracuse, but had returned to Troy by July 17 when he at last met with Rev. Dr. Halley and the elders of the Second Street Presbyterian Church.

The church set Mather down gently, only charging him with "Habitual absence from the ordinances of the Gospel" or skipping church. Mather "freely acknowledged the truth of the charges and stated that his conduct had not been such as became a Christian and that if he absented himself from communion services it was because he felt himself unworthy to be there." The elders suspended him ". . . until he gives satisfactory evidence of repentance," and ordered the sentence be read at the next Friday evening prayer meeting. Only Soft Democrat Abram Van Tuyl dissented "from this mode of publishing [the sentence], it being his opinion it should be from the pulpit on the Sabbath."[1]

A scan of Second Street Presbyterian Church "Session Minutes" of 1835–56, finds only three other suspensions or threatened suspensions. Surprisingly, one suspendee was Mather's brother-in-law Daniel Wight, expelled between 1841 and 1849 for his admission of the truth of "reports . . . unfavorable to [his] . . . Christian character."[2] In contrast to the discreet way the Session dealt with Wight and Mather's sins, it laid bare those of less well-connected church members. In July of 1849, the minutes recorded a long deposition from one Dr. Wickes, beginning: ". . . Mr. Alfred Slasson . . . could not walk straight but staggered on the sidewalk as far as I saw him which was half a block. He came from the direction of the Troy House and passed down River Street and I followed him till he entered the Alhambra. My attention was called to him at this time from the fact that he nearly ran against a lady . . ."[3]

And in April of 1853, a Mrs. Agnes Williamson confessed and begged forgiveness for "antenuptial Fornication," a phrase underlined with a jagged penstroke—the visual equivalent of a scream—in the minutes. Though the elders judged Williamson repentant and didn't suspend her, the awful, underlined phrase must have destroyed her position in the Troy church; she moved to Winooski Falls, Vermont, in 1854.[4]

But Wight's appearance on this brief list of fallen church members tells something more about Mather. Here was another Mather associate—like John G. Britton—who had a morals problem. And now we remember Thurlow Weed, as well. Weed had practically invented backroom-deal influence-peddling, thereby gaining his nickname "The Great Lobbyist." Whig contemporary and sometime-ally Horace Greeley described him this way: "Weed was of coarser mould and fibre than Seward—tall, robust, dark-featured [unfashionably tanned], shrewd, resolute, and not over-scrupulous—keen-sighted, though not far-seeing."[5]

For all his lack of scruples, according to Greeley, he was not venal, according to H. D. Stanton.[6] Weed's interests seem to have been, very worthily, friendships and a true patriotism—and less worthily, power and the wielding of power for its own sake, and sex. Weed's extra-marital sex life is revealed in a range of sources. First of all, a memoir of the New York State Assembly's "doorkeeper," *The Lobby from Thurlow Weed's Time*, is filled with nudge-nudge, wink-wink references to Albany "fleshpots" and "young lady lobbyists."[7] Author Hudson Tanner's title implies Weed played some role in this scene.

Then, Weed's own autobiography describes his involvement with the children of a good-looking woman who allegedly died in Albany in the mid-1840s. As Weed tells the story, he learned by chance, while sitting in an Albany barbershop in the winter of 1846, of an "intemperate writing master [who] had died that day of delirium tremens in his schoolroom" leaving behind a small daughter imprisoned for "several hours in a cold room with the remains of its [*sic*] deceased father." The writing master's drinking had not been his only ugly feature: he was also "a hateful dwarf" who had conned the child's mother into marriage by "representing himself as wealthy, with a plantation in Missouri." Weed adopted the girl, Mary, on the day he heard of her plight. Then over the next few years, he learned more about the child's mother:

Troy House, 1824.

We subsequently [following the adoption] learned that the mother of our adopted daughter died; that she was in person and manners attractive and ladylike, and that she had evidently been accustomed to good society. The ladies of the hotel in which she had boarded during her last illness became much interested in her. To one of them, Mrs. Lyman, she, just before her death, gave little Mary, then an infant. Mrs. Lyman, who accepted the trust, died soon afterward, leaving the infant to a second orphanage. [Where was the hateful dwarf at this point? But perhaps Weed or his editor, Harriet Weed, had lost the thread of their tale by this time.] Two months afterwards, and soon after we adopted the child, Mrs. Wood, the mother of the deceased Mrs. Lyman, brought a small trunk to us containing articles that had been carefully preserved by Mary's mother, who had committed the trunk to Mrs. Lyman . . . The trunk contained a miniature of Mary's mother, and some jewelry belonging to and worn by her in her English home, in earlier and better and happier days. It contained also two marriage certificates, the earliest one giving her family name.[8]

The *Autobiography* contains more of the saga: Weed's chance meeting with a British Navy officer who fills in details of Isabella Shore's life, for that was Mary's mother's name; the discovery of a monogrammed sheet in the trunk which confirms the officer's claim Isabella had once lived as the housekeeper of a governor of the Danish West Indies; another chance meeting of Weed's in Brunswick, Georgia, which leads him to discover two more children of Isabella's in a Charleston orphanage; and finally, Weed's return to New York State with one of the new orphans.

Who can doubt Weed was not just spinning this complicated story as a way of bringing his own illegitimate children into his legitimate family circle?[9] His full participation in a "double-standard world" even appears to beam from an undated note written by Sherman Croswell, editor of the Hard Democratic *Albany Argus*. The note thanks Weed for a painting of the Western World's iconic fallen woman, "The Magdalen." Croswell: "You could not have consulted my taste more completely in the selection of a subject . . ."[10]

Forgetting the issue of sexual morality, other qualities link Mather friends and allies. Just as Horace Greeley described the self-made man, Weed, as "of coarser mould," alleged Mather associate Myron H. Clark was not a cultivated person: "Myron H. Clark . . . belonged to the class of men generally known as fanatics. He was a plain man of humble pretensions and slender attainments. He was originally a cabinet-maker and afterward a merchant. Then he became a reformer . . . his hobby was temperance."[11]

Asahel C. Geer, probably a Calvin Mather or John C. Mather crony and certainly the son of the "Judge Geer" linked to Mather by Henrietta Robinson, was a kind of fanatic, too. Though well-educated by his father, Judge Walter Geer, who had helped found an academy in Glens Falls, Asahel was a Millerite, a believer in a religious enthusiasm which flourished mainly in depressed farm regions of New York State.[12] From the 1830s, Baptist preacher William Miller of Washington County had claimed the ability to calculate the time of the Second Coming. Some of his followers named October 22, 1844, as the exact day. But even after this date, Miller and others continued to make railway-schedule-like predictions for the world's end.

19

TRENDS

In 1854—as in 1853, the year of the murders—the Robinson affair sprang to greatest life in the spring and early to mid-summer and then faded away over later months, only to revive once more in the spring of the new year, 1855.[1] During the affair's cyclical waning period in 1854, the political fallout of the Nebraska Act intensified. In fact, the year 1854 marks the near-final splintering of the old parties, before the birth of the Republican Party in New York State in 1855[2] and rebirth of the old Democratic Party in new, narrower mold.

The Softs convened on September 6, 1854, and with no disagreement renominated Horatio Seymour for Governor and endorsed his veto of Myron H. Clark's 1853 prohibition bill. But when conservatives among the Softs put forward "a cunningly worded resolution declaring the Repeal of the Missouri Compromise [the effect of the Nebraska Act] inexpedient and unnecessary yet rejoicing that it would benefit the territories and forbidding any attempt to undo it . . . the deathlike stillness which greeted its reading shook the nerves . . ."[3] When it came time to vote on this platform plank, "the Custom House had done its [patronage] work well,"[4] and the resolution passed. But the Soft leadership had won a battle and lost the war, for anti-Nebraska Softs now left the party in disgust.

The Whigs stepped, advantageously for them, into the breach. Their convention, which opened September 20, swung toward the Woolly Heads and denounced the Nebraska Act. The Whigs also came out against all non-medicinal liquor sales, choosing ardent prohibitionist Myron H. Clark to head the state ticket as Whig candidate for Governor. But many Silver Grays had already left the party, to follow either the Hards or the Native Americans (Know-Nothings) who were about to emerge from their underground realm. In early October, the Native Americans held a "council"[5] which chose New York City lawyer Daniel Ullman to head their own slate of candidates for state office. Ironically, it was discovered during the campaign that Ullman, champion of the native-born, had been born in India. His opponents called him "the Hindoo" ever after.

The Hard and Soft Democrats actually began their campaigns with near-identical platforms on state issues—as both parties endorsed Gov. Seymour's handling of canal affairs and both favored prohibition. But Hard gubernatorial candidate Greene C. Bronson soon abandoned his anti-liquor stand. Horace Greeley: ". . . he [Bronson] first inclined to water, then to rum and water, and finally he came out all rum."[6] Whig Myron H. Clark, drawing the support of anti-Nebraska ex-Softs, won the governorship. His fellow Whigs carried the largest share of state offices, with the Soft Democrats and Native Americans acquiring the next largest shares, and the Hard Democrats coming in a distant fourth.

Did all this political reshuffling affect the Robinson affair? Perhaps, but we can't track coverage of the partisan papers very precisely because liberal Whig *Troy Daily Traveller* issues survive from October 1854 through January 1856 *only*, and the one Hard Democratic paper of the region, the *Albany Argus*, dealt with the distressing-for-them Robinson case by almost ignoring it from beginning to end. The Soft *Troy Daily Times* was reveling in the story and, to some extent, turning into an advocate for Robinson. On September 15, 1854, the *Times*, in the course of informing readers Mrs. Robinson's case would not "as supposed by some" be retried in October and "[i]t will be some time yet before Mrs. R. is retried, if at all," offered a mildly

positive glimpse of the convicted woman: "The Grand Jury visited the Jail this morning. We understand she was inclined to be courteous and agreeable,—even condescending to exhibit to the gaze of the Jury her beautiful face, and to engage in entertaining conversation. The Jury is said to have been delighted with their visit. Mrs. R, since the "chaining operation," has been remarkably docile."[7]

Then in late November, the *Times* sprang to defend Robinson from a rumor which had appeared in both the *Traveller* and the *Budget* that, "there was 'babby' born [to Robinson] in jail about whose paternity much vexed argument has resulted . . ."[8] The *Times*, which disdained quoting the *Traveller* or *Budget*, responded to the story after it was picked up by the *Albany Transcript*: "We are advised that this murderess, now incarcerated in the Troy jail, on Wednesday night presented some person with a baby! Mrs. R. has been in jail over a year!" The *Times*: "It is but proper to deny the truth of the above statement. No such issue as that intimated above has taken place; and if 'coming events cast their shadows before,' it is quite likely none will occur . . . Mrs. Robinson has crimes too great to bear already on her head, and those who fabricate such heartless stories as the above about her, are little better than the object they revile and slander."[9]

The *Traveller*, the originator[10] of the report, fired back at the *Times*: "The *Times* (which appears to have the confidence of Mrs. R.) says no such thing [a birth] will occur. We have only to say in vindication of our veracity, that we were informed that such was the case by a citizen of Troy, and one of their eminent legal lights, who appeared to be 'posted.' "[11]

From this point forward, the *Times* would consistently treat Mrs. Robinson with gentleness, while continuing to promote the Wood daughter story. The *Traveller*'s coverage would be ample—way ahead of any other paper—in the coming spring and summer of 1855, would focus on Robinson's personal wickedness, and would almost completely avoid the Wood daughter issue. The pregnancy-illegitimate birth item of late 1854 is typical of the *Traveller*'s stance.

The voice of the *Budget* is mostly silenced from mid-1854 onward, with no surviving issues after June 1854, though quotes from its 1855 articles in other journals show the *Budget*'s view of Robinson resembled the *Times*'s.[12]

The *Whig*, with a full surviving run through 1854 and 1855, varies the *Albany Argus*'s non-treatment of the Robinson affair by publishing a *scanty something* compared to the *Argus*'s *almost nothing*. The handful of *Whig* pieces on Robinson in 1855 were all much shorter than same-day stories in the *Traveller* and *Times*, and the *Whig*, like the *Traveller*, avoided the Wood controversy, except on occasion, to defend the Woods. But unlike the *Traveller* and like the *Times*, Troy's Silver-Gray paper tended to treat the convicted woman kindly.

Put in a simple way, from late 1854 through 1855, the Silver-Gray *Whig* urged indirectly and sometimes directly, "Be fair to the Woods!" while the Soft *Times* repeated, "How shocking that Robinson is a Miss Wood!" and the Woolly-Head *Traveller* decided over and over, "Robinson is an utterly low, vile woman!"

20

CHARLOTTE WOOD

On March 15, 1855—when the city was still half-bound by winter, the river navigation not yet opened, and many factories just emerging from their time of winter lay-offs—the *Troy Daily Times* revived the Robinson affair with a long article, "Who Is Mrs. Robinson?—The Question Answered—The Secret Out." After a run-through of the past year's Wood daughter theory, the *Times* announced in a dramatic finish to the piece:

> . . . we assert, upon proofs that have come to light—proof that will carry conviction to every candid mind, and before which even interested affidavits must vanish into thin air—that Mrs. Robinson, now in jail in this city, convicted of the murder of Timothy Lanagan, is none other than the identical [*sic*] Charlotte Wood, formerly of Quebec, a former pupil at the Troy Female Seminary—a sister of the Mr. Wood of Quebec, who swore that she was not his sister!
>
> If this statement is denied and the proofs are demanded, we are ready to substantiate it by evidence that cannot be shaken.

The *Whig* replied cautiously the next day, inclining to disbelief: "Certainly nothing short of positive evidence would warrant the publication of the articles . . . If so, out with it, that the public may judge. One thing is evident: unless Mr. Wood of Quebec, whose affidavit we published last summer, was incredibly deceived (which we do not believe) or unless he willfully perjured himself (which we shall believe when we see proof of the fact, not before)—either this, or the Times and Budget articles are most cruel to the feelings and good name of an already deeply wronged family, and are libelous to the last degree."[1]

The *Traveller* waited another day to more firmly pooh-pooh the new claim as: ". . . a shallow ruse on the part of her friends to create a public sympathy in her favor that might have an influence upon the Executive."[2]

The *Times* made no move to produce their "evidence that cannot be shaken," or at least not to print this evidence. And it was left to the *Traveller* to supply more updates on the jailed woman over the next weeks. On March 24: "While in the vicinity of the jail this morning, our attention was attracted to the upper window of the establishment by seeing the different persons passing look up . . . we discovered that Mrs. Robinson had her head and arm, which was covered with a white cloth, thrust out between the bars of the window of her room, and was holding between her fingers a small and irregular piece of looking glass. Occasionally she would draw her head in, a moment after to thrust it out again. At the time we left she was still entertaining herself in this singular manner . . ."[3]

On March 30:

> We learn that Mrs. R. generally manages to obtain copies of the city papers whenever they contain any item relating to herself. On such occasions, she is not backward in expressing herself in very emphatic and strong terms She has been heard to say, and in no gentle tone either, after reading some article concerning herself—"D—n these editors, I don't see what they trouble themselves so much about me for. If I had hold of some of them I'd learn them to let things alone that don't concern them." In this manner, as we are informed, she expresses her disapprobation, mingling with her observations an indefinite number of not very well selected oaths. We learn also that at times she can be very polite, and again at other occasions coarse, vulgar, and profane. She acts like a woman who may once have seen better days, and having fallen, is reckless of what she says and does. In profanity, she is said to be an adept, and oaths often fall from her lips thick and fast. In the words of our informant "she is a bad, wicked, devilish woman." Being curious to know how she passed her time, we made inquiry as to whether she was in the habit of reading much, and learned that she was not; and that if she was ever intellectually inclined, the desire appeared to be now dead in her.[4]

This picture of the jailed woman—helped along by Richard Jennyss's trial testimony on Robinson's inability to sign her name and later records describing her as semi-literate ("read[s] but a very little")—was not a good fit with

Winter fishing on the Hudson.

either Emma or Charlotte Wood, daughters of the book-rich Robert Wood and former students at the Troy Female Seminary.

But at this point, the early spring of 1855, what did people in Troy know of the two sisters? To begin with, many must have heard the rumor of a Wood family link to the British royal family. Had this whiff of scandal been enough to suggest that any glamorous woman with "a foreign air"[5] in the Troy jail was a Miss Wood? *Or* had the old scandal inspired Mather or someone else to create a scapegoat "Miss Wood" identity for the jailed woman? The persistence of the charge, shifting from one Miss Wood to another—from Georgiana (Emma Willard cited the eldest Miss Wood as the subject of the unnamed Troy newspaper's charge of June-July, 1853), to Emma, to Charlotte—really points more to an active agent "blowing" on the story and keeping it going *at all costs*.

Yet, *some* Trojans may have truly been sifting the evidence. A few trial observers had probably noticed that Charlotte Wood Eliott's age—she was born April 8, 1826[6]—made her a good fit with Henrietta Robinson, as far as Robinson's professed age, given in late April or early May of 1853, went. At that time, Robinson had told trial witness. Mary Jane Dillon, she (Robinson) was 27 years old with this fact reaching the public at large on Day Four of the trial, May 25, 1854.

But to counter this coincidence, Emma Willard and her son, Dr. John, had specialized information in the Seminary records that told firmly against the Charlotte Wood Eliott allegation. "Ledger B" in the archives of today's Emma Willard School contains an account for "Robert Wood," listing expenses for his daughters' educations, board, and extras from March 1843 through July 1844. Wood's account prior to March 1843 was in a lost "Ledger A." Charlotte's and her younger sister Harriet's course work emerges through the titles of books bought for them: Davies *Arithmetic*, *U. S. History*, Lincoln's *Botany*, Bennet's *Art Singing*, Hedges' *Logic*, Gray's *Chemistry*, Wayland's *Moral Science*, Kames' *Elements*, Neuman's *Rhetoric*, *Vie de Washington*, Dwyer's *Elocution*, plus an elementary-sounding "Base Primmer." While Ledger B gives no clue about which books went to which girl, another rougher account book, "Journal No. 1, J. H. W. [John H. Willard]," indicates in a March 31, 1844 entry that Kames' *Elements* and Newman's *Rhetoric* were for Charlotte. (April 30, 1844 and June 30, 1844 entries in the same journal assign Dwyer's *Elocution* and the Base Primmer to Harriet.)

Kames' *Elements* was *Elements of Criticism* (1762) by Henry Home, Lord Kames, an important figure of the Scottish Enlightenment. His volume explores a supposed rational response to art and was widely used as a college-level text in the nineteenth-century United States. Samuel P. Newman's *A Practical System of Rhetoric or the Principles and Rules of Style, Inferred from Examples of Writing* (1827) was another college-level text.

By early spring of 1844, Charlotte had been at the Seminary for at least two terms, according to the Seminary's printed catalogues. Actually, both her name and Harriet's on a January 1843 report to the New York State Regents show both girls had attended in 1842 as well.[7] Thus Seminary teachers were well aware of Charlotte Wood's abilities by 1844, when they assigned the girl the advanced Kames and Newman texts. Such testimony from the school records should have convinced Willard contemporaries of the sheer impossibility of Charlotte Wood Eliott as the non-writing "Henrietta Robinson" in 1853.[8] But as we will see, strange currents continued to carry the implausible story forward.

21

LIVELY SEASON

In mid-April, Robinson's sentencing was postponed yet again: "Judge Watson declined passing sentence, stating that as Mrs. R. had been convicted at a term held by Judge Harris, he [Harris] must pass judgement upon her."[1]

Watson was surely eager, like many others, to keep his distance from the Robinson affair. This could not be said of John M. Francis, the energetic and often caustic editor of the *Troy Daily Times*. He had jumped into the business with both feet by publishing the brand-new charge about Charlotte Wood in March. In May, he reaped the wrath of William Wood in the form of a $20,000 libel suit. But Francis stood his ground and printed the whole of Plaintiff William Wood's charge against him in the May 19 edition of the *Times*, thereby republishing the Charlotte Wood story yet again. "Mr. Francis, it is understood, will attempt to justify himself by proving that his statement was the truth and not a libel," commented the *Auburn Advertiser* three days later.[2]

On June 9, the Robinson defense learned their main goal of the past year, a new trial for their client, had been denied by the New York State Supreme Court, sitting in Albany. According to a *Troy Daily Times* report, Pierson had actually gotten Troy's Common Council to ask for the new trial.[3] But to no avail, and Robinson took this news hard. The *Times*:

She at first manifested symptoms of the most uncontrollable anger, stamping the floor with her feet, and launching out a torrent of invectives against all who were in any manner connected with her trial. By degrees, however, she became more moderate, and finally settled down with the exclamation, "I am glad they would not give me the new trial."[4]

The *Traveller*'s harsher, longer piece, which used the word "violent" three times in describing Robinson, didn't have the woman "settling down."

Instead, after abusing "ex-Governor Seymour, Judge Harris, M. I. Townsend, and Sheriff Price . . . her imagination flew off in another direction, and she became proud and defying." Both *Times* and *Traveller* described a celebration in the prisoner's cell. The *Traveller*: "A female who does her [Robinson's] washing happened to be in the room at the time. This woman Mrs. R. sent out to purchase different articles of food and a quantity of candles, to make merry over the decision, as the unfortunate woman asserted . . . she [Robinson] proceeded to place four lighted candles in each window of her room, after which she built up a roaring fire in her stove, and commencing cooking the food the woman had bought. The illumination soon attracted the attention of people passing in the street, and a crowd quickly gathered opposite the jail."[5]

The *Times* alone of surviving papers covered an episode which took place three days later between Judge Harris, Defense Counsel Pierson, and District Attorney Hogeboom. In "Exciting Scene in Court: Sentence of Mrs. Robinson Deferred," the *Times* described an unexpected gathering at the "opening of the Circuit Court" in the Rensselaer County Courthouse. At least it was unexpected by the public at large and by Job Pierson. As reported, Judge Harris "had felt an ardent desire that the sentence of Mrs. Robinson . . . should be got along with in as quiet a manner as possible—that sentence should be passed when the public knew little of the matter." And: "He had no desire to pander to the morbid taste for excitement, which he had seen too frequently exhibited in this community."

Thus at 2:00 P.M. on June 14, Harris sent Sheriff Price to tell Pierson "just as he was taking dinner" that his client would be sentenced at 3:00 P.M. Pierson arrived in court, almost breathless no doubt, to object to this plan because "he was extremely anxious of having a few moments conversation with her [Robinson]" before the sentencing. Pierson surely wanted to ward off an outburst by Robinson at sentencing, one that might contain who-knew-what names or allegations. Harris, who had equally surely been trying to screen any outburst with his plan, immediately agreed to Pierson's plea for the mini-postponement. Was the cooperation between liberal Whig Harris and Hard Democrat Pierson especially revolting to Soft Democrat Francis? Francis's careful detailing of the "understanding" says yes:

> Mr. Pierson: I do insist upon it—but still—
> Judge Harris: Very well then. The Sheriff will not bring Mrs. Robinson here this afternoon.
>
> Mr. Pierson: But still, I appreciate your Honor's motives in keeping the affair quiet. I have no objection to your Honor's sentencing the prisoner as secretly as possible.

Judge Harris: Probably it cannot now be done so secretly as it would have been.

Mr. Pierson: It was necessary.

Judge Harris: Any farther discussion of the matter is unnecessary. Mrs. Robinson will not be sentenced this afternoon.

Mr. Hogeboom: I wish to be allowed one moment's liberty, to repel the sharp insinuation of the gentleman upon the other side. [Whatever this insinuation was, the *Times* didn't record it.]

Judge Harris: But I would prefer that this discussion be continued no further at present.

Mr. Hogeboom: But the gentleman has said—

Judge Harris: Mr. Hogeboom, you will oblige me by continuing this no farther.

Mr. Hogeboom, seating himself: Very well, your Honor, it is not often I am thus assailed by gentlemen.

Despite the planning of judge and defense counsel, Robinson's sentencing on June 19 still gave the woman a brief public platform and so a dramatic scene for reporters. Strikingly, the *Whig* looked away from this story, offering no coverage at all. The *Traveller* and *Times* accounts diverged noticeably. As usual, the *Traveller* was more hostile towards Robinson personally, but the key difference between the two treatments was the absence of John C. Mather's name in the *Traveller* piece and its presence in the *Times*'s. The *Traveller* was definitely cutting Mather some slack.[6]

A special correspondent to the *New York Daily Times* (forebear of today's *New York Times*) supplies a third eye:

[Judge Harris] ordered the Sheriff to bring the unfortunate woman privately into court this afternoon, only the District Attorney and the prisoner's counsel being notified, but

"On eagles' wings immortal scandal flies."

Was there ever yet a secret faithfully kept? Towards afternoon, nearly all the members of the bar and many citizens were aware

Henrietta Robinson addresses Judge Harris. From H. B. Skinner, *The Life and Confessions of Mrs. Henrietta Robinson* (1855).

of the fact; and as the hour of three approached there were quite a number of persons in the Court-House. At 3, Judge Harris took his seat upon the bench, and for fifteen minutes an intense and expectant silence prevailed throughout the Court-room. At 3 ¼ o'clock, Mrs. Robinson was led in by Sheriff Price and took a seat inside the bar, next her counsel, Mr. Pierson. She was, as upon her former trial, well-dressed—but not so richly and expensively as then. She walked in with a firm and buoyant step, and smilingly greeted her counsel. She wore but one thickness of veil, instead of three or four, as on the trial—and through that veil it was easy to see she was very highly painted. "Will you sit down here," said the Sheriff, pointing to a chair. She seemed quite offended at being in the least degree hurried, and said, in a haughty and petulant tone, that they must wait till she got ready. She then sat down and amused herself—laughing, looking around the Court and talking, and appeared quite pleased with her situation . . .

> The Judge then requested Mrs. Robinson to remove her veil, which she did apparently quite willingly, exposing to view a countenance, which, it was evident, had once been beautiful. [The generally ungallant *Traveller* found "her face . . . as fascinating as it ever was."] The Judge asked her if she had anything to say why sentence of death should not be pronounced upon her. She said, interrupting him before he got through the sentence, and as if she had something laid up, which was now coming out, "Yes, a great deal to say, but I do not wish to be interrupted; I have been the victim of a conspiracy of you politicians at Albany," and much more of the same strain, when she was quieted by her counsel, and the Judge proceeded: "You have been convicted of the murder of Timothy Lanagan." "Yes! And upon false evidence! Shame! Judge, Shame!" "If you would hear me," said the Judge—"Oh, Yes, I'll hear you"—"I would advise you to cease battling with your fate, but submit to it like a true woman; but as you will not hear me, it only remains for me to pass upon you the sentence of the law, which is, that you be confined in the County prison until the 3d day of August next, upon which day, between the hours of 10 A.M. and 4 P.M. you be hanged by the neck until dead; and may God in his infinite goodness have mercy on your soul." While the Judge was saying, "You be hanged by the neck until dead," Mrs. Robinson very coolly drew her hand across her throat, and said: "A very pretty throat for a halter, isn't it, Judge?" And when he had finished, she told him, "he had better pray for his own soul" . . . [When] the Sheriff went up to her to remove her to the jail . . . she indignantly ordered him to wait until she was ready, and commenced abusing the Judge, Sheriff, and a portion of her counsel [Martin I. Townsend as is made clear in the *Times* and *Traveller* articles], until quieted by Mr. Pierson. She was then removed, but as she turned to go, she said in a commanding voice and with a proud glance, "May the Judge of Judges thus deal with you," and departed to her carriage . . .[7]

Neither the *Troy Daily Times* nor *Troy Daily Traveller* recorded Robinson's dangerously all-encompassing reference to "you politicians at Albany." The *Troy Daily Times* simply had Robinson say, "I am the victim of a political conspiracy which is calculated to crush an innocent man," and then noted: "The Prisoner still kept up a conversation with Mr. Pierson, which we were unable to hear, merely distinguishing the name of John C. Mather. The audience at this point became greatly excited. The greatest confusion prevailed."

The *Budget*'s account—partly reprinted in the *Albany Evening Atlas* of June 20—put a more direct statement into Robinson's mouth: "I have been persecuted on account of John C. Mather." The *Traveller*, as noted, avoided Mather's name. Instead, it offered the juicy tidbit: ". . . she also called someone a libertine." But this couldn't have been Mather, since Robinson was at this point casting herself *and Mather* as victims of some conspiracy. Both the *Times* and *Traveller* supplied added tidbits: on Judge Harris telling Robinson to leave off her "feigned lunacy"; and on Robinson's crying of "Shame!" frequently during the proceeding and also shouting "Pooh!" ("[She] continued to 'pooh' in a very insulting manner . . ."[8]) The *Troy Daily Times* showed their gentler touch with Robinson. In their account Robinson advises Judge Harris to "pray for your own soul, *sir*," using a polite form of address. The *Times* also toned up the *New York Daily Times*'s "May the Judge of Judges deal with you" into "Judge Harris, may the Judge of Judges be your Judge." The *Traveller*'s version—"May the judge of judges in the end pay you!"—sounds nastier than either of the other two.

The *Traveller* continued to hammer Robinson in print over the next few days. On June 20 the liberal Whig daily described, unflatteringly, the convict's arrival back at the Ferry Street Jail after the June 19 sentencing: ". . . she became angry and excited and would probably have launched forth into a torrent of invectives, if those in attendance upon her had showed her any opportunity." The piece included an account of the reporter's next-day visit to the jail and his sighting of Robinson using a hand mirror to look into the street below her cell: "As we were about entering the jail, we felt impelled to look up, and as we did so were somewhat startled at seeing Mrs. R., looking directly at us and laughing. The face that we saw was reflected in a clever-sized bit of looking glass which she was holding out the window at the time, but nevertheless presented us with a full view of her smiling countenance. We stood and looked at her a moment and a strange, shuddering feeling swept over us . . ."[9]

But this wasn't all. The *Traveller* half-filled another column in their June 20 issue with a story about "a singular individual named H. Barringer [Troy directories of 1852–53 list a "Barringer, H., painter" who worked at 7 Congress, rather near to the jail]" who had sent a letter to Robinson that morning, and the *Traveller*'s unsuccessful attempts to get the letter from the "violent and excited" prisoner: "She used language . . . that it would be impossible and improper to publish, although such conduct on her part is not unusual and almost leads us to believe that she is not in a sane condition."[10]

Regretting this last statement, the *Traveller* took pains the next day (June 21) in another article also titled "Mrs. Robinson" to pronounce repeatedly: "*She does not appear to have been intoxicated or insane* [modern italics] and no extenuating circumstance whatsoever can be found to palliate in the least the awful deed or remove from her one particle of the responsibility of having committed it. *She does not appear to have been intoxicated or insane* [modern italics] . . ."

But to step back to June 20, the liberal Whig *Albany Knickerbocker*—owned and edited by Hugh L. Hastings, a former protégé of Thurlow Weed[11]—had published one of the earliest appeals for commutation of Robinson's sentence. This appeal used language more or less lifted from Martin I. Townsend's trial defense: "Mrs. Robinson is undoubtedly a very wicked woman. But who has made her so? The very men who are now crying for her life. Women are first seduced—then comes neglect, suffering and dissipation. The latter is embraced to drown that remorse that the acts of some male villain have made eternal. Mrs. Robinson is sentenced to be hung while the wretches who taught her the way to the gallows are numbered among the 'most respectable men' in Troy."[12]

Did the reference to "the 'most respectable men' in Troy" spark an alarmed response in the *Traveller* of June 21? A line from its piece of this day sounds rather worried: "If she expiates her crime on the gallows, and should make a confession, *her story, such has been her character, would not gain credence* [modern italics]." The *Traveller* further held: ". . . it seems to us of very little consequence who she is, or whence her origin . . . Whether her doom is the gallows or the prison, it is better that she should be forgotten."

The *Troy Daily Traveller* and the *Albany Knickerbocker*, both liberal Whig publications, were not "on the same page" in the days right after Robinson's sentencing. There is no getting around this fact. The *Traveller* editor, William Avery, damned Robinson and sought to sweep her and her case into oblivion as quickly as possible. But *Albany Knickerbocker* editor Hugh Hastings was willing to prolong the agony of at least some " 'respectable men' in Troy." Were Albany Woolly Heads more confident about the Robinson scandal than Troy ones? Or was it simply that Hugh Hastings personally was more confident? While we can't identify a unified liberal Whig response to Robinson's sentencing, the *Knickerbocker*, like the *Traveller*, focused an unusual amount of attention on the affair in June and July of 1855. The *Knickerbocker* broke two brand-new Robinson stories over these months. We know the stories from reprints in the *Traveller* which itself reported one other Robinson newsbreak over the same time plus continued to cover all generally-carried Robinson stories at length.[13]

At this point, no other papers were digging over the affair in the same intensive way as the *Knickerbocker* and *Traveller*. Since all post-trial liberal Whig newspaper coverage of the business omitted Mather's name, so unlike the Soft coverage, and denied or avoided the Wood identity issue, also unlike Soft coverage, the liberal Whig stories on Robinson look a lot like a pro- or at least not anti-Mather attempt to mollify the Wood-Willard group combined with a desire to set the boundaries or focus of the story. Of course, the Silver-Gray *Troy Daily Whig* had been openly mollifying the Woods from soon after May 25, 1854, and also avoiding mention of Mather in their much briefer coverage. Maybe the liberal Whigs were a little ambivalent, wanting to control the Robinson scandal, for reasons soon to be explored, in a way that also protected Mather, but at the same time not worrying too much about damage to the Hard Democrat from their frequent stories.

But to return to unfolding events, on June 21 the *Albany Evening Atlas* claimed new Whig Governor Myron H. Clark had already decided on prison rather than hanging for Robinson: "It is said Mrs. Robinson, the murderess, had an assurance of pardon from capital punishment when sentenced. This may account for her reckless behavior."

The *Atlas* article went on to tweak prohibitionist Clark:

> It is understood that Gov. Clark will commute her sentence to imprisonment for life, with the conditions that she will not drink any intoxicating liquor.
>
> It will be recollected that she administered arsenic, in small beer, to two victims, who had never offended her. Gov. Clark pardons the arsenic but cannot forgive the beer.

The *Atlas* also came out against the capital sentence: "We believe that the execution of a woman, by hanging, would demoralize the community; and we are glad that the sentence of the law is not to be carried into effect."

Nearly all the state's newspapers joined in to oppose the death sentence.[14] Even the *Traveller*, which had been hurrying Robinson to the gallows on June 20 and 21, relented on June 2: "Ten years ago a crime of the diabolical character of which this woman has been guilty, would have been promptly expiated on the gallows. Her sex, beauty, art, her own exertions or the exertions of her friends could not have saved her from her doom beyond the period assigned by law . . . [Yet] Few now desire her to be executed, and it will not be surprising if a successful effort should be made to obtain from the executive a commutation . . ."[15]

On this same day, the *Knick*—as the *Knickerbocker* was often called by Avery, Francis, and others—came out with its first piece of investigative journalism: ". . . she [Robinson] was arrested in this city [Albany] some two years since. She then resided in Chestnut Street and was visited by a mysterious personage by the name of "Johnson." A gentleman residing next door resolved to find out who this Johnson was and for this purpose undertook to confront Mr. Johnson as he was approaching Mrs. Robinson's domicile. Mrs. R. discovered his design and immediately rushed out with a pistol in her hand, threatening to blow his brains out if he 'even dared sneak round her house again.' "

This was a more detailed account of the *Albany Evening Journal* story of May 25, 1854. The *Knick* named "Justice Parsons" as the official who "held her to bail, her bondsman being a well-known restaurant keeper in this city" and fined Robinson $10 for breach of the peace.[16] The *Knick*'s grubby, police blotter item roused little interest among Troy and Albany readers. At least, except for the *Traveller*, no other surviving papers picked up the Albany arrest story. Instead, the *Troy Daily Times* kept readers abreast of the prisoner's spiritual life, with sympathetic notices of visits by Father Havermans, on June 28, and by a Sister of Charity four days later.[17] These friendly items sparked the *Traveller*'s hostile "Mrs. Robinson at Prayer" a few weeks later: "Two sympathizing and Christian ladies, as we learn, called at the jail just a day or two since and requested to see Mrs. Robinson . . . all three knelt, had not succeeded in uttering but a few words when she burst out into a loud and hearty laugh. Mrs. R. begged them to excuse her as the circumstances reminded her so forcibly of her girlhood when she and other children used to erect an altar and kneeling round it make believe that she could not help laughing. The attempt was then given up . . ."[18]

Interestingly, the Hard Democratic *Albany Argus* would run "Mrs. Robinson at Prayer" verbatim the next day.[19] As mentioned, the *Argus* had dealt with the Robinson scandal and its damaging effects on Hard Democrat John C. Mather by essentially not covering the Robinson trial and after-events. Their reprint of the *Traveller* item points up the still-barely-alive Hard Democrat-Woolly Head Whig alliance—at least as far as the Robinson case was concerned.

On July 14, the *Knick* published its second scoop on the convict's past.[20] This piece—reprinted later in the year in a sensational pamphlet, *The Life and Confessions of Mrs. Henrietta Robinson*[21]—is worth scrutinizing in detail.

22

"ADMIRAL PAGNUM'S DAUGHTER"

The *Traveller* of July 14, 1855:

> The *Albany Knickerbocker* has just been informed by an Irish laborer of the truth of whose statement that paper appears to have no doubt, that Mrs. Robinson is a daughter of Admiral Pagnum and was born at Pagnum Castle, Longford, Ireland. The man says that some few years since Mrs. R. resided in Hamilton Street, Albany—that he with others on one occasion was engaged in digging a drain there through the street, and that while thus employed she beckoned him to come in, which he did. As soon as he got seated, Mrs. Robinson asked him if he had ever seen her before. He was not sure but believed he had. She then asked him if he were not a native of Longford, Ireland. He said he was. She then wished to know if he did not recollect Admiral Pagnum of Pagnum Hall, Ireland. He replied in the affirmative, said that he was reared in the immediate vicinity of the castle. "And did you never see me there?" she asked. He replied, "I am not sure, I think I have, but you are so altered." At this she burst out crying and wept most bitterly. During the paroxysm, she informed him that she was born at Pagnum Castle, that Admiral Pagnum was her father and that she had left Longford to hide her shame. She attributed her ruin to "young Robinson"—a son of her father's steward, who abducted her from home and brought her virtueless to New York . . .

"Pag-num" is a phonetic spelling of the family name, Pakenham, and Pakenham Hall, actually in County Westmeath near the County Longford border, Ireland, was the chief seat of the barons, later earls, of Longford from the early 18th century; another seat, Longford Castle, lies within County Longford. Pakenham Hall still stands and is still owned by the Pakenham family, but renamed Tullynally Castle in honor of its pre-Anglo-Norman-conquest past. The *Albany Knickerbocker*'s mentions of the family name "Pagnum" and the place names "Pagnum Hall" and "Longford" suddenly remind us of Henrietta Robinson's 1853 talk about Irish lords and castles. Then when we look more closely at the Pakenhams and the neighborhood of Pakenham Hall, we find some just-perceptible connections there to the Woods of Quebec.

First, the full title of the Woods' claimed royal ancestor was, from 1799, "Edward, Duke of Kent and Strathearn and Earl of Dublin." Charlotte Maria Wood's husband, Sir William Francis Augustus Eliott, held his baronetcy—he inherited in 1864—in the Duchy of Strathearn in Scotland. Edward's Irish earldom either encompassed some Pakenham lands or else lay very near them; it's notable the Pakenham earldom didn't commence till after Edward's death.[1] The duke's best friend, aide, and eventual estate executor, General Frederick Augustus Wetherall, is buried in County Meath, between County Dublin and County Westmeath, and Wetherall's eldest daughter married into the Pakenham family. Isabella Mary Wetherall married in 1813 Thomas Pakenham, second son of Admiral Thomas Pakenham who, himself, was second son of Thomas, the second Earl of Longford (suc. 1794–d. 1835). Admiral Thomas resided at Coolure House, on the banks of Westmeath's Lough Derravaragh not far from Pakenham Hall from 1785 until his death in 1836, when the house went to Isabella Mary's husband.[2]

Second, it really looks as though Quebec lumber merchant Robert Wood named his four eldest daughters—Georgiana (b. 1818), Emma (b. 1819), Charlotte (b. and d.1821), and Charlotte Maria (b. 1826)—in honor of the then highest-ranking woman of the Pakenham family and of the whole of County Westmeath. This was Georgiana-Emma-Charlotte Lygon Pakenham, wife of the second Earl of Longford and "reigning" Lady Longford from 1817 until 1835.[3]

Third, the family of Robert Wood's eldest son, Robert Hudson Wood, lived in Athlone, one of Westmeath's chief towns, during the 1850s; both of Robert Hudson Wood's children, Harriet Agnes and Robert William, born in 1857 and 1859 respectively, were baptized in Athlone.[4]

Fourth, and maybe most importantly, in the small world of Westmeath's Anglo-Irish gentry there was a single, long-established Wood family, which claimed at least one mid-eighteenth-century-born Robert Wood of about the right age.[5] The Wood family of Westmeath lived on an estate named Rosmead (or Rosemead) near the town of Castletown Delvin on the eastern borders of the county. The founder of the family was a German Protestant named Hans Albert Widman who had arrived in Westmeath (then simply the western part of Meath) in 1680 as part of Cromwell's "Protestant Plantation" in Ireland. By 1682 Widman had turned into Hans Albert Wood (on an address to King Charles II), and by 1703, Hans Albert's son appeared as "Johannes Wood, de Rosmead" on a great map or chart of the county. A Henry Widman Wood headed the family from 1802 until his death in 1847 at age 90, when his daughter Frances's husband, Admiral Hercules Robinson, took over the family headship, and within a few years—in this Potato Famine time—lost the entire estate. Rosmead was "sold in the Incumbered Estates Court in 1852 and purchased by Lord Vaux, of Harrowden, to whom it was indebted in the sum of £52,000."[6]

And here's a clue to the Rosmead Woods' extra-family relationships. In 1857 Admiral Hercules Robinson published a memoir, *Sea Drift*, written while searching for buried treasure on islands "between Madeira and the Canaries"[7] in an attempt to recoup the family fortune. While sailing between digging sites, he penned anecdotes about his sea career, though without mentioning any fellow sailors by name, except for three young men who accompanied him on a voyage to Brazil.[8] One of these three is "Elliot," introduced by Robinson to a "Don [*sic*] Luiz of Pernambuco" after Dom Luiz had "inquired of the Consul, sotto voce, what English noblemen I [Robinson] was connected with, and also my middies."[9] This "Elliot" is none other than Russell Eliott, son of the 6th Baronet Eliott and uncle of the William Francis Augustus Eliott who would marry Charlotte Maria Wood in 1846 in Quebec. Russell Eliott (b. 1802) served as a midshipman on Robinson's ship, *Favorite*, between 1817 and 1821 during its cruise to Brazil.[10] This is a surely more-than-coincidental thread joining Quebec Woods and Westmeath Woods through the Scottish Eliotts (with Edward, Duke of Kent, no doubt patron of all three families).

Also Admiral Hercules Robinson's eldest son, born in 1823, three years before Charlotte Maria Wood Eliott, was named *Henry Robinson*.[11] This is a very suggestive name in any story of Henrietta Robinson. We know the Troy murderess was not one of Robert Wood of Quebec's legitimate daughters, but was she connected to them in some way—distant or not so distant?

23

ANGEL OF MERCY

But in 1855 in Troy and Albany, the public eye did not alight with much interest on the ditch-digger's tale of Pagnums in Ireland. Instead, it was absorbed by the arrival on the Robinson scene of glamorous feminist Elizabeth Oakes Smith. In 1855 Oakes Smith was 43 years old and at the height of her fame as a writer and lecturer. She played the same role in the feminist movement of the mid-nineteenth century as writer Gloria Steinem played in that of the 1970s—at least public image-wise. Both were beautiful, fashionable women and already-established writers before joining existing women's movements, and both met suspicion from other activists. At the third "Woman's Rights Convention" held in Syracuse in 1852.[1] Susan B. Anthony condemned Elizabeth Oakes Smith because she and a friend, Paulina Wright Davis, came to a meeting wearing "short-sleeved, low-necked white dresses, one with a pink, the other with a blue embroidered wool delaine sack with wide flowing sleeves, which left both neck and arms exposed."[2]

"Susan B. Anthony spoke out boldly and said that nobody who dressed as she [Oakes Smith] did could represent the earnest, solid, hardworking women of the country for whom they were making the demand for civil rights."[3]

Anthony's attack finished Oakes Smith as a leader of the movement, but the New York City-based writer continued to speak and write on women's issues, perhaps reaching more lecture-goers and readers than Anthony herself during the 1850s, the era of Oakes Smith's greatest fame.

Elizabeth Oakes Smith was a different kind of person from the stern Anthony. She also differed from Emma Willard, the other well-known woman involved in the Robinson affair. Physically, the Maine-born writer had a doll-like beauty, even into her forties, and a slender figure unlike Willard's more stately form. Like Willard she had grown up in a Yankee family of progressive leanings, but there was no adoring father in her background. He had died at sea in her babyhood, and when young Elizabeth wanted to become a teacher, her mother, fearing she might become an old maid, married her off at sixteen to bald, bespectacled Seba Smith, a Portland, Maine newspaper editor.

Oakes Smith's autobiography makes clear she had no pleasure in her marriage, outside of her children. She had four sons, and after the work of caring for them in childhood, they helped liberate her, to some extent, from her unhappy marriage to Smith. They did this by serving as escorts so she could go into society without her husband. This liberation coincided with the family's move from Maine to New York City and both Smiths' entry into the literary world there. Beautiful Mrs. Smith, who wrote poetry, stories, and articles, was welcomed in all the literary salons of the city and soon won national fame, mainly as a poet. In 1850 and 1851 after attending the Worcester convention, she penned a series, "Woman and Her Needs," for Horace Greeley's very liberal Whig *New York Daily Tribune*. These catapulted her to greater fame, and she became a sought-after speaker. In 1852–53 she toured northeastern cities including Troy with a talk on "Cleopatra, the Woman of Passion and Power," which praised the ancient queen for her strength, political savvy, and spiritual qualities and refused to "judge her actions by the . . . moral laws of the present."[4]

From all Oakes Smith wrote of herself and from a few surviving letters, she appears as a very intelligent, tenderhearted woman who looked for emotional connection with others and beamed charm at near everyone who crossed her path. She didn't want to be a dutiful daughter like Willard. Oakes Smith wanted lovers. Since she was virtuous, she relied mostly on emotional ties with other women,[5] but she enjoyed flirtations with men, too. Her autobiography fondly recalls a note sent to her by Whig statesman Daniel Webster, then 48, when she was 24. The note, an answer to an early-morning one of hers asking for an interview, read: "In bed, but always yours, Daniel Webster."[6] And Kentuckian Whig orator Henry Clay found Oakes Smith "irresistibly fascinating . . . Her smile is the play of a sunlit fountain."[7]

But she couldn't charm the male transcendentalists, Emerson, Hawthorne, and Thoreau. They hated her seductive ways *and* women's rights' positions. An 1855 letter survives in Harvard's Houghton Library from Thoreau to Oakes Smith, warning her off from a hoped-for visit to Concord, Massachusetts.

It's surprising by this time she didn't realize how unwelcome she was there. In 1852, a year after she had visited the Emersons for some weeks in Concord, their friend and sometime-neighbor[8] Nathaniel Hawthorne published *The Blithedale Romance* in which a very Oakes Smith-like char-

acter, Zenobia, appears as a near-villainess. *Blithedale* deals fictionally with Hawthorne's true-life experiences at the early-nineteenth-century commune Brook Farm, but scholars agree no Zenobia type can be found among the "communists" there.[9] Oakes Smith, who never visited Brook Farm but had visited Concord in 1851, is Zenobia to the life—a charismatic, glitteringly-dressed, and worldly feminist who enchants both men and women and also boasts psychic powers. ("From childhood Elizabeth Oakes Smith had been endowed with a penetration not altogether pleasing to those about her, which she chose to call clairvoyance."[10])

But we don't need the Zenobia character alone to spot these male writers' dislike of Oakes Smith. In addition to his polite but re-buffing letter of 1855—which contains the phrase, "we did not fatally disagree," about their 1851 meeting—Thoreau wrote directly of the feminist writer: "My interview [with Oakes Smith] added nothing to the previous impression, rather subtracted. She was a woman in the too common sense, after all. You had to substitute courtesy for sense and argument. It requires nothing less than a chivalric feeling to sustain a conversation with a lady. I carried her lecture for her in my pocket, wrapped in her handkerchief; my pocket exhales cologne to this moment."[11]

The chill response of the Emersons, Ralph Waldo and wife, to Oakes Smith even peeps through a shined-up reminiscence of her 1851 Concord visit written in the 1880s:[12]

> Mr. Emerson did not hear me [Oakes Smith's lecture]; he was going to speak the same evening before the Lyceum at Marblehead. Mrs. Emerson with her weird grey eyes and faultless repartee . . .[13]
>
> One evening Mr. Emerson said to me, "How do you think Boston compares with New York society?" to which I am afraid I answered almost impertinently.
>
> "I must say I think New York far superior to Boston. If society represent [*sic*] humanitarian and progressive ideas, they are about equal; but it seems to me that society for genial, social purposes is almost lacking in Boston . . ."
>
> "Perhaps for that reason society in New York is more shallow and the knowledge more superficial" [said Emerson].
>
> "I have not thought so. New Yorkers have not the intense admiration for each other that Bostonians have; they are not cliquish; they are not so pedantic . . . [zinged E. O. S. back at the Concord crowd].[14]

Hawthorne's dislike for Oakes Smith is very intriguing as regards the Robinson affair. He expressed dramatically, on the page, many society-wide preoccupations, and one of Hawthorne's most powerful images is the Veil which hides something Hideous or Evil. His 1836 short story, *The Minister's Black Veil*, deals with a young minister who takes to shrouding his face with an impenetrable veil. The veil is never lifted, even at death (by his instructions), but it's gradually borne in on the reader that the covering hides some sin or shame. Another veil appears in the 1852 *Blithedale Romance*, and it says more clearly what Hawthorne feared. *Blithedale*'s innocent young heroine, Priscilla, wears the veil this time, in a disguise (forced onto her by a mercenary father) which turns her into The Veiled Lady, a medicine-show clairvoyant.

At one point in the novel, Zenobia describes a party of young gentlemen who speculated on what lay behind the Veiled Lady's veil: "Some upheld that the veil covered the most beautiful countenance in the world; others,—and certainly with more reason, considering the sex of the Veiled Lady,—that the face was the most hideous and horrible, and that this was her sole motive for hiding it. It was the face of a corpse; it was the head of a skeleton; it was a monstrous visage with snaky locks, like Medusa's, and one great red eye in the center of the forehead."[15]

The Medusa face is the giveaway. Since Freud, scholars have agreed the female gorgon's single red eye is a stand-in image or metaphor for the vulva, with the "snaky locks" pubic hair. In other words S-E-X was the fearful thing that hid behind the veil, accompanied by fears of that other mystery, death.

Hawthorne wasn't the first to worry about sex and death lurking behind sinister draperies. Mary Radcliffe's *The Mysteries of Udolpho* (1794) launched the veil image in popular fiction. Her young heroine, menaced by threats of rape and murder inside the fortress-palace of a wicked count, in one critical scene draws back the veil of an alcove to find (as she thinks) the dead body of an earlier female victim of the count. Then in 1817 Irish poet George Moore published his *Lalla Rookh*, known by both Robinson trial prosecutors and Robinson herself. What was the hideous sight that Moore imagined behind his male Veiled Prophet's veil and which caused the maiden Lalla Rookh to shriek and faint? Not just some metaphor for male sexual parts—with which Moore was comfortably familiar—but surely some mark of sex perversion or sex-linked disease, with the same idea holding true for the disfigurement of Hawthorne's minister's face. The ravages of syphilis maybe?[16]

Why were nineteenth-century people thinking about veils in this way? Maybe better standards of living with more domestic privacy were beginning to draw more of a "veil" over acts of sex and death for middle-class people, who as a result felt more anxiety about these life events. The Age of Reason (1700s) had also challenged religion's calm and certain rule over these areas. No wonder sex and death, disturbing to everyone throughout the ages, became extra-fraught with fear and mystery for many at the beginning of the nineteenth century.[17]

On another level, inhabitants of new industrial cities like Troy were also anxious about identities. It was no longer possible to know or read at a glance the wealth or social standing or respectability of all the people who passed in busy streets. The idea of the veil as something that hid true identity was very upsetting, too. People were particularly concerned about mistaking well-turned-out prostitutes for ladies. Some of this creeps into Hawthorne-Zenobia's story of the young gentlemen who wonder about The Veiled Lady. One refers to a report that "pretended to assert the identity of this strange creature [the Veiled Lady, who has—according to 1850s convention—lost any claim to ladyhood by appearing on the stage] with a young lady . . . the daughter of one of our most distinguished families!"[18] How like the Henrietta Robinson situation this is!

But there's even more. Some scholars believe that from the earliest years of the Industrial Age, or even a bit earlier, women gained more power within marriage in terms of controlling sex so as to limit births—a necessity for non-farm families.[19] Did this intimate female power, in an age without efficient birth control, heighten male anger against women? Maybe. Perhaps it also caused men to "protest too much" about the powerlessness of women, for reams of scientific theory soon arose about women's weakness and general incapability. And by the mid-nineteenth century, normal or "good" women were also seen as passionless, with only wicked or fallen women having any sexual desire. And—this is where the veil comes in again—men of the nineteenth-century couldn't help fearing, as their writings show, that a wicked, passion-filled woman lived beneath the serene exterior (veil) of a supposedly virtuous wife or daughter. Since their passionless wife theory was strained anyway, hints of the "wickedness" of those near and dear must have been surfacing all the time and causing great unease.

Knowing all this suddenly makes us realize the impact of the Veiled Murderess case. It was pushing every tender psychological button possible for the 1850s' male. A fallen woman, suspected of a great fall—from pure daughter and wife of men of the social elite—had now committed the worst of crimes. She was Woman as Demon[20]—and behind a literal veil!—the being they subconsciously worried might inhabit their own wives and daughters. And then, Henrietta Robinson's story seemed to unfold almost like a morality play, so closely did it follow antebellum notions of a fallen woman's step-by-step downward path. Contemporaries even commented on the fictional air of Robinson's case: "The whole affair of the murder, with the scenes in Court, the veiled prisoner and her mysterious conduct,—all appear more like romance than reality."[21]

The only irritating glitch in the true-life story was Robinson's brisk and saucy manner at sentencing. This did not seem at all right, even for a wicked woman, at the close of her sad drama. No wonder Judge Harris had urged her—over her cries of "Shame, shame!" and "Pooh, pooh!"—to "cease battling with your fate but submit to it like a true woman . . ."[22]

But now, in July of 1855, Elizabeth Oakes Smith stepped forward to train a different spotlight on Robinson's dilemma. Actually, Oakes Smith's first move came at the end of June, when she sent a letter to the *New York Evening Mirror* condemning the death penalty for Robinson on the feminist grounds no women had served on the Robinson jury and no women had taken any part in forming the laws which convicted her. While most Troy and Albany area papers by now urged commutation, both the pro-commutation *Troy Daily Times* and *Troy Daily Traveller*[23] condemned Oakes Smith's arguments. The *Times*: "Woman is not the only party who is a subject of the law without any voice in its enactment. Our children, all persons under twenty-one years of age and all persons of any age who are not citizens, (and these classes constitute a large portion of the population of the country) have no voice in legislation, yet are liable to suffer its inflictions. Even the poor Irishman, who, in his own graphic language, has not been long enough in the country to "understand the rules," much less to help form them, has to submit to their punishments."[24] [Francis should have included slaves on this list, too, but that would not have been a politic argument in 1855 Troy!]

Oakes Smith had let the male establishment "have it" in her *Mirror* letter, assuming the mantle of a superior female morality. This was the one area of alleged superiority granted good women by the "women's sphere" theorizers. Oakes Smith in the *Mirror*:

> I would say to hang a man in this enlightened era is a shame that might cause the angels to blush; but that is a matter for men to settle in their own way . . . If the gallows be a comely object to their eyes, let them keep it. If a poor, helpless, bound human being suspended like a dog, be a sight grateful to their eyes and comforting to their hearts, let them hang each other thereon to their hearts content; but in the name of all that is holy and pitiful and human do not place thereon a creature who had no word of sanction asked or given; whose voice is as

> much unknown in legislation as if she belonged to the planets Jupiter or Neptune . . . She, nor any, nor all women since the creation of the world, could ever have devised our monstrous penal code, bearing upon its face the ancient barbarisms of man, not of the race merely.[25]

But as Robinson's execution day (August 3) approached, Oakes Smith's plea for Robinson became less ideological and more personal—a natural result of a long visit by the feminist to Robinson in mid to late July, but maybe also an effort to reach "the executioners" in a softer way. Oakes Smith's interview with Henrietta Robinson, published in a letter to the *New York Daily Tribune* of July 28, 1855, stresses the woman's youth and victimhood. "She is perhaps thirty," finds Oakes Smith, doing away with the five to ten years other writers had laden onto age estimates. The feminist then portrays a girlish thirty-year-old, writing of "this young creature, full of health, with nerves so delicately strung" who "talked with me so candidly, often with such a child-like simplicity, laughing even over some bygone experience, and then weeping like a poor, ill-treated child . . ." Further youthful images—"her little pale hand" and "her lithe, active make"—call up an almost teenaged picture of Robinson.

As for victimhood there is no doubt in Oakes Smith mind: ". . . she has unquestionably been "more sinned against than sinning." No hand has been extended to aid and protect her in her weakness, while many have aided in her downward tendency, and with such the guilt must rest."

But before the (implied) appearance of Mather and others on the scene, Robinson's own mind and body sabotaged any happy or normal life for the woman according to Oakes Smith:

> Phrenologically her brain is low above the ears, and her coarse black hair grows down upon the forehead even lower than that upon the bust of the celebrated antique of Clite [a sculpture of Aphrodite]. She has two projections in the region of what is called Constructiveness, extending backward, which of themselves would be sufficient to throw the whole character out of balance. When you add to this brain a refined, lady-like form, round and compact, with a temperament of the highest and most excitable kind, it will be easily seen that education might retard and modify her destiny, but would hardly serve to recreate her into a reliable or very safe character.

Like many other reformers, Oakes Smith had swallowed whole the pseudo-science of phrenology, developed by a German doctor at the end of the eighteenth century, which related head shape to character. The whole area of scientific method and proof was still rather fluid in the 1850s, for scientists and non-scientists, and this allowed the intelligent Oakes Smith to float still another flawed theory, similar to the moral-physical collapse explanation of cholera: "These people [Lanagan and Luby] might not have died of poison. Our scientific men are far too ready to give this kind of testimony. Chemical tests are by no means reliable testimony. The human system is a grand chemical laboratory. We cannot, indeed we dare not, affirm that several causes may not call into action deadly chemical agents. Who shall say that the stomach may not generate fatal products; the liver secretes sugar, and the brain starch. With these known scientific data, I know of no limit to be given to the secretions either in a healthful or morbid point of view."

But Oakes Smith only threw out this last idea in passing. Her main point was Robinson's feminine frailty, with even the murderess's mental disturbance—"She is so evidently of an insane organization"—portrayed as gentle, confused, child-like. In the Oakes Smith interview, Robinson also shows the altruism and spirituality of an Oakes Smith heroine:[26] "Oh, I am so sick of the world. Look here, please, my poor husband, and ——— do not know where I am—they know nothing of all this. My father and mother are both dead; I have concealed my family name; while I live people are curious to know about me—when I am dead all will die with me. I have promised my brother to be very still; to die without betraying anything, and when I am gone I shall cease to worry and distress my family. Here I am shut out from the world, of no use in it, sick of it. Oh, let me go home to my God."

Oakes Smith commented: "There was a manly [!] courage and good sense in this forlorn desire for death . . ." She then tried to cheer Robinson with the idea of her death bringing reform: "If you are executed, you will be the last woman who will endure the penalty in our country. It will raise a storm of indignant protest, which will compel our rulers to annul the statute, at least where a woman is to be the victim." Robinson, in reply: ". . . smiled in a very sweet heavenly manner: "Then I shall do some good in my death. Is not God very good if he will permit a sinful creature like me, not only to atone for my wicked life by this violent death, but may even allow some good to grow out of it."

Elizabeth Oakes Smith showed surprise at the jail visits of Father Havermans and the Sisters of Charity ("You are a Roman Catholic!"). Responding to Oakes Smith's almost alarmed exclamation, Robinson said: "I am now. And since I have had someone to talk to me, to tell me truly about myself, and my duty to God, I am a great deal happier. The Sisters of Charity come and talk to me very kindly; they tell me not to wish to live, but to take God's mode of drawing me back to himself, patiently and willingly." Oakes Smith approved this speech: "This was very sweet, and gave even an elevated expression to her handsome but unspiritual face."

Robinson had received her visitor while "reclining upon the bed . . . [with a] plain white dress, or robe rather . . . fastened at throat and wrist, thus concealing her whole person, while a large dark-blue vail [*sic*] was thrown over her head, hiding her face partially." On Oakes Smith's request, Robinson "laid aside her vail," saying: "Oh yes, for you, but I do not like to have strangers come and stare at me. On my trial I *felt* I could not; I *could* not be looked at. *It seemed to me I should make other women ashamed*" [all original italics].

These delicate sentiments, which explained away the veil in a new, 1850s-acceptable way, may have come straight from the brain and pen of Oakes Smith. Though maybe not. Henrietta Robinson was, at times, a skilled manipulator of others, very good at telling people what she thought they wanted to hear. (Her interactions with prison doctors in 1876–1905 show this.) Anyway, a new picture of Henrietta Robinson emerges from Oakes Smith's sympathetic interview. It's almost hard to believe this is the same woman described for so many months by Troy's all-male press corps. Only in the second half of the interview does some of the manner already attributed to Robinson surface once more. This, at least, assures us of the authenticity of one long statement. When asked by Oakes Smith "to tell me truly whether you are guilty of the crime . . . ," Robinson's "eyes assumed a wild expression" and she launched forth:

> No, I am not guilty. These people were good to me; sometimes when others were unkind they were good to me. They came to see me when I was sick, and sent their children to stay with me. I never treated a human being ungratefully. My heart is a kind one. I have with my own hands taken care of rich people, and cooked up things for the poor, and have helped them as much I could. Now those enemies who accuse me know that I am not guilty—that I never dreamed of poisoning my friends. I don't know about it. [EOS: ". . . she began to talk wildly."] I had been sick: I was mad for a while because ——— gave me something that took away my senses. I try to think over a great many things that happened, and I can't understand them. I can't tell exactly how I got here. I know I'm a wicked woman, but I did not do that. I am the victim of a conspiracy. A political party wished to crush John C. Mather and Myron H. Clark, and so they took me up. They could do it, you know—I, a poor woman.

When Oakes Smith asked about her marriage, Robinson replied simply (and in a way that carries a ring of truth because the statement is not self-serving): "I was married very young and to a man I could not love. He was a good man, but I did not love him, and my first sin was in deserting my family."

Oakes Smith then judged Robinson's mental state:

> I am convinced she has no consecutive memory of the past. She thinks she talks coherently when much of what she says is a mere jargon. This mood of mind is entirely distinct from her religious one, the latter being a new one and a very harmonious one in her present exigency, enabling her to ignore the past and to look calmly into the brief space of life before her, revealing a never-ending blissful future. It seems as if she had arisen from a terrible chaos, and she dreads life lest she should again relapse into it.
>
> Turbulent as has been her career with her stormy passions, she could not recall it without a shudder; and yet she laughed wildly and gesticulated in an almost frantic manner more than once. As it regards the past, her whole mind is in fragments. She remembers indeed "a mass of things, but naught distinctively.

But Robinson was distinct enough in certain areas. She told Oakes Smith a specific story about the seduction of a young girl which ended disastrously: ". . . she told me of sufferings, mental and physical, frightful to have been endured by any human creature. One case of deceit and perjury practiced upon a young girl, worthy only of a fiend, and for which a day of retribution must come if there is a God superintending the affairs of men, she told me. The cruel deceiver was one to whom she stood in relation. Her memory seemed preternaturally vivid in this case. She told me the pity she felt for the innocent victim—her womanly pleading—the melancholy journey of the child to New-York, and her death in less than twenty-four hours after her arrival."

This was apparently an account of "third persons," of Robinson's "relation" and of the girl this relation had deceived. Oakes Smith expressed the belief Robinson's association with "these persons had maddened her." Robinson also gave Oakes Smith a specific message for the New York State Governor: "Tell him there is a political party wishing to put him out of office. They wish to crush Myron H. Clark [the Governor, himself] and John C. Mather; and if he commutes my sentence they will make political capital out of it; and I would rather die than be used as an instrument to ruin a good man. Tell him to let me die, as I wish."

In the end, Oakes Smith's pleading of July 28 had little effect, for Governor Myron H. Clark—whose name Robinson joined so intriguingly with Mather's—had issued his order commuting Robinson's sentence to life imprisonment on July 27. The news of Clark's order reached Troy papers on the same day Oakes Smith's letter, describing her Robinson interview, appeared in the *New-York Daily Tribune*. Likely—as the *Albany Evening Atlas*[27] had charged more than a month earlier—a commutation had long been in the works.

24

DEPARTURE

John M. Francis of the *Troy Daily Times* now (July 30) announced he and his paper had enjoyed an inside line to the Veiled Murderess:

> During the past two months, or since the libel suit was commenced against us by Wm. F. Wood . . . we have had frequent interviews with Mrs. Robinson, and have conversed with her freely about her history and "mystery." Immediately on being informed of the prosecution [against Francis], she lifted the veil and disclosed all of mystery that had surrounded her identity—declaring that she was unwilling, either directly or indirectly, to be the cause of inflicting injury upon the innocent [Francis]. She not only made the disclosure to us frankly, and in all apparent sincerity and truthfulness, but to many others, also, who had known Charlotte Wood in the happy days of girlhood, as a pure, beautiful and accomplished young lady, and as a pupil in the Troy Female Seminary. Mrs. R. invited many who knew her some twelve years ago while attending the Seminary, to visit her at the jail, with the view, as she averred, of establishing her identity. Several of them did visit her, and not one of them we believe hesitates to express the undoubting belief as to who she is [the "we believe" shows up the latitude in this claim]. Others, from timidity and a fear of publicity in the matter, or a dread of giving offence if they consented to become voluntary witnesses for the vindication of the truth, refused to see her at all.[1]

The *Times*'s new intimacy with Robinson allowed the paper to record her views about the commutation: "We saw and conversed with Mrs.

Robinson . . . on Wednesday evening [July 27]. She rushed wildly to the lady accompanying us, inquiring eagerly, 'What are they going to do with me?' When assured, that she would not probably be executed, she exclaimed, 'I will not go to State Prison. I want to die. Why will they persecute me more?' "[2]

When Robinson learned of her reprieve the next day, she "raved and stormed against the Governor,"[3] and then began "breaking the furniture in her room, tearing up the beds and matrasses [*sic*], and presenting them to persons in the street."[4] Then: "She . . . piled up the straw from her beds near one of the windows, and declare[d] her intention of celebrating her departure for Sing Sing by a grand bonfire."[5] The *Traveller* viewed these acts in a more serious light: ". . . she had broken up almost everything in the room, and heaped it in a pile with the intention it is thought of burning the jail and herself in it."[6]

Both *Times* and *Traveller* covered Robinson's July 30 departure from the Troy Jail and journey to Sing Sing at length, but with the *Traveller*'s coverage, typically, longer and more hostile. The *Traveller* opens:

> On our approaching the jail (at about 4:00 P.M.) we found a considerable crowd of men, women and children collected in front of it . . . Mrs. R. came down stairs, preceded by a boy carrying a clever-sized bundle, which contained the few articles she desired to retain. Her furniture and other articles she had either destroyed or given away during the morning. She herself came down alone in a remarkably easy, graceful and ladylike manner. In her right hand she carried a small bundle while with her left hand she held up her skirts. She wore the same black silk dress and scarf that she has always worn, and as heretofore her face was enveloped in that same blue veil. After descending the stairs into the hall, she turned toward the Sheriff's excellent lady, who with her daughter and several other females were standing in the back part of the hall, and lifting up her hands gave vent to a speech at once profane, vulgar and indecent, so much so that we dare not put it into print. No notice being taken of her, she passed on toward the door, muttering something but in such an inaudible tone that we could not understand it. The door being opened she was hurried into a carriage which was in waiting.
>
> The crowd at this time was pretty thick surrounding the door of the jail and the carriage. After she was seated some bareheaded Irish women collected on the side of the carriage nearest her and began to curse upbraid and ridicule her—shaking

> their fingers at her and telling her that she ought to be hung and using much other similar language . . .

On Robinson during the carriage ride to the new Union Railroad Depot on Union Street between Broadway and Fulton:[7] ". . . she drew back the veil and exposed her smiling face to the crowd . . . We say smiling and we say truly, for never a frown darkened her handsome countenance . . ."[8]

The *Times* dealt with Robinson's outburst against the Prices by only noting "[she] scolded the Sheriff and his family roundly, appearing to be in a very bad humor." On her emotions in the carriage, the *Times* found the prisoner more troubled, and thus more an object of sympathy, than the *Traveller*: "On her way to the cars, she burst out laughing, and suddenly changing into her angry mood again, fell crying."[9]

The *Times* tells the rest of the story, portraying a disturbed, disoriented, but always ladylike and pitiable woman on her way into a dark future:

> When the cars started she soon asked if they were not going to take her home to her friends, saying to the Sheriff, "You are going to take me home, ain't you?" She then described the scenery on Lake Champlain, the Islands in the River and Canada. She suddenly changed to scolding and laughing alternately. She would then look out of the cars, and break forth into rhapsodies upon the beauty and grandeur of the River scenery. Again ask if she were not going home. These changes took place several times on her passage down. In reply to one of these questions, the Sheriff frankly told her where she was going to—that he was taking her to Sing Sing. She was greatly moved and declared that she would not remain in prison long—that she should kill herself—that he would soon hear of her death.
>
> At times she seemed perfectly bewildered, and frequently when she asked if she were not going home, she seemed really in earnest in the belief that she was on her way there. Again she would speak in a rational manner. She was very much troubled about her clothes. She was afraid they would make her put on prison clothing. She wanted to wear her own clothes, and when they were gone she would get more. She wished the Sheriff to intercede with the prison officers for her. She alluded frequently to the picturesque scenery along the route, and expressed a wish that it was a fair day and she had pencil and paper to make sketches. Her actions and talk on this subject were very simple and childlike.

> When, at Poughkeepsie, she expressed a wish for some refreshments, she partook of them in a very decorous and ladylike manner. Although very few of the passengers were aware of who she was, she was under the impression that everybody knew her, and seemed very much annoyed and excited about it. She kept herself closely veiled all the time, until after dark.

Before reaching Sing Sing she appeared very much exhausted and weary. On arriving there she was quite bewildered, asking frequently where she was. When she entered the office of the prison, the Sheriff announced her name, the officer in charge not happening to be present, and a party of young ladies and gentlemen being present in the room did not greet her very cordially. [These were probably tourists viewing the prison, something then allowed.] She turned to the Sheriff and exclaimed "What queer people these are; they have no manners!" She then begged to be taken home, she did not wish to stay in such a place and among such folks. She repeated her request to be taken home, and urged the Sheriff to have her brother William come after her. She enjoined this message upon him several times. Her naming of William Wood as well as the earlier remarks about landscape along the Champlain waterway (leading north from Troy into Canada and Quebec City, home of the Woods) give us a moment's pause, until we remember Robinson's skillful role-playing with Elizabeth Oakes Smith. The prisoner had been gentle, confused, and childlike with the feminist writer, too (as well as religious-minded in a way calculated to appeal to Oakes Smith). And it was easy enough to toss out William Wood's name.

The *Times*:

> Soon the officer came in and proceeded to ask her the usual questions as to her age, birth-place, etc. At this procedure she laughed immoderately. Turning to Sheriff Price she said: "Why, the man is crazy!" The officer scolded her and commanded her to answer him correctly. She continued to laugh heartily. When he asked her age, she declared she would not tell him. In answer to the question as to her birth-place, she said she was born in Quebec. This was the only answer she would make to any of the questions put to her. He threatened her with cold water, but she only answered with a laugh. [Something like water-boarding was an approved prison punishment at this time.[10]] He finally relinquished his efforts and postponed the matter, saying to her if she did not answer next time, she would get cold water. She laughed again, saying to Sheriff Price, "that fellow is crazy!"

The officer then took a small package she had brought, and on opening and examining it, he found among some toilet articles a small rope, the size of a bedcord, and about five feet long, coiled up.

She was then escorted by the officer and the Sheriff to the Female Prison, where they met the Matron. Here, after telling her that she would be kindly cared for, and giving her other assurances calculated to soothe and quiet her, Sheriff Price took his leave, and the Prison Gate closed on Mrs. Henrietta Robinson, the "Veiled Murderess," forever.[11]

The *Troy Daily Whig* hoped for finality, too—witness the title of their July 30 story, "The Last of the Robinson Case," a piece almost laughably brief, mild, and non-specific. It summed up the events of the day: "The prisoner on leaving was dressed with characteristic neatness and good taste, and as may well be supposed her departure drew together a large crowd at the Depot. She appeared cheerful, and spared the Sheriff all trouble in regard to herself."

PART SIX

IRISH ANSWER

1851 AND THE DEEPER PAST

Thurlow Weed.
(Courtesy New York State Library)

25

SUSAN GAYNOR

With Henrietta Robinson's fate now settled—for the next 15 years or so—we pick up the Irish thread to her story, introduced in "*Admiral Pagnum's Daughter*," once more. The convicted prisoner was someone who knew—or knew of—a cluster of well-placed families (Wood, Pakenham, Robinson) from a particular corner of the world, County Westmeath in Ireland. Significantly, another "internal" clue links Henrietta Robinson of Troy with the same area. Her delirious vision in the Troy Jail after her arrest, the story of being forced into the cauldron, connects with an image from Leinster region folklore.

The first bronze cooking vessel of Ireland's Bronze Age, the large round pot or cauldron was so highly-prized it acquired magical properties in the eyes of owners.[1] Thus, the cauldron passed into Irish legend as: *one*, a "cauldron of abundance" capable of feeding any number of people; *two*, a "cauldron of resurrection" into which story heroes or heroines threw dead bodies in order to bring them to life again; and *three*, a "sacrificial cauldron" in which a king or other victim was ritually drowned. Except for some magic cauldrons in Chinese and Tartar folktales, there is no similar interest in giant, transforming pots outside Celtic folklore.[2]

And a particular cauldron story associated with County Westmeath holds the sacrificial idea plus ideas of guilt and retribution. According to this legend, Diarmaid mac Cearbhaill, High King of Ireland between 544 and 565, gave land at Clonmacnoise, just a few miles from Castletown Delvin in Westmeath, to St. Ciaran, the founder of a famed monastery. Diarmaid had acquired the land from an enemy, Flann Fion; the king had burned Flann's house down over his head, thus boiling the man to death when he sheltered from the fire in a cauldron of water. But Flann, while cooking,

Albany County Penitentiary.

cursed Diarmaid, and years later in County Antrim, the High King died in the same way: also trapped in a burning house, he leapt into a vat of ale and was fatally drowned or boiled there.[3]

A woman whose mind held an image of punishment-by-cauldron was surely an Irishwoman, and likely a native of Westmeath. In support of the Irish-born idea, in 1901 a Troy reporter would describe Robinson's speech as having "deteriorated into a coarse-sounding brogue."[4] The notion of an active, or even passive, impersonator of, first, "a Wood daughter," and then, Charlotte Wood Eliott, makes a great deal of sense. We already know Henrietta Robinson had had some brush with the law in 1851 Albany. Perhaps this had been something worse than just threatening someone with a gun.[5] If so, both the veil and yet another identity—as a Wood daughter—would have provided good shelter for the woman (and her friends!) from any negative fallout from her Albany past.

In connection with this, we suddenly remember notorious manipulator Thurlow Weed was especially close to John C. Mather in 1851, the year preceding the late December Big Letting. Weed had also omitted Prosecutor Hogeboom's statement about "Henrietta Robinson's table" in Albany from his *Albany Evening Journal* coverage of the trial. Knowing Weed's fondness for women with a British or aristocratic air (*i.e.* Isabella Shore from the *Autobiography*[6]) we suspect the gregarious Weed[7] spent at least some evenings at that Albany table in 1851. And even if Robinson had had a sexual relationship with Mather alone,[8] there was no reason for the canal commissioner to hide the ladylike (when not drinking) woman away from his friends. On the contrary, her home or lodgings offered an ideal place to entertain legislators without their wives. Also, Robinson's 1855 linking of Mather's name with Clark's tends to show she had operated in a Whig social world.

Had ultra-subtle Thurlow Weed promoted the "big lie" about Henrietta Robinson's identity—the Wood daughter story—when the new and much worse trouble of 1853 threatened to spotlight the woman's 1851 Albany life and maybe his own as well as Mather's dealings with her? Or had Mather alone launched the same false story?

Intriguingly, a single woman with a Westmeath surname got into serious trouble in Albany in 1851. Her name was Susan Gaynor. The Gaynor surname was far more Westmeath-specific than either Wood or Robinson, and an older one in the mid-Ireland county than Pakenham. A Gaynor was one of fifteen Norman lords, followers of Hugh de Lacy, who gained control in the 1200s of what became Westmeath; the Pakenhams only arrived there in the 1600s.[9] Gaynors, almost all Church of Ireland Protestants, lived throughout the county in the eighteenth and nineteenth centuries. Even as late as 1890 the name was still so concentrated in Westmeath that a "census" of surnames in Ireland found Gaynors living in only two counties outside Westmeath: County Cavan (which borders Westmeath on the north) and County Dublin.[10]

The *Albany Evening Atlas* gives the fullest account of Susan Gaynor's "trouble" of late August 1851:

> A man named John Ryan, a worthy, industrious man, who had been in the employ of Wm. Carroll, blacksmith in Montgomery st., came to his death last evening under the following circumstances: A house in Spencer st., near Montgomery, is occupied by two families, the lower part by a Mrs. Susan Gaynor. Those occupying the upper part were in the habit of sawing wood in their apartments to the great annoyance of Mrs. Gayner [*sic*], who had frequently quarreled with them for doing so. Yesterday afternoon, about 4 o'clock, they being engaged at their business again, Mrs. Gayner [*sic*], very much enraged, rushed upstairs and commenced throwing the wood out the window, regardless of all consequences, and paying no attention to who was passing at the time. At this moment Mr. Ryan was passing and received one of the sticks on the head, which struck him senseless to the ground, and causing a severe fracture of the skull. Those in the vicinity witnessing the occurrence, ran to his assistance and removed him into the house. Mr.——— Belknap [Zabina Belknap, a coal dealer at corner of Spencer and Montgomery Streets. and also, interestingly, Albany's "Chief of the Fire Police"] went up stairs and there found Mrs. Gayner [*sic*] engaged in a fight with the

> family—the result of her hasty and summary manner of removing the wood from the window. After separating the combatants, he informed Mrs. Gayner of what she had done, and brought her into the presence of the dying man. She appeared very much affected on beholding the [*sic*] him.
>
> Mr. Ryan leaves a wife and five children who reside in Montreal. He was 40 years of age. The piece of timber was 4 feet 2 inches long, 4 inches thick, 8 inches wide, and weighed about 21 pounds. Mrs. Gaynor was arrested and had a partial examination before Justice Cole [Police Justice John O. Cole] last night. This morning Coroner Winne held an inquest, and it was shown by the evidence that Mrs. Gaynor was intoxicated at the time she throw [*sic*] the stick out of the window; that she was in the habit of getting intoxicated and quarreling with her neighbors . . .[11]

On the day the *Atlas* ran their story (August 26), Thurlow Weed's *Albany Evening Journal* published its own coverage of the Spencer Street accident. Though the *Journal* was ordinarily scornful of any public bad behavior by women—as were all newspapers of the period—on this occasion, Weed's newspaper did all possible to call up sympathy for Gaynor. There was no mention in the *Journal* article of Gaynor's "habit of getting intoxicated and quarreling with her neighbors" as had appeared in the *Atlas* piece. Instead, Weed, or one of his employees, almost defended Susan Gaynor's rash act: "The family upstairs have been in the habit of sawing wood on the floor, to the great annoyance of Mrs. Gaynor, who occupies the lower story. Some of the family were thus engaged yesterday afternoon. Irritated by the repetition of what she had so often protested against, Mrs. G. ran up stairs to stop the annoyance. As the most effectual means to accomplish her purpose, she seized the stick of wood, and threw it out of the window . . ."

The *Journal* then released its own shower of sympathy: "The unfortunate woman was not aware of the evil results which had flowed from her conduct, and the parties were engaged in a scuffle [contrast this with the Atlas's "fight"] for several minutes, and until informed of the probable death of Mr. Ryan. When told of it, Mrs. G. exhibited the most intense remorse, and, after her arrest, and during her examination at the Third District Station House, she manifested the deepest grief . . . She is certainly to be pitied. Her agony is undoubtedly as sincere as it is intense . . ."

Not until the tail end of the *Journal*'s "A Man Accidentally Killed—A Sad Affair," did the writer admit "her [Gaynor's] thoughtless conduct had brought deep agony into [a] family . . . waiting intelligence from a husband and father . . ." and also quote, without comment, the coroner's report containing the phrase: ". . . said stick was thrown out by Susan Gaynor *under the excitement of liquor* [modern italics]."[12]

The timing of the woman's prison sentence dovetails neatly with Henrietta Robinson's appearance in Troy in 1852. Gaynor's indictment papers survive, labeled "Albany Mayor's Court, the People agt [against] Susan Gaynor, Indictment for Manslaughter in the 3d. degree," and signed by A. J. Colvin, District Attorney, and by J. F. Phelps, "Foreman." Penned in very lightly between the original bold black ink of these titles are brief notes: "Tried Sept. 13, 1851"; "Guilty"; and "Sentenced 6 Mo. Penitentiary."[13] Since Gaynor was hustled off to the Albany Penitentiary right away, she emerged from prison in mid-March, 1852. The springtime release date fits well with the *Troy Daily Times* information of May 26, 1853 that Henrietta Robinson had lived at 627 River Street "something over a year."[14] A just-expired prison term in Albany would also explain why a Mather-connected courtesan left Albany in the spring of 1852 to come to Troy. Otherwise, the move is a little mysterious since Mather kept his state post of Canal Commissioner with its Albany office through 1853.

More things say "Susan Gaynor" *might have been* the "other name" by which Constable John Upton knew Mrs. Robinson in 1851. Gaynor's at once haughty, at once lowdown-and-dirty behavior on August 25, 1851, recalls Robinson acts of early 1853. The deposition of Margaret Hanan, the sawer of the wood in the upstairs apartment on Spencer Street, gives the gritty details:

> This afternoon between five and six o'clock deponent and Alice Brown and Mary Collins were together in deponent's room—deponent was sawing a stick of wood in her own room—when Mrs. Gaynor came in, and said, "you parcel of whores, what are you doing sawing wood over my head"—and then she seized the stick of wood and threw it out of the window . . . Deponent followed Mrs. Gaynor to the window for the purpose of taking hold of the wood, but Mrs. Gaynor turned upon her and seized her frock by the bosom and tore it off. Deponent defended herself and Gaynor was got down, deponent was on top of her and her [Hanan's] son (Michael got on top of her [Gaynor])—and then W. Knap [Z. Belknap] came in and separated them.[15]

Interestingly, Thurlow Weed took a trip to Europe not long after Gaynor's conviction. He left Albany in mid-November 1851, and accompanied by a party of ladies—"Harriet [his daughter] went with him . . . as did an old acquaintance, Mrs. Eliza Hunter, and her daughter Frances Jane"[16]—remained abroad until July of 1852. This voyage followed the unexpected death of Weed's thirty-year-old son, James, in the spring of 1851 followed by a losing election season for the Whigs that fall. But even so, Weed's eight-month departure from the thick of things in 1851–52 looks unusual. Is it possible that having done his best for "Susan Gaynor" with the positively-slanted, August 26 write-up of the Spencer Street event, but then unable or unwilling to do anything more for the violent woman, he thought it best to put an ocean between them—especially over the time of her expected release in the spring of 1852?

Of course, there is the issue of the Spencer Street address. The story of the Irish ditch-digger places Mrs. Robinson in Albany's Hamilton Street in 1851. But it may be foolish to cling to every detail of this story. Though Hugh Hastings, editor of the *Knickerbocker* (in which the July 14 "Hamilton Street" item appeared), was an Irishman—one of very few Irish-born Whigs—and so extra-approachable by a humble new immigrant from Ireland, how much more likely it is the "ditch-digger" was just a fiction, a way of introducing information learned in another way. Specifically, some political gentleman or Hastings himself might have sat at Robinson's table in Albany and heard the Admiral Pakenham references there! Anyway, a slightly earlier *Knickerbocker* piece, the June 22 item about "Mr. Johnson" placed Robinson's Albany dwelling on Chestnut Street. All these addresses—Spencer Street, Hamilton Street, and Chestnut Street—lie about the same distance from the state capitol buildings, past and present.[17] And it is not hard to believe *either* that Editor Hastings obscured the woman's real address *or* that a quarrelsome single woman changed her lodgings often.[18]

And on the subject of obscuring things, what about the "Mr. Johnson" story itself? This was the *Knickerbocker*'s June 22, 1855 improvement on the *Albany Evening Journal*'s June 25, 1854, story. It had Robinson dragged before an Albany magistrate for threatening a neighbor with a gun. While believable, in fact just the sort of thing Robinson was likely to have done (since she committed the same act several times in Troy in 1853), why did the two liberal Whig newspapers, the *Journal* and the *Knick*, and no others (except the liberal Whig *Traveller* which reprinted the *Knick* piece), run the item in its two varying forms? Was the Mr. Johnson story floated to obscure gossip about a more serious Robinson encounter—under her "other name"—with the law in Albany in 1851?[19] A "yes" to this last question would explain so much: Robinson's obsessive veiling before conviction coupled with occasional open claims of connection with the Wood family.[20] A previous manslaughter conviction, under an alias, would definitely fill the bill as a reason for the heavy veil.

In line with all this, we begin to wonder about the notice on Judge Parsons of Albany serving as a witness in Robinson's trial (*Albany Evening Atlas*, May 25, 1854). Was this another "red herring," too, fed to the *Atlas* editor to focus attention away from Robinson's/Gaynor's appearance before Albany's other Police Justice, John O. Cole? Albany had just two police court judges at this time, S. H. H. Parsons and John O. Cole, and judging by Susan Gaynor's court papers, the two men presided over so-called "Mayor's Court" proceedings, as well, with Cole the one who heard Gaynor's September 13 trial after having taken the original depositions.

In any case, Judge Parsons helps us understand the gravity of Susan Gaynor's Spencer Street crime. The Albany Hall of Records preserves a large, red book, Parsons' "Criminal Register, 1851–1852," with handwritten notes on all the trials and other proceedings which came before Judge Parsons (but not before Cole, who must have had his own book). Not surprisingly, there's nothing on Susan Gaynor in Parsons' ledger, but the judge helpfully glued into the inside cover a newspaper article, "Statistics of Crime in Albany," beginning: "We are under obligations to Justice Parsons for the following statistics of business done at the Police Office for the year ending January 1st, 1852." The writer deplores the rise in arrests in 1851 (3,957), up nearly a third over 1850. The largest category of offense, by far, was "Assault and Battery," with 1,267 offenders; followed by "Breach of the Peace," 666; "Petit Larceny," 442; "Intoxication in public street," 421; "Vagrancy," 330; "Violations of City Ordinances," 209; "Riot and Affray," 185; "Disorderly persons neglecting to support families," 61; "Grand Larceny," 57; "Misdemeanor, violently entering houses in the night time, and disturbing the peace," 53; and then many more small categories with offenders numbering in the 20s or less. Among the single-digit groupings were: "Murder" with only two arrests; and "Manslaughter" with just three arrests.[21] Some murders and manslaughters must have escaped detection, but still, this shows what a serious crime Susan Gaynor had committed by the standards of her community. It wasn't one a powerful protector or protectors could handle out of court or make go away.

26

IMMIGRANTS AND OTHERS

The Irish environment of the 1830s and 1840s *could well have* formed a rage-filled woman with a hair-trigger temper who then ran afoul of the law in Albany, either under the name of Gaynor or some now-unknown name, and in Troy as Henrietta Robinson. Ireland's "Protestant Plantations" of earlier generations, mainly of Presbyterian Scots, hadn't planted themselves on vacant land. The original tillers of the soil had been largely forced off, to exist on patches of scrub or bog or to make costly arrangements with the newcomers. Only rigid political oppression kept a lid on the distressed natives. The desperation of the 1830s and early 1840s in Westmeath shows up in modern-day indexes to collections of Westmeath newspapers. An index to subjects in the *Athlone Advocate* of the 1830s reads: "Army; Attacks on Houses; Death Sentences—Assizes; Election Addresses; Executions; Famine; High Sheriffs; Inns; Murders; Poetry; Raids for Firearms; Ribbonmen [agrarian terrorists who slashed and mutilated farm animals]; Robberies; Threshers [maybe another agrarian terror group], Misc., . . ." One for the *Westmeath Independent*, admittedly covering all of the 1840s as well, reads: "Army; Attacks on Houses; Death Sentences; Executions; Famines; High Sheriffs; Malicious Burnings; Murders . . ."[1]

The Nugents, the chief landholders of the Castletown Delvin area of Westmeath (where the Irish Wood family lived) were extra-oppressive landlords, with reputations bad enough to survive into modern-day guidebooks of the region.[2] The Pakenhams may have dealt more gently with their tenants, but this didn't prevent a serious disturbance, the "Castlepollard massacre," from occurring in the village nearest to Pakenham Hall in 1831.[3] And in 1849 (three years into the Famine) two men murdered the "gardener to Capt. Robinson [Adm. Hercules Robinson]" at "Rosemead."[4]

This violent society created some very violent emigrants: "According to English witnesses [of the Victorian era] the Irish attacked out of sheer homicidal belligerence. Newspaper reports often implied the Irish were savages given to sudden unprovoked attacks: 'George Bennett was attacked by Irish and so brutally beaten and kicked that on Monday evening he died.' In most such cases, the Irish claimed to have been provoked by being laughed at or insulted."[5] And: "[Irish] Women accused of violent assaults often showed no remorse and in fact argued that their actions were justified . . . Anne Madigan who assaulted William Boland with a meat cleaver for taking her husband's job [said] . . . 'thanks be to God that it was no robbery I committed.' [As for gentry-class women] When gunmen fired at the carriage of Miss Louisa Ellard, a landlord's daughter who was managing her father's estate, 'she turned and fired three shots from a small revolver. She then ordered the driver to unhitch the horses and ride after the assailants . . .' "[6]

The Great Famine of 1846–52 uprooted gentry (i. e., Hercules Robinson, husband of Frances Wood, who lost the old Wood estate, Rosmead, in 1852) and their hangers-on as well as craftspeople and peasants. In 1849—the very year some claimed Henrietta Robinson first arrived in Troy[7]—Thomas Carlyle of philosophy fame traveled on a steamboat bound to Ireland where he met two "Misventurous [*sic*] Irishwomen, giving up their plan of emigration to Australia, and cowering back to Ennis in Clare." These sisters in "clean summer bonnets . . . much admired by me [Carlyle]" were " 'ladies'—you could not have hesitated, even in the poorhouse, to call them." Carlyle gave their story: "Father had been a lieutenant of foot with a pension, mother too with pension; both being dead, resources were all out; parson had advised emigration, "free passage to Australia" was certain if we would deposit £12 in advance; deposited, sold off, came to Plymouth, found the "free passage" a passage among parish paupers, shrieked (of course) at the notion of it!"[8]

Had Henrietta Robinson been a hardier émigrée of this type?

It is even possible, *though not likely*, that the murderess was an illegitimate child of Robert Wood, born of some liaison in Ireland and abandoned there—to make her way to the New World on her own, later in life. According to family tradition, "Young Robert Wood was sent to school in England in 1805 when he was thirteen years old but returned to Quebec the next year when his father [maybe foster-father] died."[9] Did he then go back again to Europe in his young manhood, to fight in the last of the Napoleonic wars in the British army or navy? This would have been a highly plausible thing for him to have done, though there is no discoverable evidence in lists of British officers to confirm the idea. But, as we have seen, some bond with the Pakenham or Wood familes of Westmeath *apparently* caused him to honor Lady Georgiana-Emma-Charlotte Lygon Pakenham through the names of his daughters and also to place his eldest son in a Westmeath-based regiment. Robert Hudson Wood was an officer with the 67th Regiment of Foot, stationed in Athlone, County Westmeath, during the 1850s and perhaps earlier as well. It's hard to imagine the existence of such a bond without some travel to the Irish county.

Yet without question, Robert married his wife—nineteen-year-old Charlotte Gray of Quebec City and "daughter of James Gray, Clerk in the Barracks Department, now at Kingston in Upper Canada"—on October 4, 1817, in Canada.[10] The couple then resided in Quebec through the births, baptisms, and occasional early deaths of all their 13 children from 1818 to 1840.[11] Charlotte gave birth to a new child every one to two years between 1818 and 1835, with Robert Wood present at every Quebec City baptism, and a July 1840 letter from 16-year-old William Frost Wood, in school in England, sends greetings to all the rest of the family in Quebec.[12] There is no sign Robert Wood left the North American colony again until January 1847, when a letter from him to his son, William Frost Wood (on Charlotte Maria's recent marriage to William Francis Augustus Eliott) places Wood and his wife in Savannah, Georgia, a city with strong trading and immigration links to Ireland at this period.[13] Only a few months later, on April 13, 1847, Robert Wood died in Savannah.

In the 1890s Martin I. Townsend would claim he had long believed his former client to be an illegitimate daughter of Robert Wood:

> I had frequently seen the Wood girls . . . when they were at school in Troy in 1833–1835 [these would have been the older two, Georgiana and Emma, not Charlotte and Harriet], and as my office was very near the seminary, I knew their features, complexion and general appearance very well, and I was struck with the wonderful resemblance which this lady [Robinson] bore to them. I had also seen Mr. Wood, the father, and the resemblance to him was equally strong. I was very sure, however, that this was not Emma Wood, because of information which I had obtained elsewhere, and from that day until within the last year I have held the opinion that Mrs. Robinson was the actual daughter of Mr. Wood, but not the daughter of his wife. But this was simply a conjecture founded only on resemblance . . . I came to the conclusion that Mrs. Robinson had not been educated among persons of intelligence and was a person of a very low order of intellect, although her manners and conversation, as far as they went, indicated that she was a lady who esteemed a correct personal carriage beyond all price.[14]

But Lawyer Townsend wasn't thinking of any overseas-born child

United States Arsenal at Watervliet.

when he floated the illegitimate daughter idea. Just a year before his comment about "the actual daughter of Mr. Wood," he said: "I should judge from her [Robinson's] account that she was a French woman,"[15] obviously implying she was a Québecoise. And from time to time in Troy and later in New York prisons, Robinson claimed either to be of French nationality or to speak French. Though aside from Townsend, no one else seems to have to have taken these claims very seriously. "She claims to be French, but is undoubtedly English by birth," commented the *Troy Daily Times*, right after the murders.[16] There is even a skeptical air about this memory of Mary Jane Dillon's: "I never heard her speak French. She told me she could speak French."[17]

Anyway, it was only too easy for a new immigrant to reinvent herself (or himself) even several times over, in booming Troy. Antebellum cities offered near-limitless opportunities for deception. Troy newspapers of the 1850s carry many accounts of swindles, large and small, which depended on "anonymous" swindlers, and female con-women were not unknown.

Late in life, Troy druggist William Hagan recalled the case of "Little Miss Frinck, the Dressmaker of William Street." In the mid-1840s, the twenty-five-year-old Frinck had regularly disguised herself as an older woman, "with her face mainly covered by a green veil [shades of the Veiled Murderess!] which was passed down over her poke bonnet and with the ends tied beneath her chin . . . [and] through the veil . . . she wore spectacles." She donned the disguise to pass counterfeit money, regularly doing so at Hagan's shop, where, as a long-time "opium eater . . . she [Frinck] purchased her weekly supply of the drug." By the chance of a lost pocketbook, Hagan traced the green-veiled woman to Frinck's house, to find Frinck just recovering from a suicide attempt [yet more depravity!] and attended by "a sanctimonious looking individual, whose throat and neck was buried in an enormous measure of white cravat, and whose appearance was very clergymanic." But it wasn't till years later Hagan finally understood Frinck's double identity and also the true identity of the "clergyman," Frinck's husband or boyfriend. The druggist re-encountered the couple in state court in Albany in the 1860s, where they were both facing life sentences for counterfeiting.[18]

Even closer to home—as far as the Veiled Murderess affair goes—was the case of Miss Abby (or Abba[19]) Goddard, the headmistress in the early 1850s of a tiny and unsuccessful girl's school in Troy.[20] Goddard didn't hide her identity but traded on her apparent respectability to bilk targets via "loans." In 1859 Trojans would read with interest of Goddard's arrest in Boston and of her many crimes, which included conning well-to-do citizens as far back as her days in Troy.[21] Goddard's exposure was yet another blow to Emma Willard's quest to improve public views of women's education.

PART SEVEN

LATER LIFE AND LEGEND

SEPTEMBER 1855–MAY 1905

Hentrietta Robinson, the Veiled Murderess.
Portrait of the 1880s appearing in *Troy Budget* of Dec. 8, 1901.

27

THE SING SING YEARS

About a week after her arrival at Sing Sing, the *Troy Daily Times* carried a report card on new prisoner Henrietta Robinson: "Mrs. Robinson, since her imprisonment there, has behaved well, and with the exception of a few eccentricities exhibited on her first arrival, she has complied with the rules of the prison, and has earned the goodwill of the worthy matron. She is somewhat annoyed, however, by visitors at the Prison, who manifest great curiosity to see her, and she endeavors to hide her face from observation. She is engaged with a sewing machine, is industrious and does her task well."[1]

Robinson's mental health was normal enough at this stage of her imprisonment, as it would continue to be for the next twenty years at least. But the *Times*'s cheery update shouldn't disguise the woman's situation in 1850s Sing Sing. The prison was then between two periods of reform (1840s and 1870s), and conditions were difficult for inmates. "Mount Pleasant Female Prison at Ossining" had been built in the 1830s in the form of a "Greek temple overlooking the Hudson." Its design and location made it almost impossible to enlarge, and the women's building, ringed with a curtain wall to separate it from the men's, was overcrowded by the early 1840s. The female prisoners worked long hours at button-making and hat-trimming (work contracted by private manufacturers) and sewing clothes for the male prisoners. A "rule of silence," relaxed in the 1840s, still officially forbade chatter between the women workers in their workshop, and punishments for female inmates included "gagging" as well as the cold water treatment Robinson had been threatened with on admission.[2]

Following the *Times*'s report, her story disappeared from the papers for a while. No wonder, as interest in the case was soon fed by recappings of the whole Veiled Murderess affair. *The Life and Confessions of Mrs. Henrietta*

Robinson, the Veiled Murderess, Who Was Sentenced to be Hung August 3d, 1855, at Troy, New York, for the Murder of Timothy Lanagan, Etc., a 24-page pamphlet published before the end of the year in Boston by "Dr. H. B. Skinner,"[3] was a collection of newspaper trial coverage introduced by the "Admiral Pagnum" article from the *Albany Knickerbocker*. The Bostonian Dr. Skinner must have found this charge more sensational than the rumors about Charlotte Wood, for he omitted all mention of the Wood-daughter controversy, the scandal of chief interest to Troy and Albany journalists. Other true-crime pamphleteers probably made money on the Robinson story as well, but their fragile products haven't survived.

David Wilson's *Henrietta Robinson*, published by Miller, Orton, Mulligan of Auburn (Cayuga County) and New York City in mid-September 1855,[4] was more ambitious than any pamphlet. This 329-page book was also a stitching together of earlier newspaper coverage, more complete than Skinner's, though Wilson left out the Pagnum material which he surely judged as distracting from or conflicting with the Charlotte Wood story. This last theory Wilson presented as established fact.[5] He also supplemented the news clippings with a fair amount of new reporting, and almost all of this involved Charlotte Wood newsbreaks. He describes an old Irishwoman from Quebec, "Mary," who visited Mrs. Robinson in the Troy jail and held the prisoner, crying "Charlotte, Charlotte, is it you, indeed!"[6] and reports memories allegedly shared by Robinson with Troy Seminary alumnae visitors to her jail cell: Charlotte Wood's near-death by drowning during one student expedition to a swimming hole near Troy; her creation (with the help of a dressmaker) of a life-sized doll which she then introduced to fellow students "with great ceremony and formality"; and her enjoyment of revival meetings in Ferry Street during her time at the seminary.[7]

We recognize all these stories as likely "riffs" on Robinson behavior reported on in 1854: the account of the doll repeats Robinson's staging of her stuffed dress during the Grand Jury visit to her cell; the swimming-hole incident reflects Dillon's trial testimony about Robinson's claimed swimming ability; and the revival meeting information reflects Robinson's dealings with Father Havermans and the Sisters of Charity. Wilson also contributed an important nugget to the growing legend of the Veiled Murderess: the story of her love, while at the seminary, for a young, unnamed gentleman of Troy and her parents' rejection of this man.[8]

David Wilson was an 1840 graduate of Schenectady's Union College, as mentioned earlier, and by the end of that decade he was a lawyer in Whitehall at the northern end of Washington County and the author of at least one long, muckraking article for *The Whitehaller* newspaper (on abuse of Irish immigrants traveling the Champlain Canal). In 1852 Wilson won election to the state legislature as a Whig but continued to write.[9] In

1853 he published two non-fiction books: *The Life of Jane McCrea*,[10] on the Revolutionary War era murder of a young Washington County girl by Indians, and *Twelve Years a Slave*,[11] the as-told-to account of a black resident of Saratoga Springs who had been kidnapped and sold into slavery in Louisiana.

Twelve Years a Slave raises the question of political allegiances. The book's very existence shows Wilson had abolitionist sympathies, for no writer of the early 1850s without anti-slavery views would have undertaken such a project. Thus Wilson was a Woolly Head Whig, a member of Thurlow Weed's political faction. Here was yet another liberal Whig writer—in addition to those of the *Troy Traveller* and the Albany *Knickerbocker*—jumping all over the Henrietta Robinson case.

Though Wilson's *Henrietta Robinson* followed other liberal Whig coverage in ample word count and sense of being "out front" in breaking new ground on the story, it swung away from *all* earlier Whig writing's avoidance of any Wood daughter story (post-May 25, 1854). Wilson also dropped the veil of protection with which *all* Whig papers had surrounded Mather. Though there is no mention of John C. Mather by name in the text, Wilson's book followed and expanded on ideas put out by the Soft *Troy Daily Times* in the spring and summer of 1855, and one edition of *Henrietta Robinson* carried a full-page portrait of the ex-canal commissioner. (A single copy of the Mather portrait edition survives, in the collection of the Rensselaer County Historical Society. The frontispiece portrait has been skillfully "tipped" or glued into the volume, yet because this page matches the volume's other pages in size and paper type, the tipping may have been done in-house by the publisher.)

There is actually a tidy explanation for Wilson's stance. The state's Softs (most of them) and the liberal Whigs, the prime anti-slavery groups, merged in late September of 1855 as the new Republican Party. Thus Thurlow Weed and his faction had lost all interest in sheltering Mather. *And* Robinson was now safely tucked away in State Prison, a fact probably connected with the other two situations. The earlier liberal Whig gentleness towards Mather—or at least absence of overt hostility—has always looked strange: as though guilt or worry over past intimacies with courtesan Robinson was the real source of this gentleness rather than political reasons. Only the Soft Democrats, men quite outside Robinson's old Hard Democrat-and-Whig social circle, had not been afraid to make the most of the scandalous story from the beginning.

In the spring of 1856 Robinson's mental condition drew new attention. On May 10 the *Brooklyn Eagle*, referring to an item in the *Boston Post* of a few days earlier, reported: "It is rumored that Mrs. Robinson, the "veiled murderess," has been transferred from the New York State Prison to the Lunatic Asylum, preparatory to her transfer to freedom. She has yet quite a capital of youth and beauty." In fact, Robinson hadn't been transferred to the Utica Lunatic Asylum, then a brand-new and humanely-run hospital. The *Eagle* also quoted the Whig *New York Express* on the subject of the possible release. The *Express* wasn't well-informed on the details of Robinson's case, but condemned any move to free the prisoner: "Give her the opportunity, do, to bring her "youth and beauty" to a better market than the Auburn State Prison [Robinson was then at Sing Sing]—even if one more husband is to have poison put in his coffee!" [Robinson hadn't poisoned her husband, of course.][12]

Some six months after this scrap of news broke, the *Troy Daily Times*, once the chief proponent of the Charlotte Wood Eliott identity, printed a startling retraction.[13] In a very short column, "Mrs. Henrietta Robinson Not Mrs. Wood [*sic*]; Who She Is," the *Times* took up the Veiled Murderess affair again:

> Public opinion was on the wrong tack. The Times was led into an error, and the judgment of almost everybody has been at fault relative to this wretched murderess. She attempted to impersonate a lady of high respectability; from a sympathy with public opinion or some other cause, respectable persons who knew the lady well while attending the Seminary here, identified the "veiled murderess" as that lady—the evidence was deemed conclusive. But lo and behold! The lady herself, coming all the way from

State prisoners.

> England as a witness, appears in our city, and is seen, known and proven to be herself—the lady of irreproachable character, instead of the "veiled murderess!"

Curiously, the announcement had little impact on the course of the affair, now turned into a lingering mystery that would be revisited by the daily press, from time to time, over the next half century. Why didn't Charlotte Wood Eliott's presence in the flesh blast the rumor, or at least go a long way towards doing this? One answer may be Wood Eliott did *not* turn up in the city, and *Times* editor Francis simply ran the item at the request of the Woods as part of the settlement of their $20,000 lawsuit against him. This would explain why no other area paper except the *Times* carried any mention of the supposed visit.

Another answer may be Wood Eliott's appearance was real enough, but at this point none of the other Troy or Albany papers wanted to take up the story again, with the *Times* alone doing so, briefly, because of the old lawsuit. The overheated political air had gone out of the Henrietta Robinson case following the election victory of the new Republican Party about a week before Francis's retraction. The Republicans had at last carried New York State, though failing to propel their presidential candidate, John Fremont, into office on the national scene. Thus with Hard fortunes at a low ebb and Mather relocated to New York City, there was little reason for further attacks on him through Henrietta Robinson. On top of this, the allegation story, involving the step-by-step fall of a pure daughter of the social elite, was a powerfully confirming one for nineteenth century people, then caught up in a swirl of fears about women and sex. The "sudden appearance" story carried none of this power or appeal.

But whether Charlotte showed up in Troy in November 1856 or not, Francis tacked an intriguing story onto his retraction:

> A gentleman residing at Sing Sing, and a former pardon officer, who has had several interviews with the "veiled murderess," and heard from her own lips, a confession of her duplicity in this matter [her alleged impersonation of Charlotte Wood Eliott] made to Governor Clark [!] at the prison, wrote us a private letter some time ago to this purport:
>
> It is an entire mistake that Mrs. Robinson is one of the Wood family. She is a native of England, and never saw one of that family until she was called upon at the jail by Wm. F. Wood. But she had learned something of them from an acquaintance of theirs in England, which aided her in practicing the deception. She was convicted of infanticide and sentenced to banishment

> to Van Dieman's Land. Through the intercession of friends, the sentence was commuted to banishment from the country. She left for the United States; on the vessel she commended herself to a respectable lady of New-York, who was a passenger returning home, by kind attentions to the lady during her sickness. The latter offered her a home, providing her with employment and sewing. But Mrs. R. remained with her benefactress but a few weeks; she went to Boston, got into bad company and pursued the life of a wanton. Occasionally, however, the New-York lady received letters from her. Our friend states that the husband of this lady was present at the prison when the interview alluded to took place between Gov. Clark and the murderess; that the New-York gentleman exhibited the letters written by Mrs. R. to his wife, and the latter acknowledged that she wrote them, and confessed that she lied in representing here that she was one of the Wood family.

Robinson's supposed confession of the infanticide to the "New-York lady" and then to Governor Myron H. Clark looks doubtful. No lone woman trying to commend herself to powerful prison visitors would admit to such a past. To be fair to Francis, he presented the English-convict tale with caution: "We discredited the story at the time [when Francis first received the letter containing it]; we supposed our friend, who is a lawyer, might possibly have been deceived for a consideration, or from too much credulity. But from the light we now have, very possibly this story is a true one."

Yet the *Times* story of 1856 would echo in a much later newspaper piece which presents an altered and more believable version of Francis's tale. Written by a folksy, "sportin' " writer named Harry Hill for a New York City paper, this second telling of roughly the same story made its way into at least one Troy paper, probably in March or April of 1881.[14] Hill identifies Francis himself—not the former pardon officer and lawyer—as the eye-witness observer. In Hill's version, there are no mentions of Robinson's supposed conviction for infanticide and banishment from the British Isles, and there is a new revelation about the "New-York gentleman's" encounter with Robinson, something learned by Francis in an additional meeting with Robinson. This revelation shows Robinson behaving exactly like a professional con-woman:

> The reporters were all the time writin' yarns about her [Robinson], and once some country editor [clearly Francis] said that she was a member of a highly respectable family from Canada. The highly respectable family from Canada went for that editor and made it

pretty hot for him with libel suits, and one thing and another, till the editor "squealed" and apologized. But he determined to get even by findin' out who "The Veiled Murderess" really was, and he got what he thought was his chance sooner than he expected. [According to Hill, "the country editor" went to Sing Sing together with Gov. Clark—Governor in 1855–57—and a New York City merchant who claimed to know the identity of the Veiled Murderess.]

When she entered the room the merchant rose up, and the V. M. rushed into his arms, as if she were his wife or mother-in-law. The merchant didn't seem quite prepared for so much affection, but he stood it like a man, and the V. M. proceeded to slobber over him, and to vent her feelin's on his shirt bosom . . . The merchant took a seat and pointed to a chair near him for the woman to sit down on. But she made another rush for him, hugged and slobbered over him once more, and then knelt at his feet, showin' her face as she did so, and a rather pretty face it was. The merchant got talkin' about his family, and when he told her that his wife was dead, the V. M. burst into a fit of tears, real tears, and did some more slobborin' [*sic*] on his shirt front. After a while the country editor stepped up to the merchant and after congratulatin' him on his meetin' such an old and dear acquaintance, asked who this woman he had just recognized, or who had just recognized him, was. The merchant told him that she had been a seamstress in his family . . . But who she had been, or what else besides his seamstress she had been, he did not know. [The merchant did know the woman's name, however. It was "Emma H.," and Francis (according to Hill) managed to locate this woman's "male friend who used to take her to singin' school," and thereby expose Henrietta Robinson's con in the Sing Sing visiting room. Her act had been convincing enough to fool both the New York City merchant, an innocent dupe, and for a time the "country editor," Francis.]

At last he [Francis] got an interview himself with the veiled murderess, and in this interview the woman coolly owned up that she had been "foolin' the New York chap."

"But why did you deceive the old gentleman?" asked the editor.

"Oh, the old fellow looked as if he wanted to know me," she replied with a laugh; "and so I didn't think it polite to let him be disappointed, especially as he had come all the way from New York to see me."

> The matron of the prison who was present at the interview, then began to scold the V. M., but she made a jest of the scoldin', and right in the midst of it, turnin' to the editor, she said: "Did you notice how I cried on the old chap's shoulder? I moistened his broadcloth for him in first-class style, didn't I?" And then she burst into a fit of laughin'.
>
> The matron sent her back into her cell, and she afterwards grew fat and disorderly, and at last crazy . . .

But to return to Francis's article of 1856, the *Times* editor reaffirmed the view of Robinson as a "lady": "That she has once and somewhere moved in refined circles; that she has enjoyed early educational and social advantages; that she was, withal, a beautiful and accomplished woman, no one who has seen and conversed with her freely can for a moment doubt." Francis summed up in true 1850s fashion: "But what a fall, and how low she has fallen! Let the veil be drawn over her and the degradation forever more" [the veil we are working so hard to raise!]

Two years later, the *Brooklyn Daily Eagle* printed a negative (*Troy Daily Traveller*-like) glimpse of the woman in prison. Mather was then a sitting New York State Representative. Excerpted from a longer article on Sing Sing which had originally appeared in the *Albany Statesman*, the piece told readers:

> She [Robinson] is treated as a partial lunatic, but the officers of the prison do not fully believe that she has lost her reason. Her last fancy is a belief in the science of witchcraft. She professes an ability to bewitch any person, when it pleases her to do so. A tall commanding figure, a haggard face with the devil's own eye, for accessories enables her to strongly impress these vagaries upon the ignorant and superstitious who are her companions . . . for an hour or two each day while the other convicts are engaged in the shops, she is left at liberty in the prison yard . . . [where she searches for] four-leafed clover.[15]

Robinson's extra recreation time suggests favored treatment, while the witchcraft business swings our minds even more firmly towards someone from a largely "pre-modern" place, like mid-nineteenth century Ireland. And the account of witchery can't be dismissed as a made-up, hostile report, since much later—1890s—doctors' notes on Robinson at Auburn Prison mention her belief in "witches, signs, omens, etc."[16] The *Albany Statesman*'s physical description is hostile, though. Other portraits of Robinson make her out as a person of "middle height" with a very feminine shape as opposed to "a tall, commanding figure," and also as someone who usually looked extraordinarily well, as opposed to "haggard."

Another fuller description covering the year 1858 makes no mention of witchcraft. The memoirs of Sing Sing Prison chaplain John Luckey, published in 1866, tell of "her [Robinson's] three years confinement in this prison" (1855–58). Luckey:

> I am by no means positive as it [*sic*] regards the question of her insanity; but am inclined to the opinion, that she is, at least, a monomaniac, or periodically deranged, and that she was so when she committed the murder . . . At any rate the same eccentricities that the testimony on her trial attributed to her are still manifested. She makes the same efforts to hide her countenance from the gaze of strangers now that she made then. She changes from the most innocent and inoffensive looks and language to the most repulsive and vehement, as suddenly now as she is reported to have done then. She assumes the ability to control the political destinies of certain candidates for office as she did then. In a word, here, where for about three years she has had no artificial stimulants whatsoever (to which the prosecution attributed any appearance of insanity on her part,) she has continued to exhibit, almost daily, the very traits of character upon which her counsel founded a plea of insanity.[17]

Luckey quotes a prison-inspector colleague: "Mrs. Robinson still keeps on her airs, and is a high-spirited, head-strong woman. Whenever a stranger enters her presence, she turns her face to the wall with an air which seems to disclose the inner working of the uppermost thought of her heart—that she is some superior being."[18]

This last image reinforces the idea of some displaced would-be gentlewoman, as do three letters which the chaplain "wrote at her [Robinson's] dictation and request," two on July 12, 1856, and the third on June 2, 1857. Luckey: "The letters being composed entirely of her own language, and uttered impromptu, speak for themselves in reference both to her sanity and education. To me, who have frequently heard her converse in the same incoherent strain, they seem to need no comment."[19]

Is Luckey saying the letters show a *disordered* intelligence, but also an *educated* one? The documents certainly seem the work of someone who had at least lived among educated people. They also suggest a clever, manipulative author. Their incoherence is not obvious to a modern reader. The 1856 letter written to "one of her counsel":

> Dear Sir,
>
> Having permission from the proper authorities, I write to you to say that my health, at present, is rather poor. I wish particularly in this communication to speak of a matter that I understand has transpired here, and which has grieved me much. I refer to a short article from one of the papers said to have been found in the yard of this prison, which however was totally false in all its essential features. Now as I have some reason to suppose that the ladies may think that I had something to do in getting up that article, I desire to have you by some means disabuse their minds in this regard, for I sincerely avow, that I have the fullest confidence in the matrons, as kind-hearted and discreet managers of the institution. They never, to my knowledge, misused or abused any of us. Those editors, therefore, who sent out such an article, must have designed nothing but mischief and slander. As I must write all I have to say to you on this half of my sheet, you will be good enough to hand what is written on the other half to Sheriff [Price].
>
> Yours, &c.,
> Henrietta Robinson[20]

If a newspaper article containing criticisms of Sing Sing personnel had made its way into the prison—something easily imaginable—Robinson, as a current focus of press interest, might well have feared the matrons would tap her as source of the story. This concern doesn't seem crazy at all. The other letter of 1856, addressed to Sheriff Price, is less clear-cut:

> Dear Sir,
>
> When the Governor was here, for fear he might be induced to pardon me, I told him that I heard at Troy, that if he pardoned me, he would be sure not to be elected again; now you know why I said this, but I wish to say to you, and you are at liberty to say it to my friends if you think it proper, that I heard no such thing; but on the contrary, I heard from yourself and others, that if he had restored me to my friends, instead of sending me to the State Prison he would have been re-elected. The Captain (who promised to endorse a certain note if I were willing) informed me, to your certain knowledge, that he would see that, should the gentlemen here use their influence to get me pardoned, they

> would thereby secure their election to any office they might be candidates for. I mistrust that this is doubted by some, but you and Coroner H. can assure them of the fact. Remember me kindly to your family,
>
> Respectfully, Henrietta Robinson[21]

Robinson's complicated scheming about the pardon, plus her belief in her continuing political influence fall on the irrational side. Yet we still don't find "incoherence."

The letter of 1857, addressed to "her attorney:"

> Dear Sir,
>
> I wrote to you some time ago, but have received no answer. This don't discourage me. I therefore take the liberty to forward another to you. I have proved you to be a kind and faithful friend, and therefore submit to you some of my present reflections. I went to our Chaplain some three months ago, with as much sincerity as I could go to my God, to acknowledge my sinfulness and to inquire what I must do to be saved. I felt all I then said, and feel the same now, regardless of what my enemies have said, and I hope to remain thus as long as I live, however I may be slandered for it and for other things. I feel that I am and have been suffering solely for the reason that I happened to be, or rather that my life and peace and freedom happened to be in the way of the prosperity of ambitious politicians. But let these miserable, whining demagogues enjoy their triumphs in crushing a poor victim; their end is nigh, and oh what an end, both in this world and that which is to come! Please answer this and let me have some good advice from you once more, while, believe me, I remain your afflicted friend,
>
> Henrietta Robinson[22]

The rapid switch from the Robinson who humbly "acknowledges my sinfulness" to the one who attacks "miserable whining demagogues" and gleefully looks forward to their bad ends looks ugly to any reader. But is it unbalanced? Luckey believed so: "She will commend and vehemently defend the Governor, the Sheriff, and the prison officers one day, and the next, without any change in their course or sympathy towards her, she will denounce them as vehemently . . ."[23]

Robinson's changeability was on view in another letter, not saved by Luckey, of about this time. Addressed to John C. Mather ("the person denominated in the newspaper articles . . . her 'protector' ") Luckey remembered it this way: ". . . the first paragraph was dictated in language expressive of familiarity and strong though subdued affection, the second contained peal after peal of indignation, maledictions and menace, and so on through the whole letter. After she was through, I, as my custom is, read it to her and enquired if it was 'all right?' I shall never forget the perfect satisfaction beaming in her countenance, while uttering the prompt response, 'Yes, sir, all right.' "[24]

Undoubtedly this last letter was uglier and angrier than the 1857 one, and not wholly sane. Yet nineteenth century psychiatry, following in the footsteps of Esquirol, was disposed to view almost any difficult female behavior as insane—and it goes without saying, the behavior of a convicted murderess. Also *never* during all Robinson's years at Sing Sing and later at Auburn and Matteawan would she be anything but charming and ingratiating to those she saw as having ultimate authority over her: the doctors.[25] If Robinson had suffered from alcohol-caused psychotic breaks, her prison abstinence was now greatly benefiting her mental health. Of course, Elizabeth Oakes Smith described Robinson's mental confusion in the Troy Jail in 1855, when Robinson had already been locked up for two years—and with Oakes Smith surely a less Esquirol-influenced witness than Luckey. Either Troy physician and deputy William Hegeman's prescriptions of rum and brandy for the prisoner—he mentioned these prescriptions in his trial testimony—had slowed Robinson's recovery or she *had never* and *would never* operate on a completely healthy plane. Probably the second case is true, but her illness remained distinctly *controlled*, at least according to the doctors who cared for her.

The year 1860 saw at least two newspaper notices on Robinson. In a round-up of recent events, the *Troy Daily Times* of March 22 reported the visit of "a gentleman" to Sing Sing. He had found Robinson "at light work," "restless," and still "entertain[ing] an idea that she is a victim of the State." That fall the *Lansingburgh Gazette* reprinted a negative item on Robinson from the *New York Times*:

> In the hat shop [at Sing Sing], on a front seat as you enter, sits Mrs. Robinson, the "veiled murderess." The lady does not rejoice in the possession of a veil at present. She wears a half smirk continually on her round face, and her hair is black and glossy, and her cheeks red; but, for all these "points," she is by no means a handsome nor even a good-looking woman. Her smirk is the smirk of a devil. She looks as utterly heartless as

> a viper—not hardened but naturally heartless. Her features, on close observation, are seen to be coarse in the extreme. She too is here for life. But it may be a circumstance worth mentioning, that out of the whole population, male and female, in the prison, this woman was the only convict for whom our reporter found himself unable to awaken any feelings of pity or sympathy.[26]

During the 1861–65 Civil War—which finally settled the issue Hards and Softs, Woolly Heads and Silver Grays, and others had been struggling over—the Henrietta Robinson story vanished from view. It raised its head again, barely, in a slightly disparaging item which ran twice in the *Brooklyn Daily Eagle*, on April 23, 1869 and on May 3, 1869: "The desire to appear attractive has gone into prison with Henriettta Robinson, the veiled murderess, in the Sing Sing Penitentiary. Her face is dressed with a cosmetic, which gives it a clear and youthful appearance, and this cosmetic she distills from a flower and root which grows in the prison yard."

Then in the early 1870s her case surfaced in a controversy over her continued imprisonment. By this point one of the chief actors in the affair, John C. Mather, had been out of office for a dozen years. After serving as Democratic Representative from Lower Manhattan (Fourth N. Y. S. Assembly District) in 1858 and 1859, his political fortunes had nosedived with those of all former Hard Democrats during the Civil War years and Reconstruction. He wasn't even living in New York City any more, where directories show he had maintained a "storage" warehouse from 1861 through 1868. In 1869 he had married a wealthy thirty-six-year-old widow, Helen Goulding, and moved with her to Watertown.[27] The couple lived in Watertown's Woodruff House Hotel from 1877 until Mather's death in July of 1885.[28]

The other politico who *may* have played a role in the Veiled Murderess affair, Thurlow Weed, was still a man of influence in the early 1870s. Wartime work for President Lincoln and the nation had led him to sell the *Albany Evening Journal* in 1864 and move his base of operations to New York City. There, he continued to wheel and deal post-war, though in a reduced way. He was now in his seventies and ailing. It's possible Thurlow Weed had something to say about prisoner Robinson's status in the 1870s, but unlikely Mather was in any position to do the same.

Sometime in 1871 or 1872, word reached Troy-area readers of attempts to win Henrietta Robinson's release. An undated newspaper clipping from a Troy scrapbook (pasted in directly after an item dated August 31, 1870):

> District Attorney Banker has been requested to furnish the Governor with information in regard to the trial and conviction of Mrs. Henrietta Robinson, the "veiled murderess," now in prison

> in Sing Sing, for whose pardon efforts are being made by some of her friends . . . It seems that some one still remembers with affectionate interest the "veiled murderess" and is endeavoring to open her prison doors and give her the delights of liberty once more ere death closes her career.
>
> The Governor has a delicate duty to discharge in considering the application for her pardon. It was the opinion of the late Job Pierson, who defended Mrs. Robinson without hope of fee or reward, that she was insane. A great many of our citizens who became interested in her case, coincided in this view. If insane, she ought not to be confined in a state prison, but should be transferred to a proper asylum. If insane at the time of the commission of the murder, and sane at the present time, would the government being doing right to keep her any longer in confinement?[29]

The final suggestion of complete freedom for Robinson received some support. Another newspaper supplied a second clipping to the Troy scrapbook-maker: "It is said that she expects a pardon. I do not think that Governor Hoffman would incur the censure of public opinion were he to grant the wish of this half-crazed woman, who for seventeen weary years has suffered the torture of an earthly hell . . ."[30] But these voices were overwhelmed by others. The scrapbook-maker included a third item: "We cannot see upon what grounds this convicted murderess [Robinson] should be let loose again upon the community. There was not the smallest doubt of her guilt . . . if the prisoner were insane when the deed was committed, what assurance is there that she may not become "insane" again? People who are liable to attacks of insanity, especially when they are of such a destructive type as that of Mrs. Robinson, ought to be kept where their monomania cannot be dangerous . . ."[31]

The *Brooklyn Daily Eagle* also took an anti-release stand, on November 11, 1872: "Henrietta Robinson, "the veiled murderess of Troy," as that fine lady is romantically named, who today is confined in Sing Sing . . . is not mad as some of the papers reported a few days ago. She is as clear-headed as ever, still retains the old time reserve, still paints her cheeks and still hopes that executive leniency will be exercised on her behalf."[32]

Just a month later Robinson's chance at freedom did slip away, though in a way that rebuked the *Eagle*'s November position. On December 19, 1872, the Brooklyn paper reported, with no mention of its earlier article, Robinson was "to be transferred to the State Asylum in Auburn" and she was "hopelessly insane." The transfer took place eight months later. On

August 29, 1873, the *Troy Daily Times* noted the move of August 28, quoting another journal's comment that Robinson's "insanity is of a mild type."[33]

There had been a men's prison at Auburn in Cayuga County since 1818, where by 1823 the "penitentiary system"—separate cells for inmates at night plus a "rule of silence" in the common workrooms during the day—had developed, influencing other prison administrations in the state and nation. From 1825 a few women felons lived in "an attic story" at Auburn, until in 1874 women felons of all mental conditions moved into "the old Insane Asylum" constructed next to the main building in 1857 (after Utica State Asylum doctors protested the number of criminally insane sent to them).[34] From 1873 through 1877 Sing Sing progressively closed its women's wing, spurring re-classification of prisoners like Robinson. On April 22, 1874, the *Troy Daily Press* reprinted an *Auburn Advertiser* item showing Robinson once again, as in her first months at Sing Sing, making a good impression on prison authorities: "Henrietta Robinson, the veiled murderess, now an inmate of the state asylum for insane criminals in this city, is rapidly improving in health and spirits under the skillful treatment of Dr. J. W. Wilkie, the efficient superintendent."[35]

About six months later Robinson was in top form charm-wise:

> "The *New York Times*, speaking of the visit of Gov. Dix to the Auburn insane asylum, says:
>
> 'Here he was introduced to Henrietta Robinson, known as the "veiled murderess" of Troy, who was convicted many years ago of killing her husband! She is a remarkably prepossessing woman, still in the prime of life, and extremely courteous. She welcomed the governor and congratulated him on his fair prospects for re-election.' "[36]

Robinson's re-classification as legally insane and move to Auburn forestalled, probably premeditatedly, her release through an amnesty for "lifers" then in the legislative works. News of the amnesty reached Troy readers in a way connecting it with Robinson on April 19, 1875. Under the misleading title, "Henrietta Robinson, the Veiled Murderess, a Free Woman Again," the *Troy Daily Times* explained:

> The bill that has just passed both houses of the state legislature in relation to convicts sentenced to prison for life, affects but only person sentenced from Troy—Henrietta Robinson, known as the "veiled murderess." The bill provides that persons sentenced for life shall be conditionally released at the end of fifteen years,

> provided their conduct has been such as to warrant clemency; that they are to have their liberty for ten years, at the end of which time, if no other charge is brought against them, they are to receive pardon . . . Henrietta Robinson is now confined in the insane asylum at Auburn, being one of three women there who will be released by the new law . . . [But] She has no friends and will probably remain in the insane asylum until released by death. A few years ago her pardon would have been gladly welcomed. It comes too late, however, and perhaps she will never realize it.

If the *Times* had generated the 1871–72 scrapbook clipping which questioned whether the state was "doing right to keep her [Robinson] any longer in confinement," Francis's newspaper no longer held this view. And Troy's rising Democratic paper of the era, the *Troy Daily Press* had weighed in about ten days earlier with a strong negative: "While she lived in this city it was generally understood that Mrs. Robinson was the mistress of a then well-known politician . . . A few days before the poison was administered to the Lanigan family, Mrs. Robinson was heard to make threats against this man's life, and it is altogether likely that if released from prison at the present time she would carry out her purpose, the gentleman being still alive."[37]

Was the Democratic *Troy Daily Press* looking out for old Democrat Mather? It's possible, but at this late date the politics of the newspapers covering, only occasionally, Robinson's case no longer interests us much. What *is* interesting is that soon after these April notices about Robinson, someone concocted a brand-new false history for the Veiled Murderess.

On June 17, 1875, the *Troy Daily Press* ran "The Veil Uplifted: Henrietta Robinson and Her Heretofore Unknown History, etc.," which reported the statements of a "Doctoress Alexander, a lady who has quite a medical reputation in St. Louis." Doctoress Alexander remembered Henrietta Robinson as a tiny, dark-eyed, dark-haired girl who had worked as a circus rider in Georgia, then married a tall, blond ringmaster, against her parents wishes, and traveled with him to New York. The doctoress further held the male victim in the Troy poisonings had been none other than the blond ringmaster. Was this crazy story just a chance piece of flotsam and jetsam churned up in the wake of the long-running mystery, or was someone trying to distract public attention from the old stories involving Mather, the Woods and the Willards, or even "You politicians at Albany"?

28

AUBURN

In the later 1870s Henrietta Robinson disappeared from the newspapers, but a more intimate record of her doings survives in the asylum doctors' case notes. On August 1, 1876, someone, probably Superintendent Wilkie himself, wrote:

> She herself endeavor[s] to promote the idea of her aristocratic origin by making allusions to the haughtiness of her family; the wealth in which she was reared; the horses she rode, etc. She prides herself on the mystery surrounding her and is never so happy as when she has been curiously examined by distinguished visitors. She says if she should notify her family they would come after her at any minute. But this she "will never do." But if she ever does go out she will give everyone a splendid present . . . She denies in toto that she committed the murder and says that she is the victim of a political conspiracy. Seymour, who was Governor at the time of her trial, she regards as her bitterest enemy; she calls him a "hell-pup" and hopes that he will be damned. She considers herself of much importance and thinks that she has political influence. If displeased at a political election, will use very profane language and at night sometimes get up, stamp on the floor and curses [*sic*] by the hour. At times imagines that her food is poisoned and at the table will pass her plate away and take that of another patient. She will take medicine only from a physician as she fears attendants may poison it. She is well preserved considering her long confinement; her complexion is fresh; her teeth good; she has almost a voracious appetite; generally sleeps well. To officers and visitors she is extremely affable,

> and patronizing sometimes; among the patients she frequently instigates mischief but so cunningly that it is difficult to detect her . . . She is extremely illiterate, not writing at all and reading but a very little . . .[1]

None of this surprises, except for one piece of information coming near the end of the entry: "Her conversation is a mixture of high-flown and convict phrases pronounced in the strongest cockney-English manner, giving one the impression that she was reared among the lower classes in England. She excuses her English by saying that she spoke only French when young and doesn't know English."[2]

How much of a clue is the "cockney-English" comment? As mentioned earlier, in 1901 a Troy reporter would describe Robinson's speech as "a coarse-sounding brogue."[3] Was her voice that of an Irishwoman who had lived for some time in London?

Robinson's health and behavior changed little in the next years. Case note of January 1, 1877: "As usual very agreeable to officers and mischievous among patients. Consumes seven large slices of bread at each meal besides other food. Appetite exceeds that of any other patient." On April 1, 1878:"Associates very little with the other patients on the ward; remains, sewing, in her room most of the time during the day." On July 18, 1878: "Is in excellent health and generally cheerful and exceedingly polite to medical officers." November 1, 1878: ". . . extremely good-natured and polite. Conversation is incoherent." June 1, 1879: "Is occasionally irritable, her irritability manifesting itself in sly attempts to induce other patients to make a disturbance on the ward." October 1, 1880: "Continues to occupy her time in making embroidery for herself and other patients." October 1, 1881:

Since last entry patient has been in very good bodily health, taking a weekly dose of castor oil which she regards as a panacea. Becomes very angry if it is by mistake omitted. Still spends her time in embroidery work and of late professes to have "regained her ideas so that she is ashamed of what she formerly considered fine work." Says: "There was a long time when I did not remember very well. I see it now." "I used to do very nice work in silk when I was younger." Attendants report that she is at times abusive to them; but she is always polite to medical officers and visitors to the ward.[4]

And on November 10, 1881: "A day or two since patient was asked by Superintendent if she knew that Gov. Seymour had succeeded at the recent election. She at once became greatly disturbed, denounced Seymour as a —— s— — — b——, etc. Her excitement was brief and she apologized for her vulgar speech afterward." [Seymour, after two terms as Governor of New York (1852–54 and 1863–65) ran and lost as Democratic presidential candidate in 1868 and then remained active in New York politics until his death in 1886.][5]

The Superintendent, then a Dr. McDonald, likely dropped the name of "Seymour" to demonstrate Robinson's "monomania" for the benefit of a visitor, Mrs. Charles H. Bailey, who wrote an account of Robinson for the *Troy Daily Times*. Bailey's article describes the "storm of passion" touched off by mention of Seymour, but then shows Robinson at her usual well-turned-out and ingratiating best:

> A white-covered bed, a cushioned rocking chair, a home made rug, and in the centre, busy with her needle, a gentle looking woman. A neat dress, something thrown about the shoulders in grandmotherly fashion, a face, the skin of which looked fair as a child's, and hair done up in an indescribable style of crimps and puffs, such as we see in oldtime engravings, and Henrietta Robinson was before us . . .
>
> A little girl with us carried her as a gift some stamped cotton. Mrs. Robinson was much delighted. Taking the little one in her lap she kissed her, and putting the baby head on her shoulder, rocked back and forth, saying: "I do love children so!"
>
> She talked to the child about her dolls in real mother fashion, and when we proposed going she said: "Oh please, let me hold the baby a few minutes longer, I do love her so!"[6]

Bailey praised McDonald and his prison and probably drew on some of the institution's case notes on Robinson, mentioning the "seven slices of bread," etc. This woman writer judged—from her own observation or from the doctors' notes: "The story of her [Robinson's] noble origin can hardly be credited, as she cannot write, and reads with difficulty."

The next year, 1882, brought the absolute departure of one principal in the scandal, John C. Mather, and of one *possible* participant, Thurlow Weed. John C. Mather died August 13 in Watertown,[7] and Thurlow Weed died November 22 in New York City. The *Troy Daily Times* gave Mather quite a respectful obituary which dealt at length with his political career, yet the piece's title, "Death of John C. Mather; A Man with a History," almost shouted the "History" was the Henrietta Robinson one. The *Times* allowed itself only one direct but understated sentence on the great scandal of the 1850s:"Mr. Mather was an intimate friend of Henrietta Robinson, the veiled murderess, and interested himself in her defense."[8]

Either John M. Francis himself, who was still going strong in 1882, or his son, Charles S. Francis, devised this devastating line which was enough to evoke the whole of the old outrageous business for Trojans.[9]

The deaths of Mather and Weed almost seemed to mark a turning point in Robinson's mental condition. On September 1, 1883, for the first time, Auburn doctors noted a change: ". . . it is quite apparent that she is gradually drifting downward towards complete dementia." Yet in many ways, Robinson remained the same. The January 1, 1884, report found her still "very pleasant and affable" and continued: ". . . she works a great deal (sewing); reads and talks but is inclined to make trouble among the patients." An April report of the same year: "Uniformly good-natured and agreeable. Skillfully resists any attempt to ascertain her history."[10]

View at Cohoes Falls.

Did Mather's and Weed's deaths act as another kind of watershed, too? It may have been only the passage of time, but after 1882, published reports on Robinson generally kept to the Charlotte Wood Eliott story—with no more critical looks at Robinson's manner (like reporter Bailey's) except from one source, her old lawyer, Martin I. Townsend. But the critiques from Townsend wouldn't surface until the 1890s.[11] In the meantime, the Robinson "field" lay open to lush, romantic re-plays of the Wilson book material, as in the Troy *Daily Telegram*'s "She Loved A Man of Troy" of September 27, 1884, reprinted from the *Syracuse Herald.*

This piece sparked a late November or early December of 1884 ("some weeks ago" as of December 22) visit to Auburn by Robinson's old lawyer: "Patient was visited by the Hon. M. I. Townsend,"[12] and Robinson "was delighted to see him and expressed herself as very grateful to him for what he had done for her; although she said she would have rather died at the time." For his part, Townsend said: ". . . he was perfectly well satisfied that she was insane at the time she committed the offence, and it had always been a source of gratification to him to know that he had saved her from being wrongfully executed."[13]

The case note covering Townsend's visit tells of a new set of false teeth for Robinson. She had gotten a first set in the summer of 1882, when her jailers had used "a small sum of money ($26.10) to her credit" to make this purchase, along with a few others, to satisfy "her various wants in excess of what would be justified in furnishing at the expense of the State."[14] But Robinson had lost these teeth "by accidentally throwing them into the watercloset." Now, as recorded directly after the account of Townsend's visit, Robinson was "provided with some new ones, made by Dr. Hudson of Auburn."[15] Was Lawyer Townsend supplying small comforts for the prisoner on his own or others' behalf?

When a fire burned 622 River Street, the Lanagans' old place of business and site of the murders, the *Troy Daily Times* ran an update from Townsend, drawn from the same 1884 visit to Robinson: "I found her feeble and silly, but having a great desire to preserve her neatness and gentility of personal appearance. She is never frantic but utterly unable to reason. The authorities informed me that she was peaceful and harmless; more like a child than a person of age and intelligence."[16]

Townsend was one of the few remaining trial participants, though John C. Mather lingered in spirit: "Mar. 24, 1885. Some time ago patient *[Robinson]* was told of the death of one of the persons with whom she was charged illegitimate intimacy with, previous to her crime, for which she is imprisoned. Since then she has had hallucinations and claims she saw him at her bedside one night and that he asked for her forgiveness for the wrongs he had done her."[17]

In the summer of 1888, New York City's tabloid-ish *World* provided a new glimpse of Henrietta Robinson, stitched into a mostly inaccurate account of her crime and trial:

> Now, at the age of 62, she is a handsome old woman, with gray hair and a decidedly aristocratic bearing. Despite the prison garb and some oddity in dress, she is not unattractive, and seems more like an old belle who has settled down to the enjoyment of the remaining years of her life in quietude rather than one who has spent thirty-three years in prison. Her time is passed in making fancy work. There was no particular reason why she should have become an insane patient except that in the asylum she would have a better home than in the penitentiary. At times her mind wanders, but there is nothing aside from this to question her sanity.[18]

The intermittent news of Robinson would soon draw two "old friends" to interest themselves in her case. The first surfaces only in the notes of the Auburn doctors. On July 28, 1890, they reported:

> She [Robinson] was visited this week by Mrs. David H. Kellogg, of Spuyten Duyvil, N. Y., who says that Mrs. Robinson was an old schoolmate of hers at the Emma Willard School at Troy; that her name was Emma Wood and she was the daughter of an Englishman who was high in court circles in Canada where he held a Government position. Her sister Georgianna [*sic*] married an English Lord and Mrs. Willard and her daughter visited her at her elegant English home. Mrs. Kellogg says she is sure of this and will write to classmates to ascertain if any remember the name and address of her sister Georgiana in Eng.[19]

The Kelloggs were one of the rich, iron-manufacturing families of Troy, and Mrs. David H. Kellogg had likely been a student at the Troy Female Seminary in the 1830s when Georgiana and Emma Wood boarded there.[20] All the information Mrs. Kellogg provides on the Wood family is absolutely correct. Yet, as outlined in Appendix I, we know beyond a shadow of a doubt Henrietta Robinson was not Emma Cecilia Wood.

The surely respectable Mrs. David Kellogg was simply wrong, and then was nurtured along in her mistake by Henrietta Robinson, in the same way Robinson had treated the New York "merchant" or "gentleman" visitor to Sing Sing discussed by John M. Francis and, later, by Harry Hill. The Kellogg incident really confirms the truth of the con-woman portrait appearing in the Francis and Hill pieces.

Within another few years, the Wood solution to the Veiled Murderess's identity would rise again, more powerfully and publicly than in Kellogg's remarks of 1890 and more powerfully even than in David Wilson's 1855 book. In the meantime, Troy's *Morning Telegram* published a long article on the aging prisoner in November of 1891, the main point of which seemed to be Robinson had finally lost all claim to good looks: "She, the fair murderess, is now a wretched bundle of wrinkled skin and bones . . ." Though the *Telegram* reporter admitted: "Her dress, while of the conventional convict style, showed every evidence of neatness and modesty. Her hair was neatly arranged, and an apron of spotless white gave her the appearance of a good old lady enjoying the last years of her life in comfort."[21]

In 1892 Robinson moved with other "insane women convicts"[22] to New York State's new facility for the criminally insane, Matteawan State Hospital in Dutchess County. She was probably in the Dutchess County hospital when, in August, the death of a Troy policeman, a twenty-year veteran of the force, recalled her crime and trial once more to Troy readers. The deceased was Timothy Lanigan, [*sic*]," one of the children of the man murdered in 1853. The *Troy Press* praised the younger Lanagan as "an efficient and careful officer . . . [who had] made many friends while an officer of the law . . ."[23] Thus the family had taken root successfully in Troy despite the loss of the father.

Robinson was long installed at Matteawan by early 1896 when the Charlotte Wood Eliott story burst on the public once more.

29

CHARLOTTE DOOLITTLE NORRIS

On January 19 New York City's *Journal* published a near full-page story, "Tragic Mystery," whose title trailed a string of subtitles: "Veiled Murderess Vows That Her Name Shall Not Be Known; She Is Believed to Be Charlotte Wood, Wife of an English Peer; Son Is Now a Well-Known Member of Parliament; Prisoner Forty-Three Years; Story of a Life Filled with Tragedy and Sorrow; Praying for Death, Which She Believes Will Soon End Her Misery." *The Journal*, like its counterpart *The World*, pumped out simply-written stories of sensational type, intermixed with harder news, to appeal to a mass readership. Large woodcut or lithograph illustrations helped the *Journal* and *World* tell their stories to readers of little schooling, many of them new immigrants with little English as well.

It's not clear why the *Journal* fastened on the Henrietta Robinson story at this moment, but the long-running mystery was tailor-made for the paper. Perhaps Charlotte Doolittle Norris, Charlotte Wood's former classmate at the Seminary whose name would surface in a *World* article of the next year, prompted the piece.[1] Anyway, the *Journal* reporter had drunk deeply of the David Wilson book before interviewing Robinson at Matteawan. The writer traveled up to the hospital—even though doctor's notes on Robinson make no mention of the interview—for he or she included one detail on appearance too bizarre to be invented: "Her teeth have fallen out lately and she deftly manipulates a peculiar arrangement of white agate buttons, which take the place of teeth and fill out the corners of her mouth, which would sink in otherwise." Yet the *Journal* gallantly found: "There are no wrinkles or crow's feet about the eyes . . . Her hair is still plentiful, and this woman who was once so beautiful that she was famous, looks more like a woman of fifty-five than the age she has reached." [Though elsewhere the reporter states: "She is a fine-looking woman, although nearer eighty than seventy years."]

Nearly one-third of the piece was made up of long, first-person statements by Robinson ("I won her confidence," claimed the reporter). Robinson in the *Journal*:

> Now I am getting old. I have forgotten my French and everything. I have done it purposely. I wanted to hide every trace of my former existence. I even use illiterate language. Don't you notice it? I used that so people would not know me and think I was educated. [What a convenient explanation for a con-woman of little education to make!] I would not have my family know of my whereabouts for anything. Why, I have a son in the English Parliament. He was living and had succeeded to his titles the last I knew, and not for worlds would I let such disgrace come upon him. [No son succeeded William Francis Augustus Eliott,

The murderess raises her veil in *The New York World* (Nov. 7, 1897)

husband of Charlotte Wood Eliott, to the Baronetcy of Stobs; William Francis Augustus had succeeded his father in 1864 and would continue as lord of his domain in Roxburghshire, Scotland, until his death in 1910 when he was succeeded by nephew Arthur Augustus Boswell Eliott.[2]]

. . . he does not know I live. He believes his mother dead. When my brother Will came to see me in the jail at Troy, I begged him not to tell the rest of my family of my shame. He alone knew of it, and I promised him that I would never reveal my identity. Many of the family are dead, I know, for I was the youngest girl, the baby of the family. [Charlotte Wood was the fourth of thirteen children, and she had two younger sisters who survived to adulthood.]

My papa was a gentleman. He was brave and such a fine man. You see he was English. I was born in England. [Charlotte Wood Eliott was born in Quebec City, Canada.] My pap was the third son [the mother of Robert Wood, father of Charlotte Wood Eliott, claimed him as her eldest child], and, of course, he had to go into the church or else serve his country. He became a middy in the navy.

My husband was the son of a man of title—a younger son—but he succeeded in time to the title after I came back to this country. [Charlotte Wood Eliott's husband was "the son of a man of title" until he succeeded in 1864, but William Francis Augustus Eliott never had any elder brothers.] . . . One of my sisters married the son of a peer and another married a peer. [None of the Wood daughters married "peers" or titled men (on their wedding days) and only one, Charlotte Wood Eliott, married an heir to a title who eventually succeeded to that title. Georgiana, the eldest sister, married the heir to a baronetcy in Buckinghamshire, but her husband died before succeeding; Georgiana's son gained the title, becoming Sir William Robert Clayton in 1866.] When I was in jail at Troy my brother came to see me with my grandmamma's lawyer. I fixed my property so that it is alright, and if ever I should be so fortunate as to be released I should be able to go to my grandmamma's old house and live comfortably. There is also some bank stock that is being cared for in the same way. When I was in Sing Sing and after my removal to Auburn I had several thousand dollars. [This is contradicted by doctors' notes of July 3, 1882 which report "she has had a small sum of money ($26.10) to her credit for a number of years."]

The *Journal*'s Robinson then explained how she received money from her family while in Sing Sing: it came by an Anglican minister, a former acquaintance, who had recognized her in the prison; he wrote regularly to "Will" who sent "checks." But, according to Robinson in the *Journal*, after her arrival at Auburn there was some problem about cashing these checks, and: "I told my brother then that I was not likely to live long. I was sick and he must not write to me or communicate with me. I have never heard since from my people."

Towards the end of the interview, Robinson, while allegedly still refusing to reveal her true birth name, offered up her childhood nickname: "Lottie."

All the statements which are misfits with the life story of Charlotte Wood Eliott confirm the prisoner was not Wood Eliott. (Though *it is possible* none of the information came from the aged prisoner. One doctor had described Robinson as bordering on "gaga" in 1883: ". . . it is quite apparent that she is gradually drifting downward towards complete dementia." And while she showed some collected behavior post-1883, with an example being the same or another doctor's note from the next year, "Skillfully resists any attempt to ascertain her history"—this example throws doubt on the interview material from another direction!)

The *Journal* article was only the first shot in a barrage of publicity. In November of 1897, the *Journal*'s rival, the *World*, published a longer, even more lavishly-illustrated story on the Veiled Murderess, with testimony from a named witness, Mrs. Charlotte Norris of Chicago, mentioned earlier. This time Robinson's state hospital record confirms a reporter's visit:

> Nov. 2, 1897. Visited today by Kate Tupper [Edith Sessions Tupper], #279 W. 113 St., N. Y. City, a well-dressed lady who said she was about to visit Chicago and Mrs. Charlotte Norris of 1837 Oakdale Ave, that city. [Norris], a classmate of Robinson's at Troy, had requested her [Tupper] to ascertain if she [Robinson] were living; she [probably Tupper] was not willing to talk freely but said that Mrs. Robinson's father was an Englishman, a Government official in Canada; that she *[Robinson]* married Sir William Elliott of England, and that she was of excellent family . . .
>
> Nov. 7, 1897. Kate Tupper proved to be a "World" reporter and published a full page alleging that the identity of Mrs. Robinson had been discovered.[3]

"Mrs. Charlotte Norris, who lives at 1837 Oakdale avenue, Chicago" speaks in the *World* piece:

The woman known as the Veiled Murderess and who is now in Matteawan Asylum . . . was for years my classmate at the Emma Willard Academy, in Troy, and as a young girl was a visitor at my girlhood home in the city of Utica. Her maiden name was Charlotte Wood, and her name and title now are Lady William F. Elliot. Of her identity there can be no possible doubt. She came to me unveiled. I recognized her instantly, and she acknowledged unhesitatingly that she was my old friend and schoolmate Charlotte Wood.

I can see no further reason for secrecy in this matter. I did not promise Charlotte that I would not tell who she was, though of my own will I have kept her true name from the public all these years . . .

She was the daughter of a rich Quebec merchant named William Wood. [This was actually the brother's name, of course.] Her mother's maiden name was Proffer. [Her mother's maiden name was "Gray."] With Charlotte I became extremely intimate, and she spent one entire vacation at my father's house in Utica . . . She told me that her father was bound that she should marry an English army officer, as her two older sisters had been forced to do since leaving school. [Both Georgiana and Emma had, in fact, married British Army officers.]

"If," she declared to me, "he does force me to marry someone not of my choice I shall run away from my husband at first chance."

In after years she kept her word . . .

After Charlotte Wood had been committed to the Troy Jail to await trial her brother called on her. Then it was that a mutual agreement was made by which the woman was to deny her identity and the brother and the rest of the family were to declare that the murderess was no relative of theirs . . .

In the summer of 1871, I went with my little daughter, with my brother-in-law, Storrs Barrows, now living in Denver, and with the clergyman of the Congregational Church of Janesville, Wis., to Sing Sing Prison to ask to see the Veiled Murderess. I, of course, in common with others, had heard the rumor that it was possible that she was one of the Wood girls whom I had known at school. I almost knew that if such were the case it was my old chum, Charlotte, now Lady Charlotte and a murderess.

Charlotte Norris then described her face-to-face meeting with Robinson and their mutual recognition, followed by a long chat: "Charlotte

Wood, Lady William Elliott, asked me of my life since school, whom I had married and twenty other questions. Then she reverted to her visits at my Utica home and inquired by name of many people whom she had met there. [Con artists often appear to "bring up" names, though actually it is their "subject" who first names the supposed mutual friends.] Not once did she refer to her crime nor to her imprisonment. Her talk, always in an undertone, was of the old days of freedom, when as a young girl she had been one of the beauties of the school and a belle of society."

Within Tupper's article, Norris also told a farfetched tale of something that supposedly took place in the summer of 1853:

> A reception was announced for one night at the Willard Seminary. When it was at its height, William Wood and his sister, Lady William Elliott, were announced.
>
> The story as told to her friends was that Lady Elliott had just arrived from Scotland and was traveling through America . . . The appearance of brother and sister at the reception stopped all talk . . . but the reception at the Willards' was barely four hours old, before brother and sister left "to go to the hotel" . . . They went as far as the jail and Lady Elliott was placed once more in her cell. How was it done? I don't know . . .

As for the last part of Tupper's piece, describing the author's own interview with Robinson, we know to a near-certainty Tupper created the murderess's responses, with all their "clutching," "panting," and "gasping":

> "You were at school in Troy?" [said Tupper].
>
> "Yes, I and my three sisters—Emma, Georgiant [*sic*] and Caroline. [The four Wood girls who attended the Troy Female Seminary were, in order of birth: Georgiana, Emma, Charlotte, and Harriet; there was no Wood daughter named Caroline.] But where is Charlotte Norris?" [said Robinson] . . .
>
> I drew my chair closer. "Your name was Charlotte, too," I [Tupper] said.
>
> The woman clutched my hand tighter. "My God!" she panted, looking round in alarm, "don't speak that name here. What do you know of me?" she demanded almost fiercely.
>
> I spoke slowly: "You were Charlotte Wood, were you not?"
>
> "Oh," said she with a gasp, "I was Charlotte Wood but I buried that name years ago. I don't want to hear it spoken. Charlotte [Norris] has told you then. I thought she would keep my secrets to the grave."
>
> She was greatly agitated . . .

The *New York World*'s view of Tupper interviewing Henrietta Robinson.

As next described, Robinson gave *unbelievably* satisfying answers to other important questions, answers confirming all Norris had claimed. Robinson said "Sir William F. Eliott" had been her "first husband," and though she didn't name Mather as her second, supplied details relating to the old affair with the canal commissioner:

> "Would to God," she cried, "I had never met him. All my trouble came from him. And yet I loved him . . . I will not tell you his

name. He was a well-known man, but he too is dead. Besides you know too much about me. Charlotte has betrayed me."

Again I calmed her and spoke of other things, but harking back again to this marriage.

"It was a conditional marriage," she said. "He wished no children. We did not live together long."

"Where were you married?"

"In Troy—in a hotel," she said. [Not in Mather's "father's house" as once claimed by Robinson to Edwin Brownell.] "The proprietor witnessed the marriage."

But despite our rejection of Tupper's personal testimony and all Tupper-reported Robinson testimony, the presentable witness, Norris, with her exact information about the 1871 visit, deserves a careful look. The little girl, the brother-in-law with the uncommon name, and the minister from a specifically-named and distant town of no importance—these things have *truth* written all over them. Even Norris's address, "1837 Oakdale Avenue, Chicago" (which can be confirmed by consulting Chicago directories of the year[4]) says authentic and verifiable.

Within another year, the Chicago woman had convinced Robinson's long-lived defense attorney, Martin I. Townsend, of her story. On June 19, 1898, Townsend composed or co-wrote an article for the Sunday *Northern Budget* which examined Norris's claims. The article included copies of two intelligent-sounding letters written by Charlotte Norris in the spring of 1898, the first to Matteawan Superintendent H. E. Allison in January and the second to Townsend in May. In the first, along with much else, Norris stated: "The story of Mrs. Robinson, or Charlotte Wood, as she is, as told in the Sunday World, is practically correct. Mrs. Robinson was my schoolmate at the Troy Seminary."

Norris also explained her actions—or inaction—after her 1871 visit: "I secured Gov. Hoffman's promise to pardon her under the condition that I secured a home for her. By the time the condition could be complied with, Gov. Hoffman was out of office and nothing could be done."

There are more things within the January letter which first seem to condemn the writer as a spinner of a false tale, but on second look, bolster Norris's credibility:

> Charlotte Wood was married to William F. Elliott, an English army officer in Quebec, within ten days of August 1st, 1848 . . . Charlotte and I had an agreement by which the first one to be married was, with her husband, to visit the other. My husband and I accordingly went to Quebec on our wedding

journey. There we found that the Wood household had been broken up, that Charlotte had married six weeks before and had gone to England with her husband. We called at the residence of a Miss Proffer, a sister of Charlotte's mother. She told us the circumstances of the marriage.

The idea of taking a long journey from Utica—Charlotte Doolittle's childhood home and the place where she married on September 11, 1848, James L. Norris[5]—to Quebec City, without sending a letter or telegram to warn the planned visitee, seems a little odd. But Quebec City was then a common destination for pleasure-trippers from eastern New York, easily reached via the Champlain Canal and St. Lawrence River. Even an unwieldy Troy "Firemen's Excursion" of "Companies Nos. 1 and 2" plus "Jones' Band" made a three-day visit there in 1853.[6] And the fact Lansingburgh-born writer, Herman Melville, traveled to the old city on his 1847 honeymoon hints that it was a popular honeymoon spot.[7]

And Charlotte Wood Eliott did have an aunt, though a married not single one, living in Quebec City with a name close to "Proffer." The true name was "Petry."[8] But most strikingly, Norris doesn't follow the David Wilson book (which in turn followed one of the 1854–55 newspaper accounts[9]) in giving December 16 [1846][10] as Charlotte Wood Eliott's marriage date. Though the December 1846 date was the right one, Norris's mistake proves at least she was *not* depending on the Wilson book for information. Instead she absorbed—probably through an actual meeting with Charlotte's Aunt Maria Petry—the date of August 1, 1848, when the young Eliotts had left Quebec. William F. A. Eliott's regiment left Canada about August 1, 1848.[11] Also Norris's comment, first appearing in the 1897 *World* article and repeated in the 1898 *Budget* piece, about Charlotte's visit to Utica acquires more weight after re-consulting the Willards' Ledger B. Robert Wood paid for two weeks' board for his younger daughter Harriet over the February vacation of 1843, but only one weeks' board for Charlotte, so perhaps the two Charlottes did spend that week together in Utica.

After H. E. Allison sent Townsend a copy of Norris's January letter, Townsend dispatched a Chicago friend to Oakdale Avenue to: ". . . make inquiries as to whether a Mrs. Charlotte Norris resided at the number indicated, and whether she was a lady of respectability. He sent me back answer . . . that he found that there was such a lady residing at the number given and that she was a person of the highest respectability."

Townsend then received Norris's May letter, naming the years she attended the Troy Female Seminary. The old defense counsel proceeded to check the seminary catalogues, finding the two Charlottes' names both present there over two semesters in 1843. He also consulted: ". . . the lady who recognized Henrietta Robinson immediately after her arrest as a Miss Wood and asked her as to the period when she knew Miss Wood, whom she supposed to be identical with Henrietta Robinson, at the Willard School, and she tells me that it was in the years 1842–'43."

And finally to top things off, Townsend wrote to yet another friend, this time in Utica, about Doolittle Norris's respectability—gaining a second positive endorsement. At the close of these investigations, the old lawyer graciously reversed his earlier position (in articles of 1891 and 1896) and ended his 1898 *Budget* piece: "This [Norris's statements plus Townsend's own investigation] seems to settle the question as to who Henrietta Robinson really is beyond cavil or query."

By this point, elder statesman Martin I. Townsend has near-convinced us of Norris's tale, too, despite Charlotte Maria Wood Eliott's 1878 death certificate plus another convincing paper from her life in Scotland (see *Appendix I*). Only twentieth- and twenty-first-century data on human psychology, a non-existent science in the 1800s, saves us. Controlled psychological experiment after controlled psychological experiment shows the almost total susceptibility of a witness like Norris. In 1871 Norris had made a difficult journey to visit "her schoolmate" in Sing Sing. This step, which pointed to Norris's strong wish to reach out to an old, though briefly-known friend and offer aid or sympathy, set her up to accept Henrietta Robinson's pose. We recall her statement as related by Tupper: "I, of course, in common with others, had heard the rumor that it was possible that she was one of the Wood girls whom I had known at school. *I almost knew that if such were the case it was my old chum, Charlotte* [modern italics], now Lady Charlotte and a murderess."

Basically the Norris situation was just the Mrs. David Kellogg one all over again, but elaborated and publicized. Charlotte Doolittle Norris, Mrs. David Kellogg, and the unnamed Seminary student of 1842–43 mentioned by Townsend were all sincere but deluded dupes, swept up by a fiction so well-spun it outlasted the purposes of the original spinner or spinners.

30

FINALE

In a way, the Veiled Murderess affair breathed its last with the articles of 1896 through 1898. They were the last big explorations of the identity question. Yet before Robinson's death in May of 1905, there was time for another eddy in the current of the ongoing story. Townsend soon retracted his endorsement of Norris, though he did this semi-anonymously. On January 27, 1900, the *Troy Record* claimed "Deputy Sheriff Atwood" had recently brought a message from Robinson to "the Man Who Defended Her When She Was Tried in This City."

> This gentleman said to a Record reporter yesterday:
>
> Yes, the officer brought me a message . . . I do not wish to be named in connection with it, however. She [Robinson] gave information that clears up much that was dark.

"The gentleman who was prominent in her defense [Townsend]" then dictated a statement putting forward the same arguments expressed indirectly (through a reporter) in 1891 and directly in the first paragraphs of his 1898 article, namely, that though Robinson resembled the Wood girls and "was a person of ladylike manner"—". . . in conversation she often showed a defect in her knowledge of the English language, which rendered it improbable that she could have been educated in the Wood family." The important information just received was simply: "Last week she stated to the officer [Atwood] . . . that her native language was French. She told him that she learned her prayers in that language, and in her private devotions uses it still."

Robinson had been claiming to speak French for years, though also allegedly saying in her 1896 *Journal* interview that she had "forgotten her

French." Remarks about French language represented no new information. Townsend just seems to have had second thoughts, unless someone—William F. Wood or Dr. John Willard?—had come down hard on the old lawyer for publicly accepting Norris's claim.

Nearly two years later, a rival Troy paper, either the *Telegram* or *Northern Budget*, essentially reprinted the *Budget* article of 1898, dishonestly getting around Townsend's repudiation by quoting Matteawan Superintendent H. E. Allison on Townsend's supposed thinking: "Mr. Townsend has since seen Mrs. Norris and I am sure that he is convinced of the truth of her story."[1]

The 1901 story, which included the comment already mentioned on Robinson's "coarse sounding brogue," was the last significant news piece on the prisoner before her death on May 14, 1905. Robinson's death from "Chronic Interstitial Nephritis & Asthma" was hastened by her increasing refusals to eat and often to drink, dating from about 1901. With a terrible justice, the one-time poisoner had developed a fear of being poisoned herself. The interstitial nephritis diagnosis may show her body was autopsied, since the shrunken, scarred kidney of this condition's end stage was not identifiable through other means in 1905. Interestingly, on June 3, 1904, less than a year before Robinson's death, a Dr. Clark of Matteawan had reported: ". . . [Robinson] says she is a member of the Royal Family in England."[2] If she truly was an unacknowledged daughter of Robert Wood, she maintained her claim to his *reputed* heritage to the very last. More likely, Robinson just continued to hold tight to a false story which had brought her extra attention and perks for years.

On Monday, May 15, 1905, the *New York Times* ran an obituary which told most of its tale in the title: "Veiled Murderess Dies with 50 Years' Secret; Henrietta Robinson, Long A Prisoner, Never Told Her Name; Slew Two at Troy in 1853; Death Sentence Commuted, Spent Last Years in Asylum Lacemaking; Seventy-eight Years Old." The writer, a "Special to the *New York Times*," describes how: "When it was apparent she was going to die, she was urged to reveal her identity, but refused. She said she had kept the secret during the half century she had been in prison and it would die with her."

The special report also covers a romantic find: "Securely sewed into her needlecase the authorities found after her death, a locket and a worn piece of newspaper, upon which was written:

> When first I saw this world of joy and pain,
> Assailed by doubt that ever will remain,
> I wondered what it meant to live to die—
> The question oft I pondered but in vain."

On more solidly factual ground, the *Times* informed readers no one had claimed the body which would be buried in the prison hospital cemetery. The obituary included the item, mentioned earlier, about Robinson's age and birthday. Four days before her death, the article claimed, Robinson had said May 10 was her birthday (not April 8, Charlotte Wood's birthdate) and she was 89 years old rather than the 79 years listed in prison records.

A day later, May 16, the *Troy Record* dedicated a front-page column to Robinson.[3] Though the paper had last—in 1900—disparaged the idea Robinson was a Wood daughter, or at least a legitimate daughter of Robert Wood, the *Record* now ran "A Dispatch from Chicago," probably something from another newspaper, affirming Charlotte Norris's old story. Oddly, though the *Record* cited the longtime prisoner's early marriage to "an Englishman of rank, Sir William F. Elliott," almost correctly naming William F. A. Eliott, it referred to Charlotte Wood as "Charlotte Ward" throughout the article. While daily newspapers are error-prone, this does seem a near-incredible mistake. Was William Wood, who would not die till the next year, still threatening lawsuits?

After Robinson's death, the affair of the Veiled Murderess slipped more and more from view. By 1925, the date of Rutherford Hayner's *Troy and Rensselaer County, N.Y.: A History*, the old scandal had turned into a story for Troy and Albany readers only. As mentioned in his introduction, Hayner accepted the Wilson-book or Charlotte Wood Eliott-identity theory, while his guest author, "Mrs. Della E. Stuart," left the identity question open. Both Hayner and Stuart avoided naming Troy's once-distinguished citizen Mather, yet Wilson's book was on many shelves, with at least one surviving copy containing the portrait of "John C. Mather."[4]

Later local writers weren't afraid to reintroduce the canal commissioner. In 1979 Jack Casey produced a six-part, fictionalized account of the crime case for the *Troy Record* which imagined an early romance between Mather and seminary pupil Charlotte Wood, among other liberties.[5] In 2004 Hollis Palmer published the first twenty-first-century account, *The Curse of the Veiled Murderess*. Palmer's lively retelling features Mather prominently, though doesn't go far into the man's politics. Palmer mostly leaves the identity question alone, focusing instead on early deaths and other troubles which beset players in the affair. Thus, in a modern replay of the nineteenth century interest in gothic horror, he finds a supernatural curse hovering over the affair.[6]

PART EIGHT

CONCLUSION

The Veiled Murderess unveiled. From H. B. Skinner's
The Life and Confessions of Mrs. Henrietta Robinson (1855).

31

WHAT REALLY HAPPENED

At the close of our journey through the Henrietta Robinson case, much is now clear. Politics drove the affair, aided by a cultural obsession with Evil Behind a Veil. The political engine was mainly Soft Democratic—and briefly, in September and October of 1855, Republican—hostility toward Hard Democrat John C. Mather. Despite this, it's near-certain Mather or friends engineered publication of both early Wood-daughter newspaper items—the June-July one of 1853 and the mid-trial one of May 25, 1854, in the *Troy Daily Whig*—in order to shift the scandal away from the Hard politician. Contemporaries certainly believed this about the second news item, and both pieces appeared in Mather-friendly Whig papers.

After the tremendous backfire of the May 25, 1854 charge as far as Mather's personal reputation was concerned, he and his newspaper allies—to different extents, the conservative and liberal Whig papers[1]—retreated from any promotion of the Wood daughter story. Mather was in a position to make trouble for the Woods and Willards. But they were in a position to make trouble for him and his allies, too. Both groups demonstrated this on May 25, 1854. The two sets of public-relations adversaries were doubtless semi-frozen with horror post-May 25, 1854, and afraid of making many moves at all, lest they rouse the wrath of the opposing group.

How much were Mather's friends in the Whig press friendly, or at least not openly hostile, to him for current political reasons and how much did their actions spring from shared guilt or worry over past links with courtesan Robinson? This is a real question. But Henrietta Robinson was a Hard Democrat and Whig problem and scandal. Only the Soft Democrats—the true outsiders in terms of past social contacts with Robinson as well as, maybe, in terms of current clout within Troy's "establishment"—were not afraid to explore her possible links with important people. (The Hard Democrats and Whigs must have had something of an upper hand in Troy in 1853–54. If not, how had they managed to pack the court which tried Robinson with so many Hards and Whigs?) Likely, the Robinson problem kept Thurlow Weed and other liberal Whigs "on the fence" longer than they otherwise would have been in terms of making common cause with the anti-slavery Softs. In other words, they couldn't act and move forward until the issue which chained them to Mather, Robinson, had finally been neutralized by her departure from Troy to a distant prison.

The charge against the Woods took off like a rocket, and went on and on, because it fit so neatly with mid-nineteenth century ideas about Sex and Women. It confirmed nineteenth century men's worst suspicions: that there was a ravening demon within even a pure daughter and wife of the social elite, and just one sexual misstep could loose this demon, setting a woman on the road to crime and insanity.[2] This conviction, which infected women too, seems to have worked almost like a form of hysteria in Troy and its news region, pulling out the testimonials from Charlotte Doolittle Norris and others.

The actual woman behind the veil was an Anglo-Irish immigrant who had spent formative years in County Westmeath, even if a turbulent life then carried her to England or Canada before her arrival in Troy. The use of the Westmeath Protestant Irish names of Robinson and Wood, and *probably Gaynor*, plus the alleged bandying about of another Westmeath Protestant name, Pakenham, say this—along with the "cauldron dream," witchcraft beliefs, and (maybe) alleged "brogue." And "Susan Gaynor of Albany" emerges as a highly logical early identity for this woman.

Henrietta Robinson was a sociopath, a bent or twisted person—partly as a result of childhood trauma?—without feeling for others, but with mostly normal perceptions and in control of her actions. At the same time, she may have suffered from what would be diagnosed today as "personality disorder" or borderline mental illness and slipped into true psychosis when drinking. Drink was often highly toxic in the nineteenth century. Many wines and liquors, particularly Robinson's favorite, brandy, illegally contained high levels of lead as a stabilizing agent.[3]

Robinson was a skilled liar, able to lead Mrs. Kellogg, Charlotte Norris, and even John Francis of the *Times*, for a bit, down the garden path of her Wood daughter pose—though these three, and others, *wanted to believe* for personal or political reasons. Her toughness and adaptability in many of her dealings with others tell us she was street-smart to the "nth degree." In other words, she was someone who had fended for herself for a long time. This quality doubly denies the old Charlotte Wood Eliott claim, if any doubts nag about C. W. E.'s death certificate and other papers. Plus

Henrietta Robinson just plain looks *too violent* and *too desperate*, too much of a relentless charmer (on occasions) and name-dropper (Adm. Pakenham, Rev. Potter, etc.) to have been a daughter of wealth, whatever the state of her mental health.

Yet there are hints of some real connection between Robinson and the Wood family, mainly the apparent Westmeath ties of both Robinson and the Woods of Quebec. If Robinson *had* used or traded on the Wood name before the murders, then others—Mather and maybe Weed—were guilty simply of "running," rather than inventing, a false story. Whichever it was, one or both men succeeded beyond any wildest dreams in putting the story over. As mentioned in *Introduction* and *Immigrants and Others*, the ease of identity-shifting in the new industrial cities of the United States provided the important pre-condition for all manipulations of Robinson's identity.

The Troy scandal echoed across the Atlantic. In the late nineteenth century, a rumor about a murderous granddaughter of Edward, Duke of Kent, filtered into some minds in Britain. How else to explain an exchange in the London-published *Notes and Queries*, dating from 1907? On February 9, 1907, one "Wm. H. Peet" wrote: "The father of Constance Kent (Road Murder, 1860) was said to be a son of the late Duke of Kent." On March 23, 1907, Peet added: "I cannot give any other authority for the suggestion that the father of Constance Kent was a son of the Duke of Kent than that of persistent rumour."[4]

Constance Kent was a middle-class English girl who confessed to the 1860 murder of a young brother. Mary Hartman has examined the case in her *Victorian Murderesses*, but nowhere in Hartman's work or in any other study is there the suggestion Constance's father, Charles Kent, was one of Edward's illegitimate children.[5] The name Kent, which would never have been given to any son of the Duke, probably just allowed the old rumor about Charlotte Wood Eliott to surface in an altered way.

Did the rumor inspire British writers? Though fallen women appear in a number of eighteenth-century and early nineteenth century novels, there is a particular kind of English novel, "the novel of sensation," which emerged only *after* the mid-1850s and which evokes the Veiled Murderess affair in an almost startling way. Two examples of the genre are Wilkie Collins' *The Woman in White* (1860) with themes of identity theft and false imprisonment in an insane asylum and Mary Elizabeth Braddon's *Lady Audley's Secret* (1862) featuring a wicked heroine who hides her own insanity-tainted identity among other crimes. Collins and Braddon actually seem to have re-cycled parts of the Charlotte Wood Eliott legend, thus weaving the Troy affair lastingly, though anonymously, into Anglo-American consciousness.

Interestingly, Wilkie Collins, who wrote about veils and impostors in his *Woman in White*, kept one woman and her children from the mid-1850s onward and then acquired a second "illegitimate wife" in the mid-1860s. Except for a brief interval in the late 1860s when Wife No. 1 left him, Collins maintained both women and their children until his death in 1889.[6] Veils and illegitimacy as well as veils and sex!

As *may have been* true in the Robinson case—if the woman *was* an illegitimate daughter of Robert Wood—the flesh-and-blood "other families" of respectable male Victorians could step from behind their veils with a vengeance. An angry illegitimate son possibly played a role in the 1892 axe murder of Andrew Borden of Falls River, New Jersey (the Lizzie Borden case),[7] and the illegitimate family of James Maybrick of Liverpool certainly played a role in the 1889 prosecution for murder of Maybrick's widow, following the man's sudden death.[8] Modern society is so free of rage-filled, unacknowledged children it's hard now to even recognize this part of the old "double world."

Our long sojourn in the nineteenth century has been a tiring, sometimes slightly frightening one. We are glad to escape back into the twenty-first century, which has its own problems, but where the air is really easier to breathe, for women especially. So many bad things have vanished from the Upper Hudson's cities, our investigation's main locale: the political turmoil spun off by southern slavery; hideous, completely misunderstood epidemics (cholera, tuberculosis, syphilis); and—just barely mentioned in this account, but very much present in contemporary newspapers—the industrial and transportation accidents which cut people in half or scalded them or ended their lives in other terrible ways. Saddest are the deaths of the boy-workers, who seemed to fall rather regularly into the wheel-pits of the water-powered factories.[9]

Of course good things have disappeared, too: the barrels of oysters and mounds of shad and sturgeon harvested from an unpolluted river; the dazzling range of other local produce in the markets, where even ordinary staples like wheat appeared in rich variety (who wouldn't want to sample one batch from a Troy market of 1851 praised as having a specially "plump, white berry"?); the city parades, which went on for hours because almost every able-bodied man marched in some association or craft group (like the German "turners" or carpenters who impressed onlookers with their white linen smocks at Troy's 1853 Fourth of July celebration); and old-fashioned pleasures (sleighing in winter, trips to the countryside to swing—then an adult pastime, target practice for militiamen, going to dancing schools or singing schools—another adult pastime, and more). Then there was the almost Wild West excitement of new industrial sites like Troy, where so much was changing everyday life. Plus the very problems and suffering within nineteenth century cities allowed some extraordinary lives to bloom, with Troy's Father Peter Havermans, the comforter of all in need, one of the most heroic of these.[10]

The investigation of one old mystery has truly opened our eyes to many things.

APPENDIX I

THE WOOD DAUGHTERS

Georgiana, the Wood daughter only briefly touched by Robinson-identity suspicions in 1853, married a second husband sometime after the 1848 death of her first, Captain William Capel Clayton of the Coldstream Guards (*Burke's Peerage and Baronetage* [London, 1913], 449). Georgiana's marriage to her second husband, J. C. de Wynter, Esq., endured until her death on January 12, 1882 at Carleton Rookery, Suffolk ("De Wynter," *London Times*, 17 January 1882, p. 1).

The second Wood daughter, Emma Cecilia, attracted far more suspicion, yet British Army records of her two husbands, Captain Anthony Alexander MacNicol of the First or Royal Regiment of Foot, and Surgeon John Mackintosh of the Royal Artillery, rule her out as a possible "Henrietta Robinson" even more firmly than a simple marriage history like Georgiana's. Emma married MacNicol in 1838 in Quebec City; in 1841, he died "after a Fit of Epilepsy" and his widow filed a pension application that found its way into MacNicol's file (Great Britain. War Office. Certificates of birth, baptisms, marriage, and death; with wills, administrations, statements of services and personal papers of officers, etc., "Bundles 325—426, McLean-MacWhirter-McLane," pp. 453–58) In 1845 Emma married Mackintosh, also in Quebec, but the couple left for Britain within a few years. In 1858 Mackintosh died of consumption in Ferry Port-on-Craig near Edinburgh, and the next year Emma filed another pension application—penned in the same precise and beautiful hand, obviously her own, as the one she submitted after MacNicol's death (Ibid. "Bundles 147–226, McDougal–McKay," pp. 623–25; these papers also contain a birth certificate for an infant, Robert Mackintosh, born to Emma in Princetown (Dartmoor) in 1851).

As for Charlotte Maria Wood Eliott, the chief Wood daughter suspect from 1855 onward, peerages claim she gave birth to a daughter, Grace

Theresa Blanche, in March 1851 when the soon-to-be-murderess was living in Albany (Bernard Burke, *A Genealogical and Heraldic Dictionary of the Peerage and Baronetage, Etc.* [London, 1890], pp. 489–90). Grace Theresa Blanche would live until 1932, dying unmarried in the family of her father's second wife, Hannah Kelsall, in Roxburghshire. There is also a death certificate for "Charlotte Maria Eliott (married to Sir William Frances Augustus Eliott, Bart. of Stobs)" who died at Crieff, County Perth, Scotland, November 29, 1878 (General Register Office, Edinburgh, Extract No. 66 from Register of Deaths for Parish of Crieff, County of Perth).

A certificate is a certificate is a certificate, and sometimes a document is created to hide a truth. Yet Charlotte died of "Bright's disease" in exactly the sort of place a wealthy Victorian might be expected to die—Crieff was a spa town catering to invalids—and attended by exactly the sort of society doctor one would expect to find caring for a baronet's lady (Account of Dr. Matthew Baillie Gairdner, who signed C. M. W. E's death certificate, in Alexander Porteous, *History of Crieff From the Earliest Times to the Dawn of the Twentieth Century* [Edinburgh, 1912], 397). The Eliotts can also point to the fact Charlotte's younger brother, James John Wood, who served in the 67th and 45th Regiments of Foot from 1851 through 1861, married in 1868 William Frances Augustus's sister, Blanche (Bernard Burke and A. P. Burke, *A Genealogical and Heraldic History of the Peerage and Baronetage, Etc.* [London, 1927], 856–58). It's hard to imagine a second marriage between the two families, the Woods and Eliotts, if Charlotte Wood Eliott was then disgracefully languishing in Sing Sing.

On top of these facts there is, in a collection of Quebec notary records, a legal document about Wood family property bearing the signatures of "W. F. A. Eliott" and "Charlotte M. Eliott" with the date July 14, 1861 affixed to the signatures by James Blackadder one of the Magistrates of the City of Edinburgh—by which time Henrietta Robinson had already been six years in Sing Sing (see Sample 2). And as if this were not enough, handwriting expert Charles Rommelt of Probst Investigations, Albany, rules that—as far as it's possible to judge from limited signature samples—the hand which signed "Charlotte M. Eliott" in Edinburgh in 1861 is the same one which created the name on a legal paper of 1847 from Quebec City (see Sample 1).

Wood family descendants also preserve the diary of a cousin of Charlotte Wood's, Frost Wood Gray, who visited Edinburgh in the winter of 1862–63, and this diary contains "many references to William and Charlotte" who acted as Wood Gray's hosts in the city (Letter, Diana Petry Apedaile to Lady Frances Eliott, 16 February 1977).

Though no charges were ever made against Harriet Wood, the sister who attended the Troy Female Seminary with Charlotte, her husband

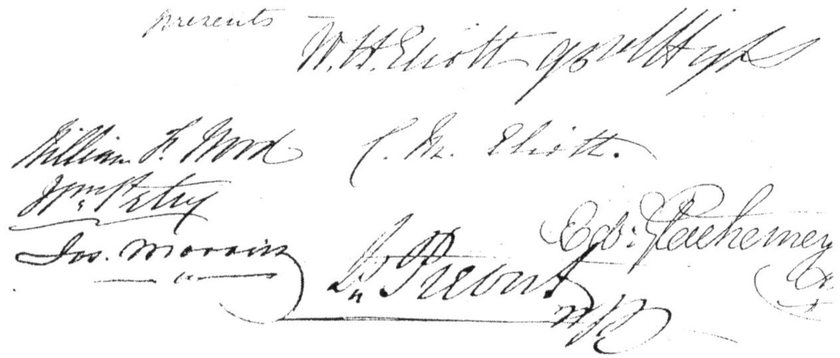

Sample 1

Signatures of "W. F. A. [with the F and A stylistically joined] Eliott 93rd Highs [Highlanders]" and "C. M. Eliott" on agreement of 11 September 1847 confirming an advance of £250 to Ensign Eliott from Charlotte's not-yet-settled inheritance from her mother. (Attached to "Obligation W.F. A. Eliot & wife in favor of the Executors of Mrs. Wood's will," 6 October 1847, No. 240, Papers of Edward Glackmeyer, Notary, Archives Nationales du Quebec).

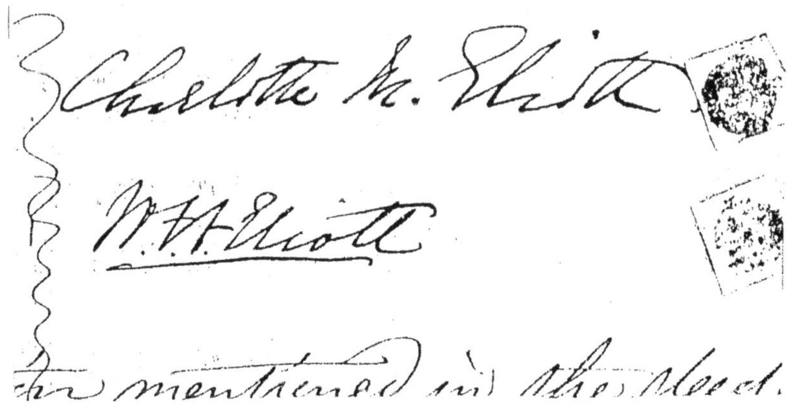

Sample 2

Signatures on the legal document signed in Edinburgh in 1861. Though Charlotte's handwriting has changed a good deal over nearly fifteen years, expert Rommelt points to the identical overlapping—actually underlapping—curl to the first stroke of the capital Ms in both samples. Charlotte's brother William does the same thing with the first stroke of his capital W, in contrast to Charlotte's husband's writing style. Rommelt also notes the large, open L in Charlotte's hand from Samples 1 and 2—again like her brother's writing—which contrasts with the short, closed L of William's hand from both samples. ("Dépot de Ratification by Mr. & Mrs. Elliot by W. F. Wood," 7 August 1861, No. 2805, Samuel Isidore Glackmeyer Notary, Archives Nationales du Quebec.)

Neil McInnes Mackay's army records document that Harriet gave birth to a daughter, Emma, in Belfast in 1870 (Great Britain. War Office. Record of Officers' Services by Regiment. Royal Regiment of Artillery, 1771–1881, vols. 359–362 "Services of Niel McInnes Mackay"). And just to leave no stone unturned, the youngest Wood daughter, Eliza, who never even attended the Troy Female Seminary and who married sometime after 1853, went on to have eight children with her husband, Rev. Humphrey Noble, minister of the Church of England. The Nobles were living in Croxton in the south of England in 1871 (W. T. N. Reeve, "Wood Family Genealogy"; "Procuration 5913, 10 November 1871, to William Enser Meiklejohn of the Royal Bank," Papers of Samuel Isidore Glackmeyer, op. cit.).

APPENDIX II

THE DUKE OF KENT BUSINESS

The story of the Canadian Wood family begins, firmly, in August 1791 when a young man named Robert Wood (*not* Robert Wood, father of the Troy Female Seminary pupils) arrived in Quebec City as a "servant" in the entourage of Prince Edward Augustus, fourth son of then-reigning George III and Colonel of the Seventh Regiment of Foot or Royal Fusiliers. This Prince Edward would become Duke of Kent in 1799. On December 15, 1792, Canada's Lieutenant Governor, Alured Clarke, appointed Robert Wood (in a document addressing him as "Robert Wood, Gentleman") doorkeeper to the Executive Council of the Province. The appointment followed two events: Wood's marriage on December 29, 1791, to Marie Dupuis "dite Caton [called Caton]," an illiterate, sixteen-year-old native of Quebec, and the birth of a baby boy to Marie the next year. After Robert Wood's death in 1806, Marie Dupuis Wood claimed seven living children of the marriage, giving the birthdate of the eldest, Robert Wood—the lumber merchant and father of Georgiana, Emma, Charlotte, and Harriet—as August 10, 1792.

Mollie Gillen, author of the *Dictionary of Canadian Biography's* "recent research," outlines all this in her *The Prince and His Lady: The Love Story of the Duke of Kent and Madame de St Laurent* [London: Sidgwick and Jackson, 1970), 25, 44, and note 38). There were five children allegedly born to Mme. de St. Laurent during her years with Edward, and according to Gillen: "Madame's own history effectively contradicts the possibility that she mothered this brood of children and left them—in spite of her known love of children and those empty years to fill after her prince's death—in forgotten silence."

On Edward:

It is impossible, too, to believe that the duke, with his strong sense of rank and privilege, would unconcernedly see the illegitimate sons of his brother the Duke of Clarence publicly received by the Queen and allow his own to remain in unacknowledged obscurity (Gillen, 267).

Yet Gillen's own research shows de St. Laurent was a worldly courtesan of thirty when she met the twenty-three-year-old prince. If abandoning her children was something demanded of her by Edward, the eighteenth-century-born-and-raised *bourgeoise* (her titles were phony) would likely have complied. But why would Edward, whose brother, the Duke of Clarence, lived openly with the actress Mrs. Jordan and their many children until late in life, hide his own illegitimate children? A compelling reason surfaces right away, having to do with Edward's standing in the royal family. "The truth was," writes Cecil Woodham-Smith, biographer of the Duke of Kent's legitimate daughter, Queen Victoria, ". . . they [Edward's parents] did not like him." George III actually disliked all his sons from the time they reached their teens, but nursed a special anger towards Edward, the tallest and probably most intelligent of the boys (Cecil Woodham-Smith, *Queen Victoria: From Her Birth to the Death of the Prince Consort* [New York, 1972].

The anger showed up in George III's reaction to a scandal caused by Prince Edward while on the Grand Tour in January of 1790. When news of the prince's affair with a woman in Geneva, Switzerland—resulting in the birth of a daughter and the mother's death in childbed—reached London papers, the king banished Edward to military service on Gibraltar. Over the next decade Edward sent letter after letter to his father seeking release from, first, Gibraltar, and then from service in Canada, and permission to return home. The 1790s were also the years when all the alleged illegitimate children were born. So given George III's reaction to this first bastard, Victoire Dubus, the constantly-petitioning prince had a big motive to hide the births of later, irregular children.

Gillen points to Julie de St. Laurent's presence at a public reception in Quebec City shortly before August 10, 1792, as disproving any Robert Wood claim to royal parentage via Edward. But this thinking ignores the "iffy-ness" of Robert Wood's birthdate (the birth record was created much later) as well as the real possibility Marie Dupuis was the true or biological mother of Wood (Gillen, 50, 270–71). Gillen's only weapons against the old tradition are a few holes in the Wood family account, mainly their acceptance of Julie's invented titles and a claim of a September 25, 1791, marriage between Edward and Julie on Malta; Edward was then in Quebec (Gillen, 273–74)

Before his death in 1946, a Lieutenant-Colonel Wood, grandson of Robert Wood, gave family records, most of which openly claim Edward as an ancestor, to the Canadian National Archives. These include one interestingly precise "fact": Robert's baptism, according to Lieutenant-Colonel Wood: ". . . took place in the Bishop's palace, Quebec, and was performed by Mgr. [sic] Charles-Francois Bailly de Messein, Bishop of Capse, and Coadjutor to the Bishop of Quebec" (St. Matthew's Cemetery Records, C-198, Archives Nationales du Quebec). Other descendants of Robert Wood also tend to believe Edward is their ancestor ("History and Genealogy of the Wood Family," typescript, William T. N. Reeve).

Even the *Dictionary* authors seem mystified by Robert Wood's boundless resources. They describe how a timber market collapse bankrupted his company in 1826, leaving him owing creditors £17,579, yet despite only gradual improvement in the timber market after 1827, he had begun to build an imposing three-storey house at Anse Saint-Michel in Sillery by the end of 1829.

In line with this, and for what it's worth, an undated booklet in the Quebec National Archives contains a statement by one Alex Addie: "I have held in my hands a document which he [William Wood; not clear if this is William Frost Wood or Lt.-Col. William Wood, a grandson of Robert Wood] signed stating that there would be no further issue, legitimate or otherwise, for which he received a large pension for life" (R. Clive Meredith, ed., *Never Really Forgotten: Essays and Reminiscences on the Cathedral of the Holy Trinity, Quebec* [Quebec City, n. d.]).

NOTES

INTRODUCTION: TROY, NEW YORK, 1853

1. *John F. Prescott's City and Business Directory for 1850–1, Etc.* (Troy: John F. Prescott, 1850), unpaged advertisements.

2. From "Troy City" in *A Gazetteer of the State of New York* (Albany, J. Disturnell, 1842), 398–400; author, editor, and publisher John Disturnell hailed from Lansingburgh, a northern suburb of Troy. Similar ideas are expressed in D. O. Kellogg, *The City of Troy: Its Commerce, Manufactures, and Resources* (Troy: Young and Hartt, 1847).

3. Rutherford Hayner, *Troy and Rensselaer County, New York: A History* (New York: Lewis Historical Publishing Co., 1925), 2:506.

4. Della F. Stuart, "Woman's Part in History," in Hayner, *Troy and Rensselaer County*, 2:407.

CHAPTER 1: RIVER STREET

1. Robinson would tell a neighbor she was 27 in late April or early May of 1853. See testimony of Mary Jane Dillon, "Rensselaer Oyer and Terminer: Trial of Mrs Henrietta Robinson for the Murder of Timothy Lannagan [*sic*]," *Troy Daily Times*, 25 May 1854, 2. (Henceforward, no page numbers cited for articles from newspapers of the 1850s; all articles appear on second pages of the four-page papers.)

2. "Mrs. Robinson, the Murderess," *Lansingburg Gazette*, 4 September 1860.

3. At the time of an 1881 interview, Robinson's hair was "done up in an indescribable style of crimps and puffs such as we see in oldtime engravings . . ." ("The Veiled Murderess," *Troy Daily Times*, 30 November 1881). Also see photograph of Robinson evidently taken in the 1880s, though not published until later ("Famous Murder Mystery Solved," *Troy Northern Budget*, 8 December 1901). It seems unlikely Robinson would have adopted this style of the 1830s late in life.

4. "Rensselaer Oyer and Terminer, etc." *Troy Daily Times*, 23 May 1854.

5. "Rensselaer Oyer and Terminer, etc." *Troy Daily Whig*, 23 May 1854.

6. David Wilson, *Henrietta Robinson* (New York and Auburn: Miller, Orton and Mulligan, 1855), 303.

7. Testimony of William M. Ostrom, "Rensselaer Oyer and Terminer, etc." *Troy Daily Times*, 24 May 1854.

8. So many slapdash or shoddy buildings were going up in the Tenth Ward that the ward would soon be famed as "a region of bad buildings" ("Some Landmarks of Early Troy, etc." *Troy Daily Times*, 20 January 1880 and 21 January 1880).

9. Karen Halttunen, *Confidence Men and Painted Women: A Study of Middle-Class Culture in America, 1830–1870* (New Haven and London: Yale Univ. Press, 1982), 39.

10. Two others were Moses Wiswall, who had a "Butt" or door-hinge factory just north of Boutwell's mill, and Samuel Sargent who operated a "Tripe Manufactory" farther north still. See U. S. Census, 1850, Rensselaer County, N.Y., Troy City, Seventh Ward, p. 310, houses 2467, 2468; *MacArthur and Wilson's Troy City Directory for the Years 1853–4* (Troy: C. L. MacArthur, 1853), 191, 205.

11. Wilson, *Henrietta Robinson*, 40.

12. Testimony of William H. Hegeman, "Rensselaer Oyer and Terminer, etc." *Troy Daily Times*, 25 May 1854.

13. Rensselaer County Clerk, naturalization record of Dennis Lanagan, book 4, 289; on 11 October 1852, Timothy Lanagan swore that Dennis (Timothy's brother) had resided in the U.S. since 8 June 1847. Timothy signed his name to this document in a fluent hand, incidentally demonstrating that he spelled his own name with three As; news accounts would often spell it "Lanigan."

14. U. S. Census, 1850, Rensselaer County, City of Troy, Seventh Ward, 284–85 (see fourteen-person household headed by 58-year-old Dennis Lanagan).

15. "Henrietta Robinson 'the Veiled Murderess'; Her Departure to Sing Sing," *Troy Daily Traveller*, 31 July 1855.

16. Unless otherwise noted, all contemporary "voices" describing the events of 1853 (within this chapter and the two following chapters) come from *Troy Daily Times* coverage of Robinson's trial ("Rensselaer Oyer and Terminer, etc.," *Troy Daily Times*, 23 May 1854–29 May 1854).

17. "Home Matters," *Troy Daily Times*, 17 February 1854.

18. Minutes of the Troy Common Council, 1838–1854, 8–9 (Troy Public Library, hereafter TPL); on 16 April 1840 the Council repealed the law that had forbidden "foreigners" to keep "a Grocery or to vend strong or spirituous liquors . . ."

19. Rensselaer County Clerk, naturalization papers of Dennis Lanagan, cited above.

20. But she never said to Dillon, "My father was an Irishman. I was born in Vermont," as erroneously reported in Wilson, *Henrietta Robinson*, 144, and repeated by some later authors, including Karen Halttunen (*Murder Most Foul*, Cambridge: Harvard Univ. Press, 1998). This statement, found in the *Troy Daily Times* coverage of 25 May 1854, was made by Dillon about herself. The entry on Henry Dillon's family in the U. S. Census, 1850, Rensselaer County, Town of Brunswick [just east of Troy], 97–98) confirms that Henry was born in Ireland and his daughters, including Mary Jane, born in Vermont.

21. Walt Whitman's *Leaves of Grass* (1853) describes respectable women in an urban environment: "On the piazza walk five friendly matrons with twined arms." There needed to be *five* to underline their virtue for readers. In practice, women of the 1850s must have been free to move independently through their own village-like city neighborhoods, with danger of shameful arrest threatening only if they walked alone outside these places.

22. Timothy J. Gilfoyle, *City of Eros: New York City, Prostitution, and the Commercialization of Sex, 1790-1920* (New York: W. W. Norton, 1994), 78–86.

23. "Last night between the hours of 12 and 1 o'clock, a fight took place in an old rookery, on that street [North Third] between Jacob and Federal Streets. Children were screaming and women yelling 'murder'—making night 'hideous.' The fight lasted full half an hour, and no Policeman made his appearance" ("Home Matters," *Troy Daily Times*, 30 March 1852).

24. This was probably Moses Warren, Sr., who had also served as a State Senator in 1828–31 and as a Sheriff of Rensselaer County. But it might have been his son, Moses Warren, Jr. (1820–1899) who was active in Rensselaer County Democratic politics, too. (The obituary of the younger Warren appears in *Troy Daily Times*, 2 August 1899.)

25. William E. Hagen, "A Troy Murder Mystery," *Troy Daily Press*, 21 October 1893.

26. New York State Office of Mental Health. Central New York Psychiatric Center, Marcy, N.Y., Henrietta Robinson's Matteawan State Hospital Record, 28 August 1873 to 14 May 1905, 13.

CHAPTER 2: MAY 25TH

1. The raised wooden sidewalks of lower River Street probably didn't extend this far north.

2. Looking at this timetable today, we wonder why the doctors gave her so little attention. Did her unmarried and penniless condition cause the doctors to abandon her? Or was there an unconscious calculation about the relative worth and importance of a male versus a female life? Later, the community as a whole would respond to the deaths of Lanagan and Lubee with a murder indictment naming the male victim only.

3. "The Double Murder: Evidence on the Inquest, etc." *Northern Budget*, 27 May 1853.

4. Untitled newspaper clipping on Ferry Street Jail, "Troy Scrapbooks," vol. 189, 53–54, TPL.

5. Janet F. Brodie, *Contraception and Abortion in Nineteenth-Century America* (Ithaca: Cornell Univ. Press, 1994), 115.

CHAPTER 3: THE NEW PRISONER

1. "Lanagan" entries in *John Prescott's City and Business Directory for 1850–1* and *MacArthur and Wilson's Troy City Directory for the Years 1853–4*.

2. "Session Minutes of the Second Street Presbyterian Church, Troy, N.Y.," vol. 1, 1834–1856, 251 (collection of the Presbyterian Church U.S.A., Philadelphia).

CHAPTER 4: INTRODUCING JOHN C. MATHER

1. Engraved, page-sized image glued into a copy of Wilson, *Henrietta Robinson*, in the collection of the Rensselaer County Historical Society, Troy (hereafter RCHS).

2. Troy's canal commissioner was not "a lineal descendant of the celebrated Cotton Mather" as an obituary would claim ("Death of Ex-Senator Mather," *Watertown Daily Times*, 14 August 1882). Cotton Mather's line died out in the eighteenth century. All the nineteenth-century descendants of the New England Mathers traced their family trees back to Increase's brother, Timothy, called "the Mather Farmer" to distinguish him from four minister brothers; see Horace E. Mather, *Lineage of Rev. Richard Mather* (Hartford: Case, Lockwood and Brainerd Co., 1890), 184 and elsewhere.

3. Katharine Chapin Higgins, *Richard Higgins . . . and His Descendants* (Worcester: Printed for Author, 1918), 372 (see information on Cornelia Mather Higgins). Loggers had given Deposit its name as they found it a convenient spot to "deposit" logs over the winter before sending them south on the spring floods to Philadelphia.

4. Delaware and Broome County Clerks' Offices, Grantor and Grantee Indices. Thaddeus Mather made a dozen real estate transactions in Broome County and more than a dozen in Delaware County). Also in 1823, when eighteen Deposit men promised cash payments toward the building of a new Presbyterian meetinghouse, Thaddeus pledged only a bit more than the median payment (Tompkins, Pa. [*sic*] Presbyterian Society Miscellaneous Manuscripts, "We the Subscribers . . . [dated] Tompkins 23 July 1823," collection of the Presbyterian Church U.S.A.)

5. In the memory of nineteenth-century Broome County residents: "He rode on a grey horse to visit the sick of the Deposit region." (Mather Family vertical file, Broome County Historical Society, Binghamton)

6. "Thaddeus Mather, administrator for estate of Joseph Cannon," Delaware County Clerk, Deed Book H:78 (23 November 1826).

7. *Biographical Review: The Leading Citizens of Broome County, New York* (Boston: Biographical Review Publishing, 1894), 15–16; See also Broome County Surrogate Court, Estate No. 88 (Henry, 1 May 1870) and Estate No. 227 (Richard, 15 June 1885).

8. W. W. Munsell, *History of Delaware County, 1797–1880* (Albany: W. W. Munsell, 1880), 307–8.

9. His younger brother, Calvin Edson, born in 1819, definitely attended, for when the academy burned in 1835 Thaddeus helped found another in the nearby Village of Franklin (ibid., 182). An older brother Richard Parker, born 1811, may have received less education; he would follow a less ambitious career path than his brothers, becoming a "merchant" in the Delaware County village of Hancock by 1836 and leaving no trace of other activities beyond the militia title, "captain." See his marriage notice, *Delaware County Gazette*, 17 February 1836. He died 7 July 1850 (Mather, 184).

10. William Seward Papers, University of Rochester Library.

11. "He . . . at the age of twenty-two removed to Troy" (William D. Murphy, *Biographical Sketches of the State Officers and Members of the Legislature of the State of New York in 1858* [Albany: J. Munsell, 1858], 77).

12. Often misspelled as "Alva" in documents, "Aloa" is a variant spelling of the herb, "aloe"; see family of "Ebenezer Porter and Eunice Kingsbury Porter" in Henry Porter Andrews, *Descendants of John Porter of Windsor, Conn.* (Hartford: G. W. Ball, 1893).

13. *A Brief Account of the Origin and Progress of the Divisions in the First Presbyterian Church in the City of Troy* (Troy: Tuttle and Richards, 1827).

14. "Session Minutes of the Second Street Presbyterian Church of Troy," 46.

15. "Democratic County Convention," *Troy Daily Budget*, 1 September 1843; the fact that Calvin Mather bought land in Stephentown, a town adjoining Berlin, in 1841 (see Rensselaer County Deeds, 54:140) helps locate John C. in Berlin in the late 1830s and early 1840s, too. The Berlin residence is also supported by Mather's absence from Troy directories in the 1830s; these yearly volumes (issued by various publishers) recorded addresses of boarders as well as householders, including those of very humble people.

16. Through dated events through the early 1840s placing John C. Mather in Troy all occur during cold weather months: his acceptance as a Second Street Presbyterian Church member on 19 November 1838 ("Session Minutes," cited above); and over twenty borrowings from the Troy Young Men's Association Library through fall/winter/spring dates in 1839–43 (Y. M. A. Library Records, vols. 1–3, 1836–43, TPL.) Summer months were the unhealthy time in antebellum cities.

17. "From Washington; Correspondence of the N. Y. Express," *Troy Daily Whig*, 10 May 1853.

18. "Legal Lights of Long Ago," *Troy Daily Press*, 20 January 1894.

19. "Death of Ex-Senator Mather," *Watertown Daily Times*, 14 August 1882.

20. "Death of Gen. George R. Davis," *Troy Daily Times*, 26 June 1867.

21. See "Loan Commissioners" notice dated November 1843 in *Troy Daily Budget*, 2 January 1844. (Davis, the state's "bank commissioner" in 1830–40, probably got Mather this job.)

22. Among many others, Mather would issue two loans to his brother-in-law Daniel Wight in 1845 (Rensselaer County Deeds, 61:264, transactions of 5 February 1845).

23. "Death of Hon. Job Peirson [*sic*]," *Troy Daily Arena*, 10 April 1860

24. Mather, 180; also see "Amos Briggs," *American Biographical Index*, microfiche no. 302 (repr. from *Appleton's Cyclopedia of American Biography*, 1888). Also Beth Klopott, "The History of the Town of Schaghticoke, N.Y., 1676-1876" (Ph.D. diss., SUNY Albany, 1981), concerning Schaghticoke Point cotton factories.

25. "Death of Hon. Job Peirson [*sic*]," *Troy Daily Arena*, 10 April 1860; First Presbyterian Church [Schaghticoke] subscription list (Briggs-Mather Family Correspondence and Papers, 1802–68, New-York Historical Society).

26. That of equally distantly-related Capt. Joseph Mather of Albany. See note 9, chapter 5.

27. Letter of 24 August 1840 addressed to "John C. Mather Esq., Schaghticoke, N.Y.," in which one C. N. Read regrets he can't attend an upcoming Whig "meeting" in Schaghticoke (Briggs-Mather Family Correspondence).

28. On 23 February 1842, "J. C. Mather of Schaghticoke" (Bethel's son) purchased three parcels, comprising over 100 acres total; he sold most of this by the end of the year (Rensselaer County Deeds, 55:66, 56:462.

29. Letter dated Albany, 19 March 1844 (Briggs-Mather Family Correspondence):

"Mr. John C. Mather, a gentleman who belongs to a highly respectable Family in a neighbouring Town, and who is himself worthy and estimable, goes South with an intention of establishing himself in business for life.

Mr. Mather is an intelligent, enterprising practical Agriculturist. His energy, business habits and integrity are proverbial. Nor is he less distinguished for his social qualities and moral virtues. I take great pleasure, therefore, in commending this gentleman to the attention and confidence of those with whom his lot may be cast. [signed] Thurlow Weed."

30. "The Forged Letter," *Troy Daily Budget*, 3 January 1843.

31. "The disturbance began in the First Ward . . ." *Troy Daily Budget*, 21 March 1837, cited in later newspaper clipping, "Troy Scrapbooks," roll 32, 60.

32. Unlike those in the *Broome County Republican*. See *BCR*, 9 July 1851: "On Sunday last we were warmly impressed or *oppressed* with the fact that the Catholic Church in this village is altogether too small for the number, constantly increasing, of its attendants . . ." And *BCR*, 11 May 1853: "The uneducated Irishman excavates canals and railroads . . . It is instructive to observe with what unerring instincts these untaught sons of toil and misfortune, upon their arrival on these shores, subside into their natural place beneath the lowest stratum of our American society . . ."

33. "Home Matters," *Troy Daily Times*, 17 November 1851; "Home Matters," *Troy Daily Times*, 17 December 1851. Other Irish jokes: " 'See there!' exclaimed an Irish soldier to a gaping crowd, as he exhibited with some pride his tall hat with a bullet hole in it. 'Look at that hole, will you? You see that if it had been a low crowned hat I should have been killed outright!' " and "An honest Hibernian had come far to see Niagara; and while he gazed upon it, a friend asked him if it was not the most wonderful thing he had ever seen, to which he replied 'Never a bit, man—never a bit. Sure it's no wonder at all that the wather should fall down there, for I'd like to know what could hinther it!" (*Troy Daily Times*, 26 December 1851; *Lansingburg Democrat*, 15 January 1852).

34. "Family of Thaddeus Mather," U. S. Census, 1850, Broome County, Town of Chenango, p. 372.

35. The rest of this interesting list: ". . . Regulators; Flock Cutters; Sheering machines; Napping d[itt]o; Card Pliers; Stripping Cards; Worsted Harness Twine; Sea Island cotton d[itt]o; Reeds of all kinds made to order, and old reeds repaired; Glass steps; Shuttle Eyes; Spindle Banding; Mule d[itt]o; Bobbins of all kinds; Clothier's Jacks; Loom and Dresser Brushes; Press Papers; Fullers' Soap; Patent Cement for Belting, etc." ("Manufacturer's Depot: At Mather's Old Stand, No. 221 River Street, etc." *Troy Daily Times*, 27 June 1851, notice dated 24 April 1851).

36. Obituary of Aloa Mather, *Northern Budget*, 14 January 1846.

37. U. S. Census, 1850, Broome County, Town of Chenango, p. 372.

38. U. S. Census, 1850, Rensselaer County, Troy City, First Ward, p. 18.

CHAPTER 5: RISE

1. William D. Murphy, *Biographical Sketches of the State Officers and Members of the Legislature of the State of New York in 1858* (Albany: J. Munsell, 1858), 77.

2. Letter of Calvin Mather, 29 October 1846, Thurlow Weed Collection, University of Rochester.

3. Letter of Calvin Mather, 20 January 1847, Hamilton Fish Papers, Library of Congress, Washington, D.C.

4. "Fifty Years After: Reminiscences of First and State Streets, etc." *Troy Daily Press*, 4 November 1893.

5. "The Municipal Government of Troy," *Troy Daily Budget*, 31 March 1849.

6. Murphy, *Biographical Sketches*, 77.

7. DeAlva S. Alexander, A *Political History of the State of New York* (New York: Henry Holt and Co, 1906), 2:126.

8. Murphy, *Biographical Sketches*, 78.

9. "Death of Hon. Job Peirson [*sic*]," *Troy Daily Arena*, 10 April 1860, 3.

10. Alexander, 149. In Mather's life, 1849 was the year he interred Aloa's body in the Albany Rural Cemetery, laid out just eight years earlier as part of a movement to create pastoral resting places for the dead. Troy had a pastoral burying ground, too, Oakwood Cemetery, opened in 1847. Mather moved Aloa from a Troy churchyard, or from Oakwood itself, as a result of some bond with the family of Captain Joseph Mather (1800–1884) of Albany. Capt. Joseph Mather was involved "in navigation on the Hudson and in railroading" (Mather, 220). As with Bethel Mather of Schaghticoke, there was no closer link between John C. Mather and Capt. Joseph than Timothy, the "Mather Farmer," of many generations before. John C. acquired burial plots next to the grave of Joseph's sister Lois Mather Raymond, buried in Albany Rural Cemetery in 1847, and near the future grave of Joseph himself.

11. The new compromises admitted California as a free state, set up other western territories without ruling on their slavery status, kept slavery in Washington, D.C., and rejected federal control of interstate slave trading while agreeing to toughen fugitive slave laws.

12. Murphy, *Biographical Sketches*, 78.

13. Those trying to get along with the slave system had hated Seward's words of 11 March 1850: ". . . we cannot be true Christians or real freemen if we impose on another a chain that we defy all human power to lay on ourselves."

14. Everyone found Granger glamorous. In the 1830s H. D. Stanton saw Granger, still dark-headed then, in the Assembly Chamber at Albany: "Granger was the attraction of the ladies' gallery. Dressed in a bottle-green coat with gilt buttons and brilliant appurtenances, he was a model of grace and beauty." (Henry B. Stanton, *Random Recollections*, 2nd ed. [New York: MacGowan and Slipper, 1886], 17)

15. Nathaniel Hawthorne, "The Canal Boat," *New-England Magazine*, 9 (December 1835}: 398–409.

16. Ibid.; Henry B. Stanton, *Random Recollections*, 18.

17. He continued: ". . . and some precautionary experiments are necessary to a stranger exposing himself to the compound effects of such an atmosphere. I would recommend the following: Enter a saloon on the towpath and call for a bowl of oyster soup; place yourself before it with your body inclined forward to an angle of forty-five degrees; seize the spoon in your right hand, and poise it on a level with your nose . . . close your eyes, open your mouth, banish thought, and let blizzard." ("Correspondence of the Democrat," Lansingburg Democrat, 4 March 1852).

18. An 1850 toll schedule for canal freight breaks down the "Lumber and Wood" cargoes carried:

"Timber, squared and round, if carried in boats; if carried in rafts; round dock sticks passing in cribs; white pine, white wood, basswood and cedar; oak, hickory, beech, sycamore, and black walnut; spruce, maple, ash, and elm; cherry; hemlock; boards, plank, scantling and sawed timber; red cedar, cedar posts; mahogany; sawed lath, split lath, hoop poles, handspikes, rowing oars, broom handles, spokes, hubs, tree-nails, fellies, boat knees, ship knees, plane stocks, pickets for fences, stuff for chairs and bedsteads, and hop poles; brush handles, brush backs, looking-glass backs, gunstocks, plow beams and handles; staves and headings and empty barrels; shingles (rafts); split posts (rafts); wood for fuel; tan bark per cord; sawed stuff for window blinds and window sashes and blinds."

Other categories—"Minerals," "Fur, Peltry and Skins," "Stone and Slate," and "Provisions"—are just as detailed, with the "bloom iron," "buffalo and mooseskins," "all stone, wrought or partly wrought," and barrels of "flour, salted beef, butter, cheese, tallow" taxed differently when traveling "to tidewater" versus "away from tidewater" (printed notice slipped into March 1850 pages of New York State Comptroller's Office, "Engrossed Minutes of the Canal Commissioners, 1849–1857," unpaged, New York State Archives).

19. Cooley referred specifically to Syracuse's "voluptuous lap" (*Speech of the Honorable James E. Cooley*, November 1, 1853, 16 [pamphlet, New York Public Library]).

20. Whig Hezekiah Seymour apparently filled two Board positions—engineer and surveyor—in 1851 and 1852, perhaps giving Mather an easier hand with the slightly smaller body.

21. Glyndon Van Deusen, *Thurlow Weed: Wizard of the Lobby* (New York: Little, Brown, 1947), 185.

22. Democrat Follett later complained of Mather's ascendancy: "The superintendents upon my division were advised by those holding high stations, to disobey my orders, and when displaced by me for being grossly disobedient to my lawful commands, were reinstated in power and place again!! . . . I was even deprived of the petty privilege—never before sought to be wrested from a commissioner—of appointing my own confidential clerk!!! . . . Still the cormorant hangers-on of the whig party were not satisfied . . ." (Frederick Follett, "The State Auditor and the Canal Commissioners," Albany Argus, 30 July 1851).

23. The *Troy Daily Times* of 24 February 1851 incorrectly cited Britton as "D. G. Britton," but this was clearly "John G."—the only Britton then listed in Troy directories.

24. "Engrossed Minutes of the Canal Commissioners."

25. "A National Democrat," in *New York Hards and Softs: Which is the True Democracy* (New York: Daily News, 1856), 19.

26. "Washington's Day Dinner," *Troy Daily Times*, 24 February 1851.

27. "Death of Calvin M. [sic] Mather," *Troy Daily Whig*, 27 June 1853.

28. The Republican writer who approved Mather's treatment of the slavery issue reveals his own obsession with it. After Mather's speech, a young fireman sang a patriotic song, and the writer commented:

"The appearance of this young hero, with his red shirt . . . and hardy limbs, on the Platform, surrounded by the Orator, the Clergy, the Revolutionary Soldiers,

Officers, and others, formed the most [illegible] and characteristic feature of the day, without we exempt the features of a 'live nigger,' who had coiled himself around a huge tree directly opposite the Speaker's stand, grinning his Ivory in the most independent manner at the scene which surrounded him. He formed the dark ground in the picture, and was worthy of the appropriate sketching of even Crookshank [sic] himself." ("The Celebration of the Fourth in Binghamton," *Binghamton Daily Republican*, 5 July 1851)

29. In addition, there was a plan to enlarge the 90-foot by 15-foot locks to 110 feet by 18 feet and deepen them to 8 feet ("Enlarging the Erie," chap. 3 in Noble E. Whitford, *History of the Canal System of New York State* (Albany: Brandow Printing, 1906).

30. John Kilham Porter, *Argument of John K. Porter, Counsel for the Managers on Behalf of the Assembly, on the Trial of John C. Mather, one of the Canal Commissioners of the State of New in the Court of Impeachments, Sept. 8, 1853, reported by Richard Sutton* (Albany, 1853), 10.

CHAPTER 6: TROUBLE

1. "Canal Contracts," *Troy Daily Times*, 12 January1852; "The Canal Lettings," 15 January 1852.

2. "Canal Contracts," *Troy Daily Times*, 20 January 1852.

3. "The Canal Board and Lettings," *Troy Daily Times*, 21 January 1852.

4. Porter, *Argument*, 3.

5. Ibid., 6.

6. *Opening Remarks of John H. Reynolds, Etc.* (Albany, 1853).

7. Porter, *Argument*, 9.

8. "In A 'Snarl,' " *Troy Daily Times*, 17 March 1852.

9. "The Canal Contracts," *New York Times*, 13 March 1852.

10. "George Law," in G. W. Bungay, *Off-hand Takings* (1854). Bungay continues: "He [Law] has vital energy enough for a village of ordinary men . . . even his oaths are plump and unctuous with energy . . . Like Thor the thunderer he makes his dent wherever he strikes, for he has force of intellect as well as bodily strength, and a generous heart beats in his broad chest." (*American Biographical Index*, microfiche, nos. 031-033).

11. In 1855 Henrietta Robinson would state: "A political party wished to crush John C. Mather and Myron H. Clark . . ." See Elizabeth Oakes Smith, "Letters From the People; A Visit to the Vailed Murderess," *New York Daily Tribune*, 28 July 1855, 6.

12. See http://www.famousamericans.net/georgelaw/ ("Virtual American Biographies," edited extracts from *Appleton's Cyclopedia of American Biography*, ed. James Grant Wilson and John Fiske, 6 vols, [New York: D. Appleton and Co., 1888])

13. Among the other directors were John S. Christie, Robert Christie, Jr., and the Troy industrialists, large-scale brewer Arba Read and stove manufacturer Titus Eddy ("Banks," *MacArthur and Wilson's Troy City Directory for the Years 1853–1854*).

14. "Home Matters," *Troy Daily Times*, 1 April 1853: "The Manufacturers' Bank, the Merchants and Mechanics Bank, State Bank and Union Bank of this

city have been selected by the Canal Board as depositories of canal tolls collected at West Troy the ensuing season."

15. "The Manufacturer's Bank," *Troy Daily Times*, 12 October 1852. Individual banks printed their own money then, inadvertently creating an immense problem with counterfeiting.

16. "Congressional," *Troy Daily Times*, 25 October 1852.

17. H. D. Stanton put the rapprochement down to Marcy's presidential ambitions and his gratitude for Barnburner support in this area. But was John C. Mather's crude division of the contracts a factor in the rapprochement, too?

18. In the exception that proves the rule, a few old Barnburners, like Mather friends James Cooley and Samuel Stover, became Hards.

19. "The Canal Question," *Troy Daily Times*, 5 January 1853.

20. John C. Mather, *Communication from the Hon. John C. Mather, Canal Commissioner, in Answer to Certain Charges, Etc., Printed by Order of the Legislature May 30, 1853* (Albany: C. Van Benthuysen, 1853)

21. "The Impeachment Case," *Albany Knickerbocker*, 23 August 1853. Follett was called "the Barnburner Canal Commissioner" in this article.

22. Says a *New York Tribune* article cited in "The Mather Impeachment Case," *Troy Daily Times*, 19 April 1853.

23. Mather, *Communication.*

24. "Messrs. Mather and Follett," *Troy Daily Times*, 9 March 1853.

25. "Washington Matters," *Troy Daily Whig*, 12 May 1853.

26. "Impeachment Case," *Northern Budget*, 15 April 1853.

27. Letter of Calvin Mather, 17 May 1853, Thurlow Weed Collection.

28. "A Political Sketch by One of the Old Masters," *Albany Evening Journal*, 10 May 1853.

29. "Death of Calvin M. [sic] Mather," *Troy Daily Whig*, 27 June 1853.

30. Hawley's letter seeks the "name and place" of an engineer whom "sometime since you were kind enough to introduce him [Mather] to" but "in the noise and confusion which sometimes attends legislation management in Albany he [Mather] lost his memorandum." Hawley asks Weed to forward the address to "H. C. Seymour and Co, St. Louis Mo." (Letter of Seth C. Hawley, 10 May 1853, Thurlow Weed Collection).

31. Letter of Alvah Hunt, 7 May 1853, Thurlow Weed Collection.

32. April, according to Brownell, though it might have been first days of May. See Brownell's testimony in "Rensselaer Oyer and Terminer, etc.," *Troy Daily Times*, 25 May 1854.

CHAPTER 7: CONTAGION

1. Assembly Journal, 1853, p. 1384, quoted in *Supplement to the Annual Report of the State Engineer and Surveyor of the State of New York, etc.* (Albany: Brandow Printing, 1906), 211.

2. "We regret to learn that Gen. Calvin E, Mather . . ." *Broome County Republican*, 29 June 1853.

3. "Death of Late Surveyor Gen. Seymour," *Troy Daily Whig*, 27 July 1853.

4. "The Cholera," *Lansingburg Democrat*, 20 July 1854.

5. "Since 1832 the cholera has twice visited Troy, in 1849 and in 1853. During the latter year it was more fatal in its effects than before." William Hagan quoted in George B. Anderson, *Landmarks of Rensselaer County, N. Y.* (Syracuse: D. Mason, 1897), 258.

6. "Eruptions and Hospitals," *Troy Daily Times*, 19 May 1853; "Street Cleaning and Health," *Troy Daily Times*, 12 May 1853; item on "Cannon Place Alley," *Troy Daily Times*, 17 May 1853; "The Troy Hospital," *Troy Daily Times*, 20 May 1853; "Housekeepers should remember . . . ," *Troy Daily Times*, 21 May 1853; "A Suggestion," 24 May 1853.

7. "The Troy Hospital," *Troy Daily Times*, 20 May 1853; he also cites smallpox in "Eruptions and Hospitals," *Troy Daily Times*, 19 May 1853.

8. "A Suggestion," *Troy Daily Times*, 24 May 1853.

9. "The Troy Whig of the 14th inst., etc." *Lansingburg Democrat*, 20 July 1854. ("The whole number of cases . . . is 179 and the number of deaths 115.") But were the newspapers undercounting deaths? In August the wife of George M. Tibbits of Troy wrote to her husband from Newport, R.I., saying, "We hear there is much cholera in Troy . . . You expose yourself very much to be in the city at this time." See Tibbits Papers, New York State Library (hereafter NYSL), box 9, folder 2, Sarah Tibbits to George M. Tibbits, 4 August 1854.

10. Dr. John Snow wouldn't link cholera cases in London to "the Broad Street Pump" until September 1854, and his findings struggled for acceptance for years after this.

11. Charles E. Rosenberg, *The Cholera Years: The United States in 1832, 1849, and 1866* (Univ. of Chicago Press, 1962), 75–81.

12. *New York Herald*, 17 July 1849, quoted in Rosenberg, Cholera Years, 120. In a further twist of belief, it was widely thought that fear itself, in particular the fear of getting cholera, could demoralize the constitution and so result in a case of the disease!

13. The pages of the *Troy Daily Times* reveal the reasons for the 1853 epidemic. Reports of greater-than-average snow and rainfall in the spring of 1853 point to an elevated water table beneath the still sewer-less city. At the same time, new immigrants poured into Troy at a rate almost equaling the growth spurt of 1845–50 when city inhabitants increased from 21,709 to 28,785. In March 1853, the Times noted a population "probably now full up to 31,000" ("Troy Population," 31 March 1853), a good guess since the New York State Census of 1855 would report 33,269. As these arrivals packed into the inner wards, new houses rose on every available lot, with new "vaults" or privies excavated behind each. Though periodically emptied, these privies tended to leak waste into the surrounding earth and water table. And in the spring of 1853 some city officials and householders made a very bad decision: "People begin to go back to the good old system of wells and pumps. Several new wells have been dug, and some old ones reopened. Among the latter we may mention the one opposite the American. Hydrant water [clean reservoir water, piped into the city since the 1830s] is good in its way: but Ross's and the Ferry and

Fourth street pumps would obtain a larger suffrage. The corporation some years ago endeavored to get rid of these old stand-bys, but the million would not permit it." ("Home Matters," *Troy Daily Times*, 1 June 1853)

14. The *Post* issues for 1853 haven't survived, but since neither *Budget*, *Times*, nor *Whig* ran the article(s) referred to by the Willards, and since the Post's successor, the *Troy Daily Traveller*, took the lead in reporting on the Robinson case in 1854–55, it's near certain the Post ran the piece objected to in the Willards' 9 July 1853 letter.

15. "Who Is Mrs. Robinson," *Troy Daily Budget*, 12 June 1854.

16. "Who Is Mrs. Robinson? The Question Answered; The Secret Out." *Troy Daily Times*, 15 March 1855.

17. "Mrs. Robinson—Who Is She?" Troy Daily Times, 8 June 1854; "Who Is Mrs. Robinson?" *Troy Daily Budget*, 12 June 1854 and others.

18. Letter of John Willard quoted in "Is Mrs. Robinson Miss Wood?" *Troy Daily Whig*, 8 June 1854.

19. Emma Willard letter of 1815 quoted in Alma Lutz, *Emma Willard: Daughter of Democracy* (Cambridge, Mass: Riverside Press, 1929), 58.

20. Lutz, *Emma Willard*, 65.

21. These are the official dates of the Wood girls' attendance at the Seminary as reported in the school catalogues; their attendance actually overlapped these dates slightly (Troy Female Seminary Catalogues, 1832–1845, Emma Willard School Archive; W. T. N. Reeve, "Wood Family Genealogy," typescript, 1997 [Reeve is a descendant of Harriet Wood]).

22. "A Famous Girls' School," *New York Tribune*, 31 October 1897.

23. Lutz, Emma Willard, 199.

24. Letter of Thurlow Weed to Francis Granger, 29 May 1838, NYSL. This letter also contains gossip about the family of William Beach, one of Henrietta Robinson's lawyers in 1854–55: "Beach heard of the elopement of his daughter here as he was returning from New York. She was his favorite and has thrown herself away upon a fool." Weed's interest in personalities was obviously one of his charms. New York State Whig William Seward wrote of Weed in this same year: ". . . the sweetness of his temper inclines me to love my tyrant." (Seward quoted in Alexander, *A Political History of the State of New York*, 31)

25. Lutz, Emma Willard, 121.

26. Ibid., 237.

27. "Emma Willard Family Papers," Special Collections and Archives, Amherst College. See "Temporary Finding Aid," 2. This describes an undated Letter W005, now misplaced, from John H. Willard to Emma Willard "Responding to a letter not preserved, in which EW apparently asked to return and again take over running the school . . ."

28. These are items from the 1827 inventory only ("Inventaire des biens de la communeauté d'entre R. Wood et Charlotte Gray," 22 February 1827, No. 37, Papers of Edward Glackmeyer Notary, Archives Nationales du Quebec). The 1847 inventory lists many more furnishings and volumes. ("Inventaire de la succession de dépente Dame Charlotte Gray, veuve de feu Robt. Wood," 4 October 1847, No. 242, Papers of Samuel Isidore Glackmeyer Notary, Archives Nationales du Quebec)

29. Isabella Lucy Bird, *The Englishwoman in America* (London, 1856; repr. Univ. Wisconsin Press, Madison, 1966), 260–65; Amelia M. Murray, Letters from the United States, Cuba and Canada (New York: G. Putnam, 1856), 72–82.

30. "The Trial of Mrs. Robinson for Murder," *Troy Daily Whig*, 25 May 1854.

31. "Account of Robert Wood," Ledger B, unpaged, School Archives, Emma Willard School, Troy.

32. Marianna O' Gallagher et al., "Robert Wood," *Dictionary of Canadian Biography, 1836–1850* (Toronto: Univ. of Toronto Press, 1988), 7:922–23.

CHAPTER 8: LONG HOT SUMMER INTO FALL

1. "Is Mrs. Robinson Miss Wood," *Troy Daily Whig*, 8 June 1854.

2. "Attempted Suicide by Mrs. Robinson," *Troy Daily Budget*, 25 July 1853; "Another Poisoning Case: Attempted Suicide by Mrs. Robinson," *Troy Daily Whig*, 25 July 1853.

3. Rensselaer Oyer and Terminer, etc.," *Troy Daily Times*, 25 May 1854.

4. *Herkimer County at 200* (Herkimer: Herkimer County Historical Society, 1992), 186–88.

5. "Rensselaer Oyer and Terminer, etc.," *Troy Daily Times*, 25 May 1854.

6. "Mrs. Robinson, the Alleged Murderess," *Troy Daily Times*, 11 October 1853.

7. At least he was there on the final day: "Mr. Mather was greeted with cheers on leaving the court . . ." (A National Democrat, *New York Hards and Softs: Which is the True Democracy* (New York: Daily News Job Office, 1856), 47.)

8. "Commissioner Mather At Home," *Albany Argus*, 8 September 1853.

9. *New York Hards and Softs*, 46.

10. Story was quite rough and ready, himself. A glimpse of him in the New York State Legislature in 1850: "A Mr. Story [Minor C. Story] called a Mr. Burroughs [Silas M. Burroughs, in 1853 one of Mather's Senate critics] a liar. When the latter sent a tumbler at the head of the former, whereupon Mr. Story started for Burroughs with the intention of striking him, but was prevented from doing so by the interference of several members . . . I jestingly proposed that we let them fight, for I never knew dogs to be parted, but that they would fight again afterwards . . ." (Letter of W. H. Robertson, Albany, 17 February 1850, Westchester County Historical Society, Elmsford).

11. "Democratic Sentiment; The Bolters," *Albany Evening Atlas*, 20 September 1853.

12. The *Troy Daily Times* was not a Freesoil paper in the early 1850s, though a legend to this effect (see Samuel Rezneck, *Profiles Out of the Past of Troy, New York, Since 1789* [Troy, Greater Chamber of Commerce, 1970], 188) arose due to Francis's later allegiance to the 1855-formed New York State Republican Party; this allegiance would be highlighted by an attack on the *Times* offices by anti-draft rioters in 1863.

13. "Democratic Sentiment; From the Oramel, Alleghany Co., Era," *Albany Evening Atlas*, 20 September 1853.

14. *New York Hards and Softs*, 47.

15. "Mather's Acquittal," *Troy Daily Times*, 17 September 1853.

16. Ibid.

17. "The Impeachment Case: Public Opinion from the Rochester Union," *Albany Evening Atlas*, 20 September 1853.

18. "Democratic Sentiment; Otsego Democrat," *Albany Evening Atlas*, 20 September 1853.

19. "Democratic Nominations," *Albany Evening Atlas*, 16 September 1853.

20. "The Impeachment Case," *Albany Evening Atlas*, 20 September 1853.

21. "The Coons Coming Again!" *Troy Daily Budget*, 15 September 1842.

22. *Speech of the Hon. James Cooley Before the Democracy of Syracuse in Mass Meeting Assembled on Tuesday Evening, Nov. 1, 1853* (New York: John F. Trow, 1853), 31–32.

23. "James T. Brady," *Troy Daily Budget*, 5 November 1853.

24. "A Split Among the Hards," *Troy Daily Budget*, 24 October 1853; "The Troy Whig's Candidate for Governor," *Troy Daily Budget*, 13 June 1854; see also "Death of John C. Mather: A Man with a History," *Troy Daily Times*, 15 August 1882 ("As the time for the Democratic state convention in 1852 drew nigh, Mr. Mather's name was proposed in many quarters for the office of governor.")

25. "Engrossed Minutes of the Canal Commissioners."

26. "Session Minutes of Second Street Presbyterian Church," vol. 1, 258.

27. Ibid., 271.

CHAPTER 9: LIMBO TIME

1. "Settlement of a Libel Suit," *Troy Daily Times*, 17 February 1854.

2. "The Troy Whig's Candidate for Governor," *Troy Daily Budget*, 13 June 1854.

3. Through the *Troy Daily Times*, we can almost see the change in public opinion in process. A play of Harriet Beecher Stowe's "Uncle Tom's Cabin" had drawn large crowds to the Troy Museum, the second floor theater located above the ground floor stalls of the Fulton Market building, from at least as early as 1852. "Home Matters," *Troy Daily Times*, 2 November 1852 ("Death of Uncle Tom' is still being played at Museum. It is having a good run."); "Home Matters," *Troy Daily Times*, 29 November 1852. The play was then revived in 1853 ("No 'let-up' to the rush at the Museum to witness 'Uncle Tom's Cabin,' " reads the *Times* of 23 April 1853) a revival which ran until 3 April 1854, when the *Times* reported the "last night of Uncle Tom."

4. "Impudence of the Whigs," *Troy Daily Budget*, 10 October 1853. There are many other references to Mather's placement of the ads in the *Whig* in contemporary papers.

5. "Home Matters," *Troy Daily Times*, 11 October 1853.

6. "The Troy Whig's Candidate for Governor," *Troy Daily Budget*, 13 June 1854; see also *Troy Daily Whig*, 2 June 1853, and "The Mather Impeachment Case, "*Troy Daily Whig*, 23 June 1853, and "The Mather Impeachment Case," *Troy Daily Whig*, 1 July 1853 for further friendly mentions of Mather by the *Whig*.

7. See *Troy Daily Traveller* issue of 21 July 1855 for "Mrs. Robinson At Prayer" article as well as another page two article praising the Hards in some recent skirmish with the Softs.

8. Alleged by Henrietta Robinson.

9. "Home Matters: Mrs. Robinson's trial for murder . . ." *Troy Daily Times*, 24 February 1854, citing an earlier *Atlas* article.

10. "Home Matters: In the Circuit Court . . ." *Troy Daily Times*, 29 February 1854.

11. Ibid. (". . . there is no doubt but the trial will be put over to the April term.")

12. "On Tuesday, the District Attorney . . ." *Lansingburg Democrat*, 4 April 1854.

13. *Burke's Peerage* (1890), 490; William R. O'Byrne, *A Naval Biographical Dictionary Comprising the Life and Services of Every Living Officer in Her Majesty's Navy, Etc.* (London: John Murray, 1849), 331.

14. Curiously, April 8 was Charlotte Wood Eliott's birthday.

15. W. H. Jeffery to G. M. Tibbits, 8 April 1854, Tibbits Family Papers, box 104, folder 1, NYSL

16. "Is Mrs. Robinson Miss Wood," *Troy Daily Whig*, 8 June 1854.

17. Wilson, *Henrietta Robinson*, 67–68.

CHAPTER 10: DAY 1—OFFICERS OF THE COURT

1. "County Court, Court of Sessions, etc.," *Troy Daily Times*, 22 May 1854.

2. "Home Matters; County Court, Court of Sessions and Adjourned Oyer and Terminer," *Troy Daily Times*, 22 May 1854.

3. Mather would essentially admit this connection to the elders of his church on 17 July 1854. Session Minutes of the Second Street Presbyterian Church, vol 1, 171.

4. "Democratic Whig Nominations," *Albany Evening Journal*, 27 October 1846.

5. This was yet another big issue for antebellum New Yorkers: the battle between large landholders, like the Van Rensselaers of Rensselaer County and tenants trying to break archaic leases.

6. "Death of Judge Harris," *Albany Evening Journal*, 2 December 1875, reprinted in *Memorial of Ira Harris* (Albany: 1876), 11–12. Harris's daughter Clara was actually a guest in Lincoln's box at the Ford Theater on the night of the President's assassination in 1865.

7. "The Whig thinks, etc.," *Troy Daily Budget*, 29 October 1853. In this article the *Budget* accuses the *Whig* of slyly disparaging Bingham, then Whig candidate for District Attorney.

8. "The Tory Whig's Candidate for Governor," *Troy Daily Budget*, 13 June 1854.

9. F. B. Hough, "Henry Hogeboom," *American Biographical Notes* (1875) in *American Biographical Index* (microfiche).

10. "Assemblymen," *Troy Daily Times*, 6 January 1852.

11. Rezneck, *Profiles*, 114.

12. George B. Anderson, *Landmarks of Rensselaer County, N.Y.* (Syracuse: D. Mason, 1897), 164.

13. "Home Matters; William A. Beach, Esq., of Troy . . ." *Troy Daily Times*, 4 August 1853; it's just possible Beach was a Whig; a William Beach appears on an 1852 list of New York State legislators, as a Whig representing the 24th District (Cayuga County). See *Troy Daily Times*, 6 January 1852.

14. G. J. Clark, *Life Sketches of Eminent Lawyers*, 2 vols. (New York, 1895) in "William Augustus Beach," *American Biographical Index.*

15. "Whig District Convention," *Troy Daily Times*, 10 September 1851; "The Ward Tickets," *Troy Daily Times*, 3 March 1852.

16. C. Lanman, *Biographical Annals of the Civil Government of the United States,Etc.*, (1876) in *American Biographical Index.*

17. Washington County-raised Walter Geer had worked as a tanner in Schaghticoke in his twenties and then relocated up the Hudson to Glens Falls in Warren County, where he expanded his tanning business into general merchandise and lumber. Walter Geer played a big role in the growth of Glens Falls as a promoter and builder of the Glens Falls Feeder Canal and donor to the Second Presbyterian Church and Glens Falls Academy. The "judge" came from his 1821–26 service as a Town of Queensbury (Warren County) magistrate. Briefly a member of the state assembly in the 1830s, he kept a hand in politics and a hand in the nearby urban center of Troy until his death in July 1855. See Walter Geer, *The Geer Genealogy: A Historical Record of George and Thomas Geer, etc.* (New York: Brentano, 1923), 315–16.

18. "Commissioner Mather At Home," *Troy Daily Times*, 8 September 1853; "Home Matters; Our woolly-head neighbor, etc." *Troy Daily Times*, 10 September 1853; "More Brotherly Harmony!" *Troy Daily Times*, 18 September 1853; "Local Summary; Second Ward 'Union and Harmony' Meeting," *Troy Daily Budget*, 3 March 1854. Interestingly, Jennyss had studied law in Job Pierson's office. "Obituary [Richard C. Jennyss]: Death of One of the Oldest Members of the Rennselaer County Bar, etc." *Troy Daily Times*, 7 July 1898.

19. Giles B. Kellogg, also from Williamstown and another Soft, was his partner.

20. R. A. Parmenter, "A Lawyer's Tribute," *Troy Daily Times*, 22 June 1898.

21. John Francis of the *Times* was not an *open* opponent of slavery until late 1854 at the earliest; in July of 1854, in condemning the "repeal of the Missouri Compromise and the re-opening of the slavery agitation," he called this action "an insult to . . . every man who respects the good faith of the nation, who would maintain the integrity of the Union, who loves his country better than chattel niggers . . ." ("Hardshell Convention," *Troy Daily Times*, 11 July 1854).

22. R. A. Parmenter, "A Lawyer's Tribute," *Troy Daily Times*, 22 June 1898.

23. Charles W—, "Legal Lights of Long Ago," *Troy Daily Press*, 20 January 1894.

24. A glancing analysis of records from the late 1830s reveals Townsend as one of the busiest book borrowers of the Troy Young Men's Association Library (Records of the Y. M. A., "Library Records," vol. 1, 1836–39, borrowers #295, #788, TPL). He continued to borrow through the 1840s and 1850s, and probably beyond, but this writer didn't investigate those borrowings. John C. Mather borrowed few books in all, and these mainly in 1838–41 (vol. 2, 1839–40, 88, borrower #1033).

25. Martin I. Townsend, *Prehistoric Structures of Central America: Who Erected Them?* (Troy, 1895); Martin I. Townsend, *The English Townsends; The Tancreds Crusaders; The Townsends of Watertown, Mass; The Townsends of Hebron, Conn. and of Hancock, Mass.* (Troy: T. J. Hurley, 1899).

26. "Scraps from the Journal of Martin I. Townsend, Esq., in Europe in the Year 1850," *Troy Daily Budget*, 31 May 1850; 1 June 1850; 3 June 1850.

27. "Famous Murder Mystery Solved," *Troy Northern Budget*, 19 June 1898, 12.

28. Ibid.

29. "Home Matters; The veil of mystery . . ." *Troy Daily Times*, 15 June 1854, quoting the *Albany Evening Atlas*. And at just this time, the anti-Mather *Troy Daily Budget* reported: "Mrs. Robinson has been in possession of means sufficient for her defence [*sic*] which she has claimed she received from her family" ("Who Is Mrs. Robinson?" *Troy Daily Budget*, 16 June 1854.

30. "Rensselaer Oyer and Terminer, etc." *Troy Daily Whig*, 23 May 1854. Also "Rensselaer Oyer and Terminer," *Troy Daily Budget*, 23 May 1854.

31. We have portions of its trial coverage ("Condensed from the Traveler") in the *Albany Evening Journal* of 25 May 1854, 26 May 1854, and 27 May 1854.

32. "Rensselaer Oyer and Terminer, etc." *Troy Daily Times*, 23 May 1854.

33. Wilson, *Henrietta Robinson*, 72.

34. "Abolition of Capital Punishment," *Troy Daily Times*, 18 February 1852.

35. "Rensselaer Oyer and Terminer, etc.," *Troy Daily Times*, 23 May 1854.

36. "Hardshell Convention," *Troy Daily Times*, 11 July 1854.

37. "Death of Hon. Alanson Cook," *Troy Daily Press*, 26 October 1880.

38. Wilson, *Henrietta Robinson*, 73.

39. The *Times* reported Robinson had lived on River Street "something over a year" ("Horrible; Double Murder By Poisoning," *Troy Daily Times*, 26 May 1853.)

40. Ibid.

41. "Rensselaer Oyer and Terminer, etc." *Troy Daily Times*, 23 May 1854.

CHAPTER 11: DAY 2—THE DOCTORS

1. Ibid.

2. Ibid.

3. Anderson, *Landmarks of Rensselaer County*, 180.

4. William A. Guy was the author of *Principles of Forensic Medicine*, published in London in 1844. Robert Christison was a baronet by the time his *A Treatise on Poisons*, first published in Edinburgh, came out in the United States (1845). Matthew Orfila, a Spaniard, published *Traite des Poisons* in Paris in 1813; he was the first to develop a forensic test for arsenic in the 1840s. T. Romeyn Beck published the first edition of his later updated *The Elements of Medical Jurisprudence* in Albany in 1823.

5. "Rensselaer Oyer and Terminer, etc.," *Troy Daily Times*, 23 May 1854.

6. Ibid.

7. Rensselaer Oyer and Terminer, etc.," *Troy Daily Times*, 24 May 1854

8. Ibid.

9. Ibid.

10. Ibid.

11. His testimony was (and is) unclear about the number of visits and when they occurred, save for the last one on the evening of the 25th, just prior to Robinson's arrest. It may be that Robinson had purchased the arsenic on the evening of the 21st and then stopped in at the drugstore an hour or so later on her way to Mather's boardinghouse. But some of Ostrom's testimony seems to place the arsenic purchase on another "Saturday evening [visit] when I saw a revolver or the muzzle of one in her dress," about one week earlier, "within two or three days of the 10th of May."

12. "Rensselaer Oyer and Terminer, etc.," *Troy Daily Times*, 24 May 1854.

CHAPTER 12: DAY 3—THE VEIL

1. Ibid.

2. "The Trial of Mrs. Robinson for Murder at Troy,"*Albany Evening Atlas*, 25 May 1854.

3. Wilson, *Henrietta Robinson*, 103.

4. Ibid., 105.

5. "Rensselaer Oyer and Terminer, etc.," *Troy Daily Budget*, 24 May 1854.

6. Bontecou had only uttered, "I conversed with her in jail," when Harris gave his new order about the veil (ibid.)

7. Ibid.

8. "The Troy Poisoning Case," *Albany Evening Atlas*, 24 May 1854

9. "Rensselaer Oyer and Terminer, etc.," *Troy Daily Times*, 24 May 1854.

10. "Rensselaer Oyer and Terminer, etc.," *Troy Daily Budget*, 24 May 1854.

11An article submitted to the *Buffalo Medical Journal* of July 1852 by a Lockport, New York doctor gives a picture of the rough-and-ready science involved:

"I poured the contents of the stomach into a vessel, and boiled them for fifteen minutes, when, in company with Dr. Worcester, I proceeded to test the fluid . . . Our apparatus was simply a Florence flask, with a cork nicely adjusted, through which passed a glass tube, furnished at its upper end with a jet of fine bore.

. . . [after introducing] 3 ss. of the fluid from the stomach, applied a lighted taper to the gas as it came over, when we at once got the dull white flame of arsenic. A plate of porcelain was brought over the flame, when it was immediately coated with a thick, metallic crust of arsenic, and so abundant was it that we have no hesitation in saying that, from one-half ounce of fluid we might have coated a surface of eighteen inches square with metallic arsenic. Not wishing to inhale the black suffocating smoke which it so abundantly produced, we were obliged to throw open the windows . . .

The wife of the diseased [*sic*], with several domestics were under arrest, and the court was waiting for us; yet, in a hurried manner, we instituted several other tests.

. . . Upon . . . [additional] fluid we instituted the ammoniacal nitrate of silver test, and readily produced the characteristic lemon yellow precipitate, which soon passed to a dark brown, on exposure to the light."

We next proceeded with the ammoniacal sulphate of copper test in the same manner, and readily produced the grass green precipitate. We burned a portion of the powder as obtained from the stomach, upon charcoal, and obtained a distinct garlic odor." (A. M. Leonard, "Case of Poisoning from Arsenic," *Buffalo Medical Journal and Monthly Review*, 8 (1852): 68–70.)

12. In June 1855, the *New York Weekly Tribune* reported on 25 people poisoned "by eating custard in which arsenic had been placed" ("Bridal Party Poisoned," *New York Weekly Tribune*, 9 June 1855, 1); a decade earlier political partisans in Yorkville, N.Y., it was charged, had poisoned 36 horses "by putting arsenic in their drinking trough." ("Diabolical Act, 36 Horses Poisoned," *The Huntress* [Washington, D.C.] 21 June 1845). Poison was not especially a woman's weapon at this time. In

July 1853, as Henrietta Robinson lay in her Troy jail cell, an Albany County judge pronounced a death sentence on a man from nearby Bethlehem, John Hendrickson, who had fatally poisoned his 19-year-old wife ("Hendrickson Trial," *Troy Daily Budget*, 9 July 1853). There was also the 1845 case of Henry Green, mentioned earlier, and Troy newspapers of the early 1850s contain notices about other wife-poisoners: John Erpenstein of Newark, N.J. ("A Murderer's Prayer," *Troy Daily Times*, 1 April 1852—Erpenstein killed other family members too); Henry Hawes of West Troy ("The West Troy Poisoning Case," *Troy Daily Budget*, 28 July 1853); and Charles Saunders of Saratoga Springs ("The *Saratoga Whig* says . . ." *Lansingburg Democrat*, 20 July 1854). All these murderers used arsenic, except Hendrickson who had, unusually, employed aconite.

13. "Rensselaer Oyer and Terminer, etc.," *Troy Daily Budget*, 24 May 1854.
14. "Rensselaer Oyer and Terminer," *Troy Daily Times*, 25 May 1854
15. Ibid.
16. Ibid.
17. Ibid.
18. Ibid.
19. Judge Ira Harris' Charge to the Jury in *Troy Daily Whig*, 29 May 1854.
20. At least it shocked Judge Harris (ibid.)
21. "Rensselaer Oyer and Terminer, etc.," *Troy Daily Times*, 25 May 1854.
22. Wilson, *Henrietta Robinson*, 142.
23. "Rensselaer Oyer and Terminer, etc.," *Troy Daily Times*, 25 May 1854
24. Ibid.

CHAPTER 13: DAY 4—BOMBSHELL

1. "The Trial of Mrs. Robinson for Murder," *Troy Daily Whig*, 25 May 1854.
2. "Rensselaer Oyer and Terminer, etc.," *Troy Daily Whig*, 26 May 1854.
3. "Rensselaer Oyer and Terminer, etc.," *Troy Daily Times*, 25 May 1854
4. Ibid.
5. "Rensselaer Oyer and Terminer, etc.," *Troy Daily Budget*, 25 May 1854
6. "Rensselaer Oyer and Terminer, etc.," *Troy Daily Budget*, 27 May 1854.
7. "Famous Murder Mystery Solved," *Troy Northern Budget*, 19 June 1898, 13.
8. "The Troy Whig's Candidate for Governor," *Troy Daily Budget*, 13 June 1854.
9. "Almost certainly," since 1853 *Post* issues haven't survived. As mentioned earlier, a process of elimination points to the *Post*, since the item *didn't appear* in any other of the Troy dailies.
10. While the *Whig* published positive notices on Mather beginning 2 June 1853, this followed a spate of harshly negative notices in mid-May (see 10 May 1853, 12 May 1853, etc.)
11. "The Old Court House; George Tibbits," *Troy Daily Times*, 5 June 1895.
12. "In the year 1853 at the annual election for officers [in January] George B. Warren, jr. and J. B. Tibbits were opposing candidates for the presidency. The canvas was very exciting. Money was freely used to purchase tickets for voters, and the strife grew so great at the polls that a riot was feared. Three thousand votes were cast amid scenes of great excitement and Mr. Warren was elected . . . the

strife had been so bitter and the animosity engendered between rival candidates so strong, that many persons withdrew from the affairs of the association." (Anderson, *Landmarks of Rensselaer County*, 353)

13. In line with this, while Troy newspapers of the 1850s lambasted one another all the time, they were never as violent in their attacks as the *Argus* (Hard) and *Evening Atlas* (Freesoil-Soft) of three times more populous Albany.

14. Either father or son; both were Troy Democrats.

15. Engrossed Minutes of the Canal Commissioners, 1849–1857, entry for 19 December 1851, "Lettings."

16. "Rensselaer Oyer and Terminer, etc.," *Troy Daily Times*, 26 May 1854

17. There exists a letter (about a property matter) from a John A. Upton to George Patterson dated 23 February 1862 (Patterson Papers, University of Rochester Library). George Patterson was one of Thurlow Weed's close associates. But it doesn't seem likely Upton was coming forward as a tool of Weed's in the 1854 trial; Weed's newspaper, the *Albany Evening Journal*, gave scant notice to Upton's testimony and no notice to the longer speech by Prosecutor Hogeboom about Upton's testimony.

18. "Rensselaer Oyer and Terminer, etc." *Troy Daily Times*, 26 May 1854.

19. Ibid.

CHAPTER 14: DAY 5—SOME ANTEBELLUM LORE

1. Wilson, *Henrietta Robinson*,, 192.

2. Ibid., 165. (What was the terrible story of Conway and Groesbeck, we wonder?)

3. Ibid.

4. Robert M. Ireland, "Frenzied and Fallen Females," *Journal of Women's History* Winter, (1992): 98–99.

5. See "Rensselaer Oyer and Terminer, etc." *Troy Daily Budget*, 26 May 1854 ("He adverted to the case of Phelps . . .") David Wilson may have confused this reference with another Phelps murder case in his account of the trial (see his p. 165). A John Phelps murdered his wife in West Troy in April 1854, but was not tried until November 1854 (see Troy Daily Times, 21 November 1854).

6. "Law Cases Bearing on the Subject of Insanity: Trial of Adeline Phelps, alias Bass, for the Murder of her Father, Elihu Phelps," *The American Journal of Insanity*, 11 (1854–55): 63-64.

7. Ibid., 68.

8. Ibid., 69.

9. Thomas M. McDade, ed., *The Annals of Murder: A Bibliography of Books and Pamphlets on American Murders from Colonial Times to 1900* (Norman: Univ. of Oklahoma Press, 1961), 307–8.

10. Wilson, *Henrietta Robinson*,, 165–66.

11. "Rensselaer Oyer and Terminer, etc." *Troy Daily Budget*, 26 May 1854.

12. Jean-Etienne-Dominique Esquirol, *Mental Maladies: A Treatise on Insanity* (1845; repr New York: Hafner, 1965), 362.

13. Esquirol's honest empiricism didn't allow him to find women always more subject to madness than men. He pondered over the fact that "in France the

proportion of [insane] women is much greater than in England," yet noted that in his own Salpêtrière Hospital "there were received during twelve years, one hundred ninety-one men, and one hundred forty-four women." He also found—not usefully to modern eyes—that in the Salpêtrière chestnut-haired and brown-eyed patients predominated and that: "In general, those who have black hair, who are strong, robust, and of a sanguine temperament, are maniacs and furious . . . Those whose hair is of a flaxen color, who have blue eyes, and a lymphatic temperament become maniacs and monomaniacs; but their insanity passes readily into a chronic state, and degenerates into dementia . . . Those who have red hair, are furious, traitorous and dangerous." (Esquirol, *Mental Maladies*, 38)

14. Also cited in such American works as: Isaac Ray, *A Treatise on the Medical Jurisprudence of Insanity* (1838) and Edward Jarvis, *Causes of Insanity* (1851).

15. "Rensselaer Co. Oyer and Terminer, etc.," *Troy Daily Budget*, 26 May 1854.

16. Ibid.

17. Ibid.

18. Wilson, *Henrietta Robinson*, 177.

19. Ibid., 180.

20. Ibid., 191.

21. Robert M. Ireland, "Frenzied and Fallen Females," 95–112.

22. Wilson, *Henrietta Robinson*, 182.

23. This rumor wouldn't appear in print (*Troy Daily Times*) until 31 May 1854, but had surely circulated in Troy earlier.

24. Wilson, 187–88.

25. The idea of "diminished capacity" was not introduced into New York State law until the mid-20th century. Currently, a New York State jury finding of diminished capacity, from drugs or alcohol or some other cause, rules out a conviction for murder, replacing it with a manslaughter one.

26. He (and Townsend, too) may have known the French and British writers only through the work of Maine's Isaac Ray, who published A Treatise on the Medical Jurisprudence of Insanity in 1838. Van Santvoord cited a particular case found in Ray: "A man may suppose his leg is of glass, and on all other subjects be of perfectly sound mind. There is one such case reported. This is monomania . . ." (See Wilson, *Henrietta Robinson*, 183)

27. Wilson, *Henrietta Robinson*, 186.

28. Ibid.

29. One example: a serial, "The Destroyer and His Victim," about a male seducer (*Troy Daily Times*, 12 March 1853–22 March 1853).

30. Wilson, *Henrietta Robinson*, 189.

31. Moore, *Lalla Rookh*; see also Wilson, *Henrietta Robinson*, 291.

32. Ibid., 182.

33. Ibid., 182.

34. Ibid., 191.

35. None of the other Troy or Albany papers carried this apology to Mather.

36. Both public and private business often ran late in antebellum Troy—we remember Robinson's 9:00 P.M. visit to Ostrom's Drugstore—at least during spring and summer months.

CHAPTER 15: DAY 6—VERDICT

1. "Rensselaer Oyer and Terminer, etc.," *Troy Daily Whig*, 29 May 1854.
2. Ibid.
3. Wilson, *Henrietta Robinson*, 205.
4. Ibid., 209.
5. Ibid.
6. "Rensselaer Oyer and Terminer, etc.," *Troy Daily Times*, 29 May 1854
7. Wilson, *Henrietta Robinson*, 218–19.
8. "Rensselaer Oyer and Terminer, etc.," *Troy Daily Times*, 29 May 1854.
9. "Rensselaer Oyer and Terminer, etc.," *Troy Daily Whig*, 29 May 1854.
10. "Rensselaer Oyer and Terminer, etc.," *Troy Daily Times*, 29 May 1854.
11. Was Phelps's age and unattractiveness balanced out in jurors' subconscious minds by the cruelty of her victim-father in disinheriting her?
12. "Mrs. Robinson, the Veiled Murderess: Her Departure for Sing Sing," *Troy Daily Traveller*, 31 July 1855.
13. "Only Living Juror," *Troy Northern Budget*, 22 October 1899.
14. Ibid. A further hint of Irish strength in Troy proper *may* be found in the *Troy Daily Times* of June, 1854: ". . . two gentlemen named Potter and Gunsalus, residents of the Village [Cohoes], were riding through Cohoes, Saturday afternoon when they were stopped by some Irishmen, and a white hat which one of them wore, was taken from his head and trodden upon by the Irishmen, remarking at the same time that they supposed he was a "d—d know nothing." Some if not the entire party were arrested . . ." (*Troy Daily Times*, quoted in *West Troy Advocate*, 28 June 1854). Nativists, the "Know Nothings," often wore round, white hats with the brims turned up all around. But the significance of the Cohoes incident is that no similar incident was ever reported as occurring in Troy. No one was foolish enough to wear a round, white hat in the street there.
15. Augustus J. Thébaud, *Three-Quarters of a Century, 1807–1882: A Retrospect* (New York: U. S. Catholic Historicval Society, 1904), 3:110–11.
16. See "A Princely Gift," *Troy Daily Times*, 17 May 1855; also NYSL Catalogue "bio" on George Tibbits family.
17. Thébaud, *Three-Quarters of a Century*, 112.
18. The *Troy Daily Times* and *Troy Daily Whig* often printed these, and it is strange today to confront Beman's ideas: in his sermons, native-born Protestants become democratic underdogs resisting the country's takeover by Old European hierarchy and aristocracy, represented by deceptively humble new immigrants.
19. Beman was a *quiet* abolitionist in terms of his published sermons in Troy newspapers of 1853–55. Anti-Catholicism was his real issue across these years.
20. J. Matthew Gallman, *Receiving Erin's Children: Philadelphia, Liverpool, and the Irish Famine Migration, 1845–1855* (Chapel Hill: Univ. of North Carolina Press, 2000).
21. "Account of Robert Wood," Ledger B, unpaged, Emma Willard School Archives, Troy.
22. "Henry Burden," in Troy Scrapbook No. 170, pp. 109–110 (clipping marked January 1891).

23. Thébaud, *Three-Quarters of a Century*, 120. Also see "Home Matters," *Troy Daily Times*, 25 February 1853 for a pro-management account of this accident.

24. Elizabeth Oakes Smith, "Letters from the People–A Visit to the Veiled Murderess," *New York Daily Tribune*, 28 July 1855.

25. Calvin's link to pro-Nativist George Law and John C.'s own sometime connection with the Nativist *Troy Daily Whig*, plus a few other "straws in the wind" support Robinson's claim about Mather's connection to Clark.

26. John C. Mather, *Closing the Canal Locks on the Sabbath: Remarks of Hon. John C. Mather of New York, Etc . . . in Senate, Tuesday, March 29, 1859* (Albany, 1859), 4.

27. William Abbott: "We were supposed to be all good fellows and temperate. One day we were at dinner and had mince pie. One of the men declared there was brandy in the pie, and then we wanted to know how he, a temperate man, could tell there was brandy in the pie. It took that juror sometime to explain matters to our satisfaction . . ." ("Only Living Juror," *Troy Northern Budget*, 22 October 1899).

28. "Rensselaer Oyer and Terminer, etc.," *Troy Daily Times*, 29 May 1854

29. Wilson, *Henrietta Robinson*, 239.

30. Ibid., 239–40.

31. "Rensselaer Oyer and Terminer, etc.," *Troy Daily Times*, 29 May 1854.

CHAPTER 16: SETTLED BUT NOT SETTLED

1. Ibid.

2. Alleged technical flaws in empaneling the Grand Jury, flaws in the indictment, and the claim that one juror had "expressed the opinion prior to the trial that Mrs. Robinson was guilty." *Troy Daily Times*, 29 May 1854

3. Ibid.

4. "The Trial and Conviction of Mrs. Robinson," *Troy Daily Times*, 29 May 1854.

5. *Troy Daily Times* item cited in "A woman who was . . . ," *Auburn Advertiser*, 9 June 1854.

6. "The Trial and Conviction of Mrs. Robinson," *Troy Daily Times*, 29 May 1854.

7. "Mrs. Robinson; The Veiled Lady," *Utica Morning Herald*, 30 May 1854 (quoting *Troy Daily Whig* of 25 May 1854); "Mrs. Robinson; Convicted of Murder!" *Lansingburg Democrat*, 1 June 1854 (quoting *Troy Daily Whig* of 25 May 1854).

8. "The Whig is trying to make out . . ." *Troy Daily Budget*, 31 May 1854.

9. "Having got through . . . ," *Troy Daily Budget*, 30 May 1854.

CHAPTER 17: BREAKING OF THE STORM

1. "Is Mrs. Robinson Miss Wood?" *Troy Daily Whig*, 8 June 1854. (The *Quebec Gazette* published Wood's note on 6 June 1854.)

2. Ibid. Willard's letter also provided the Wood sisters' addresses:

"Georgianna, the eldest, is living in London. She is the widow of William Capel Clayton, the eldest son of Sir William Robert Clayton, Bart, of Harleywood, Marlow, England.

Emma, the second, is the wife of Dr. McIntosh, recently surgeon of the Royal Artillery, son of the late celebrated Dr. McIntosh of Edinburg, and she is now living in Scotland.

Charlotte, the third daughter, is married to the eldest son of Sir William Francis Elliott, Bart, of Stob's Castle, Roxburgshire, Scotland, in which country she and her husband reside.

Harriet, the fourth daughter, resides in Dublin, with her husband Capt Mackay, of the Royal Artillery, who is now stationed in that city. Capt. Mackay is the son of the late Col. Mackay of Bighouse, Scotland. Maria, the youngest daughter, who was never at the Seminary, is now residing with her sister, Mrs. Mackintosh."

3. "Famous Murder Mystery Solved," *Troy Northern Budget*, 19 June 1898.

4. "Who Is Mrs. Robinson?" *Troy Daily Budget*, 12 June 1854.

5. Ibid.

6. See payments for the two newspapers in John Willard's Cash Book No. 6, 3 March 1853, Emma Willard School Archives, Troy. Emma Willard fell in with the *Troy Daily Whig*'s "conservative" views on slavery; see Anne Firor Scott, "The Ever-Widening Circle: The Diffusion of Feminist Values from the Troy Female Seminary, 1822–1872," *History of Education Quarterly* 19: 1–20.

7. No relation of Martin I. Townsend. See listing of City Officers in *MacArthur and Wilson's Troy City Directory for the Years 1853–4* (Troy: C. L. MacArthur, 1853).

8. "The Troy Whig's Candidate for Governor," *Troy Daily Budget*, 13 June 1854.

9. Though the prosecution never admitted Mather's involvement with Robinson, they surely realized that Upton's testimony had clinched this fact for the jury.

10. Willard tried to defend himself in a letter to the *Times* the next day: "There are at this time about one hundred and fifty young ladies in the Seminary, whose evenings for study must be entirely lost whenever a band is performing in its immediate vicinity. The summer examination is now within about three weeks of its commencement; there is to be a large visiting committee of distinguished gentlemen and ladies from abroad, to whom, for the credit of the city as well as of the Seminary, it is desirable, etc." ("Mr. Willard's 'Objections,' " *Troy Daily Times*, 25 May 1853) Francis's criticism of Willard seems a bit hard since he (Francis) then blasted the relocated concert's attendees: "Last evening the experiment was tried of giving the public a musical entertainment al fresco. Judging from the effects it produced, it is our candid opinion that a judicious application of cow-hides to the rabble assembled around Washington Park, administered with extreme unction by an able-bodied corps of policemen, would have been quite salutary . . . The crowd of tatterdemalions who infested the highways last evening . . . conducted itself less like a company of human beings than the bears and paving-stones are reported to have done under the influential lyre of Orpheus . . . Brats, urchins, and the rag-tag and bob-tail incontinently felt inspired with the spirit of liberty and independence . . . Such a screeching, yelping and howling assailed the ear on all sides . . ." ("Music for the Millions," *Troy Daily Times*, 25 May 1853.)

11. "Home Matters: Who Is the Veiled Murderess?" *Troy Daily Times*, 12 June 1855.

12. *Atlas* quoted in "Home Matters; The veil of mystery . . ." *Troy Daily Times*, 15 June 1854.

13. "Who Is Mrs. Robinson?" *Lansingburg Democrat*, 15 June 1854.

14. "Who Is Mrs. Robinson?" *Troy Daily Budget*, 16 June 1854.

15. Letter of W. Wood to "My Dear Bea," dated "32 Green Street, Park Lane, June 5/[18]96," courtesy of Lady Frances Eliott.

16. "Who is Mrs. Robinson?" *Troy Daily Budget*, 16 June 1854.

17. Ibid.

18. Rensselaer County Deeds, 60: 185 (Oliver Boutwell to John G. Britton, 10 April 1844). Boutwell had originally purchased the property from the Troy Hydraulic Co., developers of the State Dam canalway, on 20 June 1837, but then had gotten into financial trouble. The above deed describes some confusing transactions involving Chancery Court and a James Corning, but the upshot was Britton got the property in 1844.

19. Rensselaer County Deeds, 73: 133 (John G. Britton to Oliver Boutwell, 4 December 1849).

20. In January of 1854, Britton died leaving a son of the same name. The *Troy Daily Times* of 17 May 1855 records a surprising item about John G. II: "We noticed a day or two since the arrest of John G. Britton, in this city, on a charge of grand larceny . . . [later exonerated]" Yet it is likely that the 15 June 1854 *Budget* reference to "John G. Britton" meant the recently-deceased father (with this person being the same John G. who went to the dinner and bought the cottage) because Troy directories of the early 1850s only list a single "John G. Britton."

21. The lack of praise for moral or religious qualities in his obituaries is striking compared with other obituaries of the day. See "Home Matters: Death of John G. Britton—Meeting of the Bar," *Troy Daily Times*, 24 January1854; "Death of John G. Britton," *Lansingburg Democrat*, 26 January 1854. The *Lansingburg Democrat* even seemed to apologize for their own Britton eulogy by running a short item below the obituary, which urged readers to "speak kindly and deal gently with our fellow-men, whatever their condition of circumstances, whether poor or despised, erring or refractory . . ." The item included these lines of poetry:

> "It is a little thing to speak a phrase
> Of common comfort, which by daily use
> Has almost lost his [*sic*] sense; yet on the ear
> Of him who thought to die unmourned, 'twill fall
> Like choicest music."

22. "Who Is Mrs. Robinson?" *Troy Daily Times*, 16 June 1854.

23. "Mrs. Robinson—Mr. Wood" *Troy Daily Budget*, 17 June 1854.

24. "Who Is Mrs. Robinson?" *Troy Daily Times*, 17 June 1854.

25. "Who Is Mrs. Robinson?" *Troy Daily Times*, 6 July 1854; Renssley's affidavit was sworn before William Hegeman, by this date Troy Commissioner of Deeds.

26. "Serious Assault on Sheriff Price by Mrs. Robinson," *Troy Daily Times*, 10 July 1854.

27. "Troy Scrapbooks," vol. 189, p. 54 (undated newspaper clipping from the late nineteenth or early twentieth century).

28. Ibid.

CHAPTER 18: MORE MATHER

1. Session Minutes of the Second Street Presbyterian Church, 271.

2. Ibid., 118, 196.

3. Ibid., 193–94.

4. Ibid., 248, 259.

5. Greeley quoted in Alexander, *Political History*, 2:22.

6. Henry B. Stanton, *Random Recollections*, 2nd ed. (New York: Macgowan and Slipper, 1886), 19.

7. Hudson C. Tanner, *The Lobby and Public Men from Thurlow Weed's Time* (Albany: 1888), 26. Tanner's stories are heavy on allusion, given the Victorian-era publication of his book.

8. Harriet Weed, ed., *Thurlow Weed's Autobiography* (Boston: Houghton and Mifflin, 1884), 1:564–65.

9. Ibid., 1:563–69.

10. Letter of Sherman Croswell to Thurlow Weed (undated but among letters of 1852–53) Thurlow Weed Collection, University of Rochester.

11. Alexander, *A Political History of the State of New York*, 199. And let's not forget the "mastodon," George Law.

12. "An Indignant Millerite," *Troy Daily Times*, 21 July 1852.

CHAPTER 19: TRENDS

1. A cycle which obviously had something to do with court session schedules (and maybe election times).

2. One year after its organization in some Midwestern states.

3. Alexander, 197.

4. Ibid.

5. Alexander, 201.

6. Ibid., 210.

7. "Mrs. Robinson's Case," *Troy Daily Times*, 15 September 1854.

8. "False Issue," *Troy Daily Traveller*, 28 November 1854.

9. "A New Issue in the Mrs. Robinson Case," *Troy Daily Times*, 26 November 1854.

10. There are no surviving *Budgets* from this period to establish which paper had the "scoop." But the *Traveller* article of 28 November 1854 seems to say the *Traveller* initiated the story.

11. "False Issue," *Troy Daily Traveller*, 28 November 1854.

12. See "Who Is Mrs. Robinson; The Mystery Revived," *Troy Daily Whig*, 16 March 1855.

CHAPTER 20: CHARLOTTE WOOD

1. "Who Is Henrietta Robinson? The Mystery Revived," *Troy Daily Whig*, 16 March 1855.

2. "Mrs. Robinson," *Troy Daily Traveller*, 17 March 1855.

3. "Mrs. Robinson," *Troy Daily Traveller*, 24 March 1855.

4. "What Mrs. Robinson Says of Editors," *Troy Daily Traveller*, 30 March 1854.

5. "Horrible; Double Murder By Poisoning," *Troy Daily Times*, 26 May 1853. The article further states: "She claims to be French, but is undoubtedly English by birth."

6. Baptism of Charlotte Maria Wood, 2 July 1826; this record also gives her date of birth, 8 April 1826. ("Birth, Marriage, and Death Records," Cathedral of the Holy Trinity, Quebec City, Archives Nationales du Quebec).

7. There was a lag time before new students appeared in the official school catalogue. Another seminary student, Charlotte Doolittle of Utica (who would step forward, sensationally, in the 1890s to claim a friendship with the Veiled Murderess) does not appear in either 1842 catalogue, yet the January of 1843 accounting to the New York State Regents describes Doolittle's mastery of two full terms of coursework from the previous year.

8. It's only fair to note that seminary reports to the New York State Regents of 1843–45 say something went a little wrong with Charlotte's career as a student. The 1843 accounting finds Charlotte and Harriet Wood on a list of students, who because of "insufficient age, studies, etc." have not mastered any subject. The two Wood daughters fell into this category again in January 1844. The next year the seminary submitted their information to the Regents in February. This report, covering student performance of 1844, shows Harriet—younger than Charlotte by three years and a student at the Seminary for fewer terms than her sister—as knowledgeable in Newman's *Rhetoric*, Gray's *Botanical* through "Leaves," and Mrs. Phelps' "Botany for Analysis." But Charlotte had still mastered nothing, a situation that once troubled this writer, but the "blank record" probably has no significance—indicating only the older Charlotte's greater involvement in Troy's social world, if anything.

CHAPTER 21: LIVELY SEASON

1. "Motion in the Case of Mrs. Robinson," *Troy Daily Traveller*, 12 April 1855.

2. "Who Is Mrs. Robinson," *Auburn Advertiser*, 22 May 1855.

3. "Mrs. Robinson; The Reception of the Intelligence from Albany; An Illumination," *Troy Daily Times*, 11 June 1855.

4. Ibid.

5. "Mrs. Robinson; New Trial Denied," *Troy Daily Traveller*, 11 June 1855.

6. The *Traveller* of 19 June also contains an article, "No Harmony Between the Hards and Softs," which takes the Hards' part in their ongoing intra-party battle, demonstrating the continued life of the old Woolly Head-Hard link.

7. "The Mysterious Murderess," *New York Daily Times*, 21 June 1855.

8. "Henrietta Robinson, the Veiled Murderess Sentenced to Death," *Troy Daily Traveller*, 19 June 1855.

9. "Mrs. Robinson," *Troy Daily Traveller*, 20 June 1855.

10. Ibid.

11. Chauncey Depew, *My Memories of 80 Years* (New York: Scribner's Sons, 1924), chap. 20.

12. Quoted in "Hanging Women," *Lansingburg Democrat*, 21 June 1855.

13. Thurlow Weed's *Albany Evening Journal* ran nothing on Robinson after June 1854, a slightly curious fact open to different interpretations. One interpretation: the *Knick* and *Traveller* "carried water" for the *Journal* on the Robinson case, to allow Weed to keep a low profile.

14. The *Troy Daily Times* was already able to list a handful as of 22 June 1855 (see their "Mrs. Robinson" of this date). See "Should A Woman Be Hung," *Utica Daily Herald*, 24 June 1855, for one of the few adamantly pro-hanging articles.

15. "The Law's Delay," *Troy Daily Traveller*, 22 June 1855.

16. Quoted in "Troy and Vicinity: The sentence of Mrs. Robinson . . ." *Troy Daily Traveller*, 23 June 1855.

17. "Mrs. Robinson was visited yesterday . . ." *Troy Daily Times*, 29 June 1855; ""Mrs. Robinson was visited in her cell . . ." *Troy Daily Times*, 2 July 1855.

18. "Mrs. Robinson At Prayer," *Troy Daily Traveller*, 21 July 1855.

19. The *Troy Daily Times* characteristically leapt to Robinson's defense, admitting that Robinson had laughed, "But she did not 'break down' in her devotions, as represented. The ladies say that the prayer was an earnest and eloquent one, in which she manifested much feeling, and in most appropriate language she feelingly implored Divine assistance and forgiveness." ("It is true, etc." *Troy Daily Times*, 22 July 1855)

20. "The Albany Knickerbocker has just been informed . . . ," *Troy Daily Traveller*, 14 July 1855.

21. Dr. H. B. Skinner, *Life and Confessions of Mrs. Henrietta Robinson, the Veiled Murderess, etc.* (Boston: H. B. Skinner, 1855). A single copy of this pamphlet survives, at University of Missouri Law School.

CHAPTER 22: "ADMIRAL PAGNUM'S DAUGHTER"

1. Neither peerages nor atlases seem to have information on the limits of Edward's nineteenth-century earldom. Re Pakenham earldom, see Edmund Lodge, *Peerage of the British Empire at Present Existing, Etc.* (London: E. Lodge, 1839), 361–62.

2. *This* Thomas Pakenham's older brother—through a complicated twist of inheritance which also involved a name change to "Conolly"—had already acquired the estate and house of Castletown in Co. Kildare. Bernard Burke, *A Genealogical Dictionary of the Peerage and Baronetage of the British Empire* (London: Harrison, 1876), 741–42; William Courthope, ed., *Debrett's Complete Peerage, etc.* (London: J. G. and F. Rivington, 1838), 563–64; Lodge, *Peerage of the British Empire*, 361–62.

3. Ibid., 361.

4. Great Britain. War Office. Records of Officers' Services by Regt. South Hampshire Regt. of Foot, "Statement of the Services of Robert Hudson Wood" (Church of the Latter-Day Saints' Family History Library (hereafter LDS) Film No. 917273).

5. *Grand Juries of the County of Westmeath from the Year 1727 to the Year 1853 with An Historical Appendix* (Ledestown: John Charles Lyons, 1853), 1:326–28.

6. Ibid., 269.

7. George Smith, "Founder," and Leslie Stephen and Sidney Lee, eds., *Dictionary of National Biography* (Oxford: Oxford Univ. Press, 1917–1922) "Hercules Robinson," 17: 17.

8. In fact, Robinson mentions no personal names of any sort throughout his memoir, except for these three.

9. Hercules Robinson, *Sea Drift* (London: F. Pitman, 1858), 334.

10. William R. O'Byrne, *A Naval Biographical Dictionary Comprising the Life and Services of Every Living Officer in Her Majesty's Navy, Etc.* (London: John Murray, 1849), 331.

11. "Rosmead" in Bernhard Burke, *A Genealogical and Heraldic History of the Peerage and Baronetage, Etc.* (London: Harrison and Sons, 1913), 165.

CHAPTER 23: ANGEL OF MERCY

1. Oakes Smith had also attended the second one in Worcester, Mass., in 1850, but not the first one in Geneva, N.Y., in 1848.

2. Ida Husted Harper, *Life and Work of Susan B. Anthony* (Salem, N.H.: Ayer Co., 1898–1908) 2:72.

3. Ibid.

4. "Representative Women: Cleopatra," *New York Daily Times*, 21 October 1852.

5. "To Miss Mary Lee . . ." Letter of E. O. Smith, Brooklyn, 20 March 1852, mss. A5646, Schlesinger Library, Harvard University.

6. Mary Alice Wyman, ed., *Selections from the Autobiography of Elizabeth Oakes Smith* (Lewiston, Me.: Lewiston Journal, 1924), 50.

7. Mary Alice Wyman, *Two American Pioneers: Seba Smith and Elizabeth Oakes Smith*, (New York: Columbia Univ. Press, 1927), 207.

8. Admittedly, Hawthorne wasn't living in Concord between 1845 and 1852; he only returned there in 1852, after Oakes Smith's fall of 1851 visit (see Philip McFarland, *Hawthorne in Concord* [New York, Grove Press, 2004]). But the Oakes Smith-Zenobia resemblance is so striking Thoreau and the Emersons must have told story after story of the "dreadful" Mrs. Smith to Hawthorne.

9. Arlin Turner, "Introduction," *The Blithedale Romance* (New York: W. W. Norton, 1958), 13. Suggestions that Zenobia may have been based on Margaret Fuller, a feminist of very plain looks, show how completely Oakes Smith has been wiped from the movement's history.

10. Wyman, *Elizabeth Oakes Smith*, 53.

11. F. B. Sanborn, *Henry D. Thoreau*, quoted in Wyman, *Two American Pioneers, Etc.*, 200.

12. She was then in financial straits and worked up the material for a never-given lecture.

13. *Selections from the Autobiography of Elizabeth Oakes Smith*, 135.

14. Ibid., 143–44.

15. Nathaniel Hawthorne, *Blithedale Romance*, ed. Arlin Turner (New York: W. W. Norton, 1958), 127–28.

16. Syphilis is very present in both discreet and open advertisements for cures in the Troy and Albany papers of the 1850s. For its psychic impact, see John D'Emilio and Estelle B. Freedman, *Intimate Matters: A History of Sexuality in America* (New York: Harper and Row, 1988, 141). But many critics have suggested homosexuality as Hawthorne's minister's issue; see http://hawthorneinsalem.org/.

17. Karen Halttunen, *Murder Most Foul*, 41–42, 58–59.

18. Hawthorne, *Blithedale Romance*, 125.

19. Carl N. Degler, *At Odds: Women and the Family in America from the Revolution to the Present* (New York: Oxford Univ. Press, 1980), 180–85, 291–92.

20. Nina Auerbach, *Woman and the Demon: The Life of a Victorian Myth* (Cambridge: Harvard Univ. Press, 1982).

21. "The Trial and Conviction of Mrs. Robinson," *Troy Daily Times*, 29 May 1854.

22. "The Mysterious Murderess," *New York Daily Times*, 21 June 1855.

23. "Mrs. Oakes Smith in a letter . . . ," *Troy Daily Traveller*, 11 July 1855.

24. "Woman's Rights and Wrongs," *Troy Daily Times*, 30 June 1855.

25. "To the Editor . . . ," *New York Evening Mirror*, 28 June 1855.

26. Like the saintly Bertha and Lily of E. O. Smith's *Bertha and Lily, or The Parsonage of Beech Glen* (New York: J. C. Derby, 1854).

27. "It is said Mrs. Robinson . . . ," *Albany Evening Atlas*, 21 June 1855.

CHAPTER 24: DEPARTURE

1. "The 'Veiled Murderess,' " *Troy Daily Times*, 30 July 1855. Francis also zinged Dr. Willard and the Woods, again, in this article: "We have no desire to open afresh the heart-wounds of an afflicted family [the Woods], nor add another pang, even in self-vindication and in exposure of unjustifiable conduct, to the keen sufferings they must already have experienced, and are now enduring. But for a prompting cause in this city [Dr. Willard], having its origin in erroneous conceptions of respectability and duty, and a most indiscreet exposure of itself to the severity of public criticism, we do not believe that even family pride, high as it is held and tenaciously as it is cherished by the wealthy and the high-born English, would have induced such conduct."

2. Ibid.

3. *Traveller* quoted in "Mrs. Robinson's Sentence Commuted," *Lansingburg Gazette*, 31 July 1855.

4. "The Sentence of Mrs. Robinson Has Been Commuted," *Troy Daily Times*, 28 July 1855.

5. Ibid.

6. "Troy Traveler of Saturday" quoted in "Mrs. Robinson's Sentence Commuted," *Lansingburg Gazette*, 31 July 1855.

7. Through 1853 all trains from Albany, Saratoga Springs, and points farther afield (disengaged from their engines on the Albany County side of the Green Island Railroad Bridge and drawn by horses across this bridge and down River Street) had off- and on-loaded passengers in an open street depot before the Troy House hotel at the corner of First and River Streets. Union Depot, a covered railroad terminal,

opened in February of 1854, pointing up again what a watershed time 1853–55 was in Troy's history, with major infrastructure changes (including the closing of an old horse-powered ferry across the Hudson in 1854) occurring in tandem with the political ones (break-up of the Whig and old Democratic Parties) and social ones (success of the new manufacturing elite, as seen in George B. Warren Jr.'s victory in the Y. M. A. election of 1853).

8. Title of article not noted, *Troy Daily Traveller*, 31 July 1855.

9. "The 'Veiled Murderess,' " *Troy Daily Times*, 30 July 1855.

10. See *Lansingburg Democrat* of 13 May 1852: "The Showering or 'Hydropathic Torture,' sometimes administered as a punishment to rebellious convicts in the State Prisons is thus described: 'The stream of water is about one inch in diameter, and falls from a height of seven or eight feet. The head of ther patient is retained in its place by means of a board clasping the neck; the effect of which is, the water striking upon the board rebounds in the mouth and nostrils of the victim, almost producing strangulation. Congestion, sometimes of the heart or lungs, sometimes of the brain, not infrequently ensues; and death in due season releases some sufferers from further ordeal of the Water Cure.' "

11. "The 'Veiled Murderess,' " *Troy Daily Times*, 30 July 1855.

CHAPTER 25: SUSAN GAYNOR

1. E. Estyn Evans, *Irish Folk Ways* (New York: Devin-Adair Co., 1957), 75

2. Jean Chevalier, ed., *Dictionnaire des Symboles: Mythes, Reves, Coutumes, Gestes, Formes, Figures, Couleurs, Nombres* (Paris: Robert Laffont, 1969), 79–180.

3. Daithi O Hogain, *Myth, Legend, and Romance: An Encyclopedia of the Irish Folk Tradition* (London: Ryan Publishing, 1990), 158–60.

4. "Matteawan Hospital: Star Prisoner is Henrietta Robinson, the Famous Veiled Murderess," *Northern Budget* or *Sunday Telegram*, 8 December 1901 (clipping, Troy Scrapbook No. 189, 123).

5. Threatening someone with a gun was a very minor infraction in antebellum Troy and Albany, one probably often handled with little or no police or judicial record-keeping, especially in the case of a well-connected offender. A *Troy Daily Budget* article of 1849 makes this clear:

"We would advise parents to exercise the utmost care and circumspection over their boys . . . We are led to these remarks by an incident that occurred at the Alhambra [a Troy saloon] last evening. A son of a respectable citizen—a lad of only about fifteen years—came into the Alhambra early in the evening very much intoxicated. He attempted to raise a "row," when he was checked by Mr. Rockwood, who ordered him to leave the house. He refused to do so, placed his hands in pockets and drew a pair of pistols at Mr. R. threatening to shoot him. The youngster was secured and sent home to his parents.

"That boy, unless his parents take him in charge, and train him up right, will ere long bring sorrow to them and shame and disgrace upon himself." ("Local Summary: Bad Boys," *Troy Daily Budget*, 5 February 1849)

6. How natural that frontier-born John C. Mather and onetime printer's apprentice Thurlow Weed both liked women who had something they did not: a

good deal of social polish, and specifically a *British* polish. Henrietta Robinson possessed this—"she . . . is undoubtedly British by birth" ("Horrible Double Murder by Poisoning," *Troy Daily Times*, 26 May 1853).

7. Weed was often a host, himself:

". . . he [Weed] having invited many members of the Legislature and other distinguished individuals to his house. There were Gov Fish, Judge Ira Harris [future judge of Henrietta Robinson's Supreme Court murder trial], John A. King of Queens, Seth C. Hawley [major player in the Big Letting of 1851], David D. Field and many others. About 10 the folding doors were thrown open and a table loaded with choice eatables and drinkables of the finest flavor presented to our view. Oysters, grapes, a peculiar kind of diminuative [*sic*] apple, cream andc of the edibles; Champaigne, various kinds of wine andc composed the liquors [Weed was not pro-prohibition]. In the front parlor was a portrait of Bishop Hughes [Roman Catholic Archbishop John Hughes] and others; in the back parlor were portraits of ex-Gov. Seward, T.Weed and others. Left at 11 o'clock. This was a party exclusively for gentlemen. As Clerk Prindle says, 'This was a stand up party.' "

It's possible John C. Mather attended this January 1849 party as well as another, also given by Weed, the next month. ("William H. Robertson Diary, 1847–49" in *Quarterly Bulletin of the Westchester Historical Society* 23 (1947): 32–33.)

8. Recent studies of two antebellum fallen women—high-class New York City prostitute and 1836 murder victim Helen Jewett (Patricia Cline Cohen, *The Murder of Helen Jewett: The Life and Death of a Prostitute in Nineteenth-Century New York*, New York: Alfred A. Knopf, 1998) and New Orleans "kept woman" of the 1840s Madaline Edwards (Dell Upton, ed., *Madaline: Love and Survival in Antebellum New Orleans*, Athens: Univ. of Georgia Press, 1996)—reveal these women had multiple clients or protectors, and the clients often enjoyed comradely relationships with one another, with the comradeship formed or strengthened by the men's position as fellow lovers of the same woman. Also one contemporary newspaper comment suggests multiple lovers or clients for Robinson: "There is strong circumstantial evidence to prove that this woman was a Miss Wood . . . that she left her parents and was for some time the mistress of an individual *or individuals* [modern italics] in this city . . ." ("The Robinson Trial," *Troy Daily Times*, 26 May 1854).

9. Samuel Lewis, *Topographical Dictionary of Ireland* (London, 1837; repr., Baltimore: Genealogical Publishing Co., 1984), 695–96.

10. *Special Report on Surnames in Ireland: Appendix to 29th Report of the Registrar General in 1894* quoted in Donal F. Begley, *Irish Genealogy: A Record Finder* (Dublin: Heraldic Artists, Ltd., 1987), 325.

11. "Localities; Melancholy Occurrence," *Albany Evening Atlas*, 26 August 1851.

12. "A Man Accidentally Killed; A Sad Affair," *Albany Evening Journal*, 26 August 1851.

13. "Albany Mayor's Court, The People agt. Susan Gaynor, etc." Indictments, 1851–54, Box 97-00908-0000, Albany Hall of Records.

14. Anson Bingham then corroborated this timeline at trial: ". . . the prisoner, on the 25th of May last, resided in the extreme north part of the city, and had resided there previously, a year or more, keeping house."

15. Ibid. (attached deposition sworn before "J. O. Cole, Police Justice" and signed "Margaret (her X mark) Hanan.")

16. Glyndon G. Van Deusen, *Thurlow Weed: Wizard of the Lobby* (Boston: Little, Brown, 1947), 189.

17. All three streets are east-west-running. Hamilton and Spencer then ran down to the riverfront (or nearly so) but are separated by about ten blocks, with Spencer some blocks north and east of the Capitol and Hamilton some blocks south and east. Chestnut was in a newer part of the city, about as far west of the Capitol as Spencer and Hamilton were north and south of it. The three addresses (knowing only the street names without street numbers) form three (linear) "points" of a rough triangle containing the Capitol at its center.

18. Writer believes it was the second case—for a particular reason. She found among a box of 1851 Mayor's Court records in the Albany Hall of Records a series of undated depositions concerning a "Susan Gaynor of Hamilton Street" who had attacked two other women living in the same house and, rather unbelievably, had also injured someone by throwing a log out her window. Later, on discovery of the August incident and recognition of the Westmeath connection, the writer tried to find these papers again, but had misplaced their box number. After searching through many boxes, she concluded the papers had somehow been misfiled. She is also convinced that John Upton's name was on these papers as constable-on-the-spot.

19. The original, less-detailed version of this story appeared in Thurlow Weed's *Albany Evening Journal*.

20. Even if John Francis's 30 July 1855 statement about Robinson's "admission" to him is not believed—along with the *Times*'s account of Robinson's "William Wood" remark on the train to Sing Sing—there is still William H. Jeffery's 1854 letter with its "she [Robinson] . . . went into particulars respecting my history and connections with her Father (that is, Mr. Wood) . . ."

21. Writer failed to note number of "box" where this ledger is to be found; the newspaper clipping clearly comes from a January issue of an Albany paper, probably from whichever paper then had the state contract.

CHAPTER 26: IMMIGRANTS AND OTHERS

1. Maladry Moran, "Records of Athlone and District Extracted from Dublin Newspapers," vol. 2, 1780–1850 (ms. at Genealogical Office of Ireland), LDS microfilm 100214; or John B. Burgess, "Athlone Newspapers" (ms. at GOI), LDS microfilm 1472323.

2. Brendan Lehane, *The Companion Guide to Ireland* (London: Collins, 1973), 114.

3. "The Trial of the Castlepollard Policemen . . . involved in the Castlepollard massacre . . . in May 1831," LDS microfilm 1279276.

4. Item from *Freeman's Journal*, 9 July 1849 in Moran, "Records of Athlone."

5. Carolyn A. Conley, *The Unwritten Law: Criminal Justice in Victorian Kent* (New York: Oxford Univ. Press, 1991), 160. And: "Though the Irish made up only 5 percent of the population of Kentish London, they were involved in 30 percent

of the assault cases heard in the Kentish sessions . . . Motives in Irish assaults were rarely mercenary. The Irish in Kent were involved in 39 percent of assaults cases stemming from brawls but only 4 percent of assaults with intent to rob" (Ibid.)

6. Peter L. Stearns, Abstract (Proquest) of Carolyn A. Conley, "No Pedestals: Women and Violence in Late 19th-Century Ireland," *Journal of Social History*, Summer 1995: 801.

7. "At this period [Robinson's first arrival in Troy], Mrs. Robinson was twenty-three years of age . . ." (Wilson, *Henrietta Robinson*, 35; a newpaper account of 1854, misplaced by author, also contains a more specific reference to her arrival in 1849).

8. Thomas Carlyle, *Reminiscences of My Irish Journey* (New York: Harper Brothers, 1882), 23–28.

9. W. T. N. Reeve, "Wood Family Genealogy."

10. "Wood married Gray," 4 October 1817, Birth, Marriage, and Death Records, Cathedral of the Holy Trinity, Quebec City, Archives Nationales du Quebec.

11. Baptism of Georgiana Wood, 20 September 1818; of Charlotte Maria Wood, 15 July 1821; of William Frost Wood, notation of private ceremony on 8 August 1824 plus notation of "Wood received into the church" on 2 July 1826; of Charlotte Maria Wood, 2 July 1826; of Harriet Wood, 27 July 1828; of James John Wood, 11 April 1830; of Phoebe Sarah, 9 May 1831; of George Augustus Leslie Wood, 22 January 1833; of Maria Eliza Wood, 8 June 1834; of Eldridge Gray Wood, 24 July 1836; of Alexander Clayton Wood, 28 June 1840; and burial of Charlotte Maria Wood, 18 December 1821. These baptisms took place from a month to nine months after the actual births (Birth, Marriage, and Death Records, Cathedral of the Holy Trinity).

12. Collection of W. T. N. Reeve.

13. Ibid.

14. "Famous Murder Mystery Solved," *Troy Northern Budget*, 19 June 1898, 12.

15. "Her Identity A Mystery Still," *Troy Daily Press*, 9 November 1897 (clipping in RCHS copy of Wilson, *Henrietta Robinson*)

16. "Home Matters: Horrible; Double Murder by Poisoning," *Troy Daily Times*, 26 May 1853

17. "Rensselaer Oyer and Terminer, Etc.," *Troy Daily Times*, 25 May 1854.

18. W. E. Hagan, "In the Apothecary Shop," *Troy Daily Press*, 27 August 1890.

19. She appears on the 1850 census as "Abba Goddard," the 31-year-old head of a small, all-female household, which then contained two young girls who might have been students. This snapshot of the household also showed a 5-year-old daughter, named "Abba Goddard" (U.S. Census, 1850, Rensselaer County, Troy City, First Ward, 48)

20. Her advertisements for students are scattered through some of the same Troy newspaper issues dealing with the affair of the Veiled Murderess.

21. "More Operations of the Female Financier, Abby A. Goddard," *Boston Daily Traveller*, 30 July 1859 and "More of Miss Goddard, the Female 'Operator.' " Both articles appear as clippings in Troy Scrapbooks, roll 32, 170a–171a. Stacy Pomeroy Draper of RCHS has uncovered much else of interest about Goddard, unfortunately not included here.

CHAPTER 27: THE SING SING YEARS

1. "Mrs. Robinson at Sing Sing," *Troy Daily Times*, 9 August 1855.

2. Nicole H. Rafter, *Partial Justice: Women in State Prisons, 1800–1935* (Boston: Northeastern Univ. Press, 1985), 16–19. Mount Pleasant Female Prison was less hellish than many women's prisons of day, though, because run by matrons rather than male guards. "A corrupt administration at the Indiana state prison [of this era] operated a prostitution service for male guards, using the forced labor of female prisoners." (Estelle B. Freedman, *Their Sister's Keepers: Women's Prison Reform in America, 1830–1930* [Ann Arbor: Univ. of Michigan Press, 1981], 16.)

3. Dr. H. B. Skinner., *The Life and Confessions of Mrs. Henrietta Robinson, the Veiled Murderess!* (Boston: H.B. Skinner, 1855).

4. "Who Is Mrs. Robinson?" *Troy Daily Times*, 5 Septermber 1855 ("The work will appear within a week or two.")

5. Though Wilson protected himself from Wood lawsuits by never stating in his authorial voice that Henrietta Robinson *was* Charlotte Wood Eliott; he simply highlighted (and endorsed as sensible) all information pointing in this direction.

6. Wilson, *Henrietta Robinson*, 283.

7. Ibid., 16, 287–88.

8. Ibid., 17–18.

9. David Wilson alumni file, Special Collections, Union College, Schenectady; Sue Eakin and Joseph Logsdon, eds., *Twelve Years A Slave* (Baton Rouge: Louisiana State Univ. Press, 1986) xiii.

10. David Wilson, *Life of Jane McCrea, with an Account of Burgoyne's Expedition in 1777* (New York: Baker, Goodwin, 1853)

11. Solomon Northup, *Twelve Years a Slave: Narrative of Solomon Northup, a Citizen of New York Kidnapped, Etc.* (Auburn: Derby and Miller, 1853). Modern scholars have found this work very accurate about persons, places, and dates; see Eakin and Logsdon, xvi.

12. "The Rights of Women," *Brooklyn Eagle*, 10 May 1856.

13. "Mrs. Henrietta Robinson Not Mrs. Wood; Who She Is," *Troy Daily Times*, 12 November 1856.

14. "The Veiled Murderess: An Episode in the History of Henrietta Robinson [Harry Hill's Reminiscences in the *New York Mercury*]," undated clipping in Troy Scrapbook No. 167, pp. 167–168, TPL (clipping follows item dated 31 March 1881).

15. "Sing Sing State Prison," *Brooklyn Daily Eagle*, 20 July 1858.

16. State of New York, Mattewan State Hospital. "Case Notes of Prisoner 301, Henrietta Robinson, admitted 28 August 1873, discharged 14 May 1905," 16.

17. John Luckey, *Life in Sing Sing Prison, As Seen in a Twelve Years' Chaplaincy* (New York: N. Tibbals, 1866), 330.

18. Ibid., 331.

19. Ibid., 334.

20. Ibid., 332–33.

21. Ibid., 333.

22. Ibid., 335–36.

23. Ibid., 334.

24. Ibid., 335.

25. See Luckey, *Life in Sing Sing*; Matteawan State Hospital, "Henrietta Robinson." The Matteawan records are very detailed about her behavior.

26. "Mrs. Robinson, the Murderess," *Lansingburg Gazette*, 4 September 1860.

27. Mather, 184; also see U. S. Census, 1860, Wayne County, Town of Palmyra, 807, for "Helen Goulding," head of household, age 28, with a personal estate of $40,000. See listings for Helen Goulding in New York City directories (Doggett's and Rode's) from 1862 to 1867–68; the 1862–63 directory identifies her as the widow of Joseph Goulding.

28. Information from Watertown directories provided by Jeannie Brennan, Genealogical Department, Flower Memorial Library, Watertown.

29. "The 'Veiled Murderess' Once More," clipping, Troy Scrapbook No. 171, 3, TPL.

30. "Henrietta Robinson, the noted "Veiled Murderess"; Something of Her Early History," Troy Scrapbook No. 171, 17.

31. "The Veiled Murderess; Should Henrietta Robinson Be Pardoned?" Troy Scrapbook No. 171, 3.

32. Article title not noted, *Brooklyn Daily Eagle*, 18 November 1872, 12.

33. "A Crazy Criminal's Crime," *Troy Daily Times*, 29 August 1873 (clipping, Troy Scrapbook No. 171, p. 24).

34. "Auburn Correctional Facility Sub-Agency History Record," New York State Library Catalogue (on-line).

35. "Henrietta Robinson, the Veiled Murderess . . . ," *Troy Daily Press*, 22 April 1874 (clipping, Troy Scrapbook No. 171, 101).

36. Clipping, Troy Scrapbook No. 174, 4 (Item following "The Concluding Chapter in a Story of Real Life," *Troy Daily Times*, 13 October 1874).

37. "Our Temple of Justice," *Troy Daily Press*, 8 April 1875.

CHAPTER 28: AUBURN

1. Matteawan State Hospital, "Henrietta Robinson," 12–13

2. Ibid., 13.

3. "Matteawan Hospital: Star Prisoner is Henrietta Robinson, the Famous Veiled Murderess," *Northern Budget* or *Sunday Telegram*, 8 December 1901 (clipping, Troy Scrapbook No. 189, 123).

4. Matteawan State Hospital, "Henrietta Robinson," 13.

5. Ibid., 13–14.

6. "The Veiled Murderess," *Troy Daily Times*, 30 November 1881.

7. "Death of Ex-Senator Mather," *Watertown Daily Times*, 14 August 1885.

8. "Death of John C. Mather; A Man with a History," *Troy Daily Times*, 15 August 1882 (clipping, RCHS)

9. John M. Francis, a staunch Republican from the later 1850s on, filled three foreign service posts under Republican national administrations between 1871 and 1888—United States' Minister to Greece, United States' Minister to Portugal, and "envoy extraordinary and minister plenipotentiary to the Austro-Hungarian

Empire"—so he may have been abroad in August of 1882. See Samuel Rezneck, *Profiles Out of the Past of Troy*, 189.

10. Matteawan State Hospital, "Henrietta Robinson," 14.

11. "The Veiled Murderess," *Troy Morning Telegram*, 25 November 1891; "A Tragic Mystery," *Troy Daily Press*, 22 January 1896.

12. Matteawan State Hospital, "Henrietta Robinson," 14.

13. Other items purchased in 1882 were "a rug, hassock, tooth-brush, washbowl and pitcher, material for covering a rocking chair, etc."

14. Matteawan State Hospital, "Henrietta Robinson," 15.

15. Long after Townsend's death, a newspaper would refer to "her [Robinson's] lawyer who visited her at regular intervals and who admitted that his services had been paid for by 'certain influential personages' whom he was not at liberty to name" ("Histories Mysteries: Number 88," *Beacon Herald*, 11 Janaury 1923—clipping inserted in Robinson's Matteawan file).

16. "Fire Destroys the Scene of Henrietta Robinson's Crime," *Troy Daily Times*, 6 September 1886 (clipping, RCHS)

17. Matteawan State Hospital, "Henrietta Robinson," 15.

18. Reprinted in "The Veiled Murderess," *Troy Press*, 30 July 1888 (clipping, RCHS)

19. Matteawan State Hospital, "Henrietta Robinson," 16.

20. Though "Mrs. David Kellogg" fails to appear in the listing of married names of students in *Emma Willard and Her Pupils or 50 Years of Troy Female Seminary, 1822–1872* (New York: Mrs. Russell Sage, 1898).

21. "The Veiled Murderess," *Troy Morning Telegram*, 25 November 1891.

22. New York State, State Commission of Correction, *Women's Prisons, Past and Present and Other New York State Prison History* (Elmira: Summary Press, 1932), 27.

23. "A Tragedy Recalled," Troy Press, August, 1892 (clipping, RCHS)

CHAPTER 29: CHARLOTTE DOOLITTLE NORRIS

1. Though, curiously, the name of one of Admiral Hercules Robinson's (of Castletown Delvin) sons was then (1896) appearing in American newspapers. This was Sir Hercules Robinson, a younger brother of the "Henry Robinson" mentioned earlier. Sir Hercules was in the process of remaking the family fortunes through government service; he was Governor of the "Cape Colony" at South Africa and involved in political struggles leading up to the Boer War of a few years later. His name featured in a *New York Journal* headline beginning "Hammond to Escape Severe Punishment . . ." on 21 May 1896.

2. Bernard Burke and A. Burke, *A Genealogical and Heraldic History, etc.* (London: Burke Publishing, 1927).

3. Matteawan State Hospital, "Henrietta Robinson," 17.

4. See entries in both 1895 and 1896 Chicago directories; the address was actually "1857 Oakdale Avenue," but the one altered digit must represent either a newspaper typo or some attempt to shield Mrs. Norris from unwelcome visitors.

5. Extracted Marriage Record from First Presbyterian Church, Utica, N.Y., LDS microfilm 534223.

6. "The Firemen's Excursion," *Troy Daily Times*, 23 September 1853.

7. Jay Leyda, *Melville Log: A Documentary Life of Herman Melville* (New York: Harcourt Brace, 1951). See entries for August 1847.

8. This woman's (Maria Gray Petry's) husband, William Petry, was godfather to some of the Wood children, including James John, baptized 11 April 1830.

9. Writer failed to note which newspaper printed the item, later reprinted in Wilson, but is confident it appeared in one of the articles from 1854–55.

10. David Wilson, *Henrietta Robinson*, 289. With this date supposedly gleaned from "the old files of a Quebec newspaper." See also "Vital Records: *Troy Daily Whig*, 1834–1848," unpaged ms., 1980, TPL; this contains the extract: "Charlotte Maria Wood m. William F. A. Eliott, Jan. 16, 1847." This notice didn't appear in the *Whig* in 1847 or 1846, however, but was almost certainly drawn, with the year incorrectly cited (either by the 1980 compilers or by the Troy newspaper) from one of the pieces of Robinson coverage of 1854.

11. The 93rd Sutherland Highlanders debarked in Leith, near Edinburgh, on Aug. 30. See Roderick Hamilton Burgoyne, ed., *Historical Records of the 93rd Sutherland Highlanders, etc.* (London: Richard Bentley and Son, 1883), 87.

CHAPTER 30: FINALE

1. "Matteawan Hospital: Star Prisoner is Henrietta Robinson, etc." *Troy Sunday Telegram* or *Northern Budget*, 8 December 1901 (clipping, Troy Scrapbook No. 189, pp. 123–24); Townsend lived until 1903.

2. Matteawan State Hospital, "Henrietta Robinson," 19.

3. "Mystery Cleared Up: 'Henrietta Robinson' Was Really Charlotte Ward," *Troy Record*, 16 May 1905, 1.

4. Copy of Wilson, *Henrietta Robinson*, in collection of RCHS.

5. Jack Casey, "The Veiled Murderess," *Troy Record*, 1 April 1979, 8 April 1979, 15 April 1979, 22 April 1979, 29 April 1979, 6 May 1979.

6. Hollis Palmer, *Curse of the Veiled Murderess* (Saratoga Springs: Deep Roots, 2004).

CHAPTER 31: WHAT REALLY HAPPENED

1. As mentioned earlier, the Hard Democratic paper, *Albany Argus*, just avoided the scandal.

2. Philip W. Martin, *Mad Women in Romantic Writing* (New York: St. Martin's Press, 1987), 40–45; Sandra M. Gilbert and Susan Gubar, *The Mad Woman in the Attic* (New Haven: Yale Univ. Press, 1978); Jane M. Ussher, *Women's Madness: Misogyny or Mental Illness?* (Amherst: Univ. of Mass. Press, 1991), 86–88.

3. Richard Weeden, *Poison in the Pot: The Legacy of Lead* (Carbondale: Southern Illinois Univ. Press, 1984), 49, 57.

4. W. J. Thoms, ed., *Notes and Queries* (London), Tenth Series, 7 (1907): 115, 125.

5. Mary Hartman, *Victorian Murderesses: A True History of Thirteen Respectable French and English Women Accused of Unspeakable Crimes* (New York: Schocken

Books, 1977), 85–129. The work of another modern investigator, Joyce Egglinton, *Circle of Fire: Murder and Betrayal in the "Swiss Nanny" Case* (New York: William Morrow, 1994) indicates—without directly referring to the Kent case—that the Kent family nursemaid was the likely culprit in the murder of Charles Kent's son (see Egglinton, 345–55).

6. Catherine Peters, *King of Inventors: A Life of Wilkie Collins* (Princeton: Princeton Univ. Press, 1991).

7. Arnold R. Brown, *Lizzie Borden: The Legend, the Truth, the Final Chapter* (Nashville: Rutledge Hill, 1991), 297

8. Hartman, *Victorian Murderesses*, 286–338.

9. "Fatal Accident; Boy Killed," *Troy Daily Times*, February 2, 1852; "Narrow Escape," *Troy Daily Times*, July 14, 1851. Troy newspapers record several other incidents of this exact type that the author failed to note.

10. Havermans may have even been the "French catholic clergyman" who attended Timothy Lanagan in his last hours, as well as a visitor to Robinson at the Ferry Street Jail. But somehow he never seemed part of this story, no doubt because he stood completely outside both the lies and the foolish struggle for reputation that was key to the affair.

INDEX